Women Overseas

Women Overseas

Memoirs of the Canadian Red Cross Corps

(Overseas Detachment)

edited by
Frances Martin Day,
Phyllis Spence
& Barbara Ladouceur

RONSDALE PRESS
1998

RONSDALE PRESS LTD.
3350 West 21st Avenue
Vancouver, B.C., Canada
V6S 1G7

Set in New Baskerville: 11 pt on 14
Typesetting: Julie Cochrane
Printing: Hignell Printing, Winnipeg, Manitoba
Cover Design: Julie Cochrane
Cover Art: Voluntary Aid Detachment WW II poster (courtesy of the Canadian
    Red Cross)
Frontispiece: Catherine MacDonald Waters

Ronsdale Press wishes to thank the Canada Council for the Arts, the Department of Heritage, and the British Columbia Cultural Services Branch for their support of its publishing program.

CANADIAN CATALOGUING IN PUBLICATION DATA

Women overseas

Includes bibliographical references and index.
ISBN 0-921870-61-2
1. World War, 1939–1945—War work—Red Cross.   2. World War,
1939–1945—Personal narratives, Canadian.   3. World War, 1939–1945—
Participation, Female.   4. Korean War, 1950–1953—War work—Red Cross.
5. Korean War, 1950–1953—Personal narratives, Canadian.   6. Korean War,
1950–1953—Participation, Female.   7. Canadian Red Cross Society—
Biography.   8. Nurses—Canada—Biography.   I. Day, Frances Martin, (date)
II. Spence, Phyllis, 1943–   III. Ladouceur, Barbara, 1949–
D807.C2W65 1998   940.54'771'092271   C98-910864-3

DEDICATION

Here at the fondly remembered
(now mythical) "Strollers Club," we propose
a toast to all the 641 dear friends and companions
of the Canadian Red Cross Corps
for the laughter, tears and total involvement
during the war years.

ACKNOWLEDGEMENTS

This book could not have become a reality without the encouragement and assistance of many people. We are especially grateful to Phyllis Elder Matheson, Past President of the Overseas Club, Victoria, for her ongoing support and invaluable historical knowledge; Jane Rogers, President of the Overseas Club, Victoria, for her belief in the historical importance of the stories in *Women Overseas*; Jean Hill, Overseas Club Archivist, for graciously helping us to locate Canadian Red Cross Corps photographs; Ann M. Butryn, Manager, Office Services/Librarian of the Canadian Red Cross, for providing her expertise and arranging for permission to use the World War II Red Cross poster on the cover of *Women Overseas;* and Marjorie Andrew, National President of the Overseas Club, for her help in verifying historical details.

We deeply appreciate the ongoing support of our families and friends, their interest, understanding and help in preparing the manuscript. Our heartfelt thanks also to Ronald and Veronica Hatch for sensitively and skillfully leading their troops of editors and Canadian Red Cross Corps members through the exciting journey that this project has involved.

Most importantly, we give a standing ovation to the members of the Vancouver Island Overseas Club who shared their compelling stories with us. We thank them for their wholehearted support in inviting us to their meetings, welcoming us into their homes and lending us their photographs and mementoes.

CONTENTS

FOREWORD

In *Women Overseas,* thirty-one members of the Canadian Red Cross Corps recall their experiences as overseas volunteers during World War II and the Korean War. Most of these women came of age in the midst of war and all of them rose bravely to the challenge of overseas service.

Love for their country and in many cases love for their men who were already serving overseas were often the driving forces that motivated women to leave the relative safety of Canada to accept Red Cross postings in war-torn England, continental Europe and Asia. Through these vivid narratives we learn how it feels to cross U-boat infested oceans, to survive daily bombings and severe food shortages, to witness death and destruction, and to acquire the *carpe diem* spirit and courage exhibited by so many "ordinary" people during war. We hear the voices of the Red Cross Corps sing "O Canada" and "The Maple Leaf Forever" when they first land in England and then again in France to join the soldiers who preceded them. We listen to the cheers of the French people and Canadian soldiers as the Red Cross Corps members travel along the "Maple Leaf Up," the main highway from Normandy to Germany during World War II. We visit the Maple Leaf Clubs in London where thousands of Canadian soldiers enjoyed a taste of home on their leaves from the war. We learn that the maple leaf was a proud symbol of Canadian courage and solidarity decades before it first appeared on our flag. After reading these stories, the Canadian flag with its large red maple leaf proudly recalls the courage of those who died for the peace that Canadians have enjoyed for over five decades.

While the red maple leaf signifies Canadian nationality, the red cross symbolizes an international organization that comes to the aid of all nations. The concept of the Red Cross was created in the midst of war. In 1859, Jean Henri Dunant, a Swiss businessman, happened to be travelling in Italy when he arrived in Solferino in time to witness the aftermath of a battle between the armies of Austria and Napoleon III. He organized volunteers to set up emergency hospitals for the wounded soldiers of both armies. In 1862, Dunant's book *Un Souvenir de Solférino* (A Memoir of Solferino) recommended that all countries organize volunteer groups to care for the victims of war. Through Dunant's efforts, delegates from sixteen nations met in Geneva, Switzerland, in 1863, and the following year a treaty was drafted that called for the protection of wounded troops and those caring for them in wartime. In honour of Jean Henri Dunant, the Swiss flag with its colours reversed was adopted as the Red Cross symbol. Throughout the twentieth century there have been many international conferences to define and extend the principles of the first Geneva Convention.

Since its birth in Europe over a hundred years ago, the Red Cross has grown into a worldwide network of national Red Cross Societies, with the International Red Cross headquartered in Geneva. It assures that the principles of the Geneva Conventions are adhered to by all nations and officially recognizes the national Red Cross Societies. The League of Red Cross Societies in Geneva develops, promotes and assists Red Cross Societies throughout the world.

The Canadian Red Cross came into being in 1896 when Surgeon-General G. S. Ryerson placed a Red Cross symbol on a medical supply wagon used to assist the wounded in the Northwest Rebellion. The Canadian Red Cross subsequently provided aid to wounded soldiers in the Boer War (1899-1902) and World War I (1914-1918). After World War I, the Canadian Red Cross began peacetime relief programmes, and in 1927 it was officially recognized as an independent national society by the International Committee of the Red Cross. Four years later, the Canadian Red Cross took on the administration of the National Emergency

Fund which provided assistance to Canadians living in poverty as a result of the Depression. During World War II, the Canadian Red Cross set up the National Workroom, the Women's War Work Committee, the National Purchasing Committee, the National Enquiry Bureau and the Maple Leaf Clubs in London.

The Canadian Red Cross Corps was founded by the National Council of the Canadian Red Cross Society in June 1940 when World War II had reached its first critical phase with the collapse of the French Army. It was initially called the Women's Volunteer Services Corps and women were recruited through newspaper advertisements. At this time women all across Canada were responding to the war effort. While some joined the armed forces, others were attracted by the volunteer and humanitarian ideals of the Red Cross. Training and volunteer work with the WVSC was scheduled in the evenings and on weekends so that women could continue their daytime jobs or their studies. In late 1941 overseas postings were organized and the name was changed to the Canadian Red Cross Corps; it remained a women-only volunteer service.

Evelyn Chambers of Montreal had earlier organized the Canadian Women's Transport Service which provided driving services for the army in Canada and overseas. Millie Hutchison, another prominent Montrealer, had coordinated the training of VADs (Volunteer Aid Detachment) to assist with the non-medical needs of hospitalized servicemen in Canada and overseas. These services formed the basis for the first two sections of the Corps to be mobilized—Transport and VAD. Later the Office Administration, Food Administration and General Duties Sections were added to the Canadian Red Cross Corps. Thousands of women served in the Corps throughout Canada, and 641 of them were recruited for overseas duty during and after World War II. They became known as the Canadian Red Cross Corps, Overseas Detachment. They maintained their volunteer status in order to observe the obligations inherent in the Geneva Convention. Each section of the Canadian Red Cross Corps had its own distinctive uniform, but khaki was the colour of the uniform worn overseas, with the exception of the blue uniform worn by the VADs and escort officers.

Major General Basil Price, already in England, was appointed to the position of Overseas Commissioner for the Canadian Red Cross Corps. Mrs. Lee was the first Corps Commandant, followed by Isabel Pepall. They received the various requests for overseas Corps workers from the Canadian Army and passed them on to the commandants of the Red Cross Corps throughout Canada. The commandants subsequently drew up lists of qualified Corps members in their jurisdiction who were ready and willing to go overseas, with candidates being selected on the basis of this information. During the years from 1942 to the mid-1950s, members of the Canadian Red Cross Corps, Overseas Detachment, were to serve in England, France, Belgium, Holland, Germany, Italy, Korea and Japan.

The first detachment of eighteen members of the Canadian Red Cross Corps braved the dangerous wartime Atlantic crossing in December 1942. As the war raged on, more Corps women were sent to England—138 in 1943, 293 in 1944 and 192 from 1945 to 1947. Corps members were granted the courtesy of officer's rank, but no pay. The Canadian Red Cross Society provided each member with $5.00 a week; otherwise the Corps members were self-supporting. In joining the Corps, many of the women gave up good jobs or interrupted their university studies to take on overseas volunteer work that was dangerous and much more demanding in time and energy than the paid jobs they left behind. In doing so, they affirmed the extraordinary spirit of volunteerism that women have always exemplified.

As the stories in *Women Overseas* indicate, the work of the Canadian Red Cross Corps, Overseas Detachment, was diverse—far beyond the original plan. Some served in Canadian military hospitals as welfare and handicraft officers, others as transport drivers and general duties officers in various clubs in London. The Canadian Red Cross headquarters was in Burlington Gardens, around the corner from Piccadilly Circus. A large number of the Corps worked here, preparing and sending out parcels for prisoners of war and assembling the layettes to give to English pregnant women married to Canadian servicemen. Others worked with the blind and disabled, and some were seconded to the British Red Cross as ambulance or transport drivers, or to the British Emergency Medical Service Hospitals as nurse's aides. When World War II ended, three Corps members were assigned to operate a postwar civilian relief depot in Normandy. Other members acted as escort officers for the war brides and their children on their voyage to their new homes in Canada. During and after the Korean War, new members were recruited and posted to welfare and handicraft officer positions at military bases in Korea and Japan where they helped to keep up the morale of the Canadian soldiers serving there.

Perhaps the most striking quality that runs through all the stories is the perseverance of the Corps members. Merely to qualify for overseas duty as a volunteer, they had to complete a stringent training programme in hospitals or in centres where they learned such skills as driving and servicing large vehicles. In addition, they had to put in at least 200 hours of voluntary service in Canada for the war effort. When they were eventually given their notice to travel to England, many were asked to leave at very short notice. Once they were overseas, they were often sent to postings that were altogether different from what they had expected. The hours they worked may well seem unnaturally long to present-day readers, but the Corps members worked these hours willingly. Their tenacity seems to have been matched only by their good humour, and it is a delight to read about the pleasure they found in their work and the camaraderie that formed among them.

While the women all shared in the same volunteer spirit, each memoir speaks in an individual voice. The Corps members had very different experiences of the war—some served at Red Cross headquarters in London, some in hospitals, others were near the front lines in France, Belgium and the Netherlands. In the first story, Phyllis Elder Matheson dramatically recounts her Red Cross training, the long, perilous ocean voyage to England, the trauma of war written on the faces of the British and the diverse responsibilities she took on, including driving duties during bombings and blackout conditions. Like the other women in this book, she juxtaposes the inevitable feelings of deprivation and fear with the sense of humour and spirit that enabled people to face the daily horrors of life in war-torn Britain: "The housewives had started sweeping up almost before the last of the dust had settled; they had hung the dusty curtains out on the line, tacked bits of cardboard over the broken windows and brushed the plaster dust out of their hair."

In another story Frances Martin Day conveys the double-edged grief of a woman who loses her husband to the war before she can join him overseas and then decides to leave her son behind when she travels to her Red Cross posting overseas: "My life seemed over. I was stunned and numb to the point I couldn't feel anything. . . . I decided to go, not only to be busy enough to ease my sadness, but there was a war to be won."

Jean Ellis Wright's narrative recalls her work at various mobile military hospitals in Europe, caring for the wounded soldiers brought in from the battle fronts. Her memories come alive in compelling, emotionally charged details. "One lad asked me where he was, then said, 'Please—take my . . . boots off.' He hadn't had them off for two weeks, and his socks were stuck to them. I washed his face in a little pan of water, then washed his feet. He gave a sigh of relief, opened his eyes and whispered, 'Ahhh . . . thanks.' This was a precious moment for me."

Jane Rogers' memoir highlights her work as a cook at the Junior Officers' Club in London. There she meets the formidable Miss Duff, an intimidating presence in several of the women's stories. Her lively narrative is filled with self-effacing humour as she recalls her misadventures and affirms a growing mutual respect between Miss Duff and herself. As she declares early on, "In our innocence, we thought we would be the dieticians, plan the meals, and teach the English cooks how to cook the Canadian way. Was I in for a surprise!"

Audrey Copping remembers her work at St. Dunstan's, a British rehabilitation centre for soldiers blinded in the war. What starts out to be a two-week assignment goes on to the end of the war, with her full involvement in the rehabilitation activities. Later she becomes an assistant to Lady Fraser at St. Dunstan's and teaches blind patients, including a blind man with no hands, to type.

The last of the World War II memoirs is Claire Watson Fisher's inspiring account of the Civilian Relief Programme, designed by Ambassador and Madame Vanier, which was instrumental in distributing clothing and supplies to devastated Normandy in the months after the war's conclusion. In *Women Overseas,* story after story expresses the gratitude of those who received parcels from Canada, including prisoners of war, families of soldiers and the people in Europe who suffered during the war. Fisher remembers the joy of French children who received clothes from Canada, and she quotes one letter written by a nine-year-old French girl: "Long Live Canada, I love Canada and my pretty pink dress. I send many kisses and say thank you."

Several of the Corps members also took part in a historic initiative that began on February 3, 1947 in Vancouver—the development of the Canadian Red Cross Civilian Blood Donor Service. In fact, the Red Cross had been actively collecting blood from 1940—in response to a request from the military for blood for war casualties. Within the Civilian Blood Donor Service, the women's responsibilities included driving to remote parts of Canada often in the midst of harsh winter weather, to set up clinics and deliver blood where it was needed.

Three of the memoirs in *Women Overseas* describe events during and after the Korean War, a conflict that began five years after the end of World War II. Accordingly, these narratives are placed in the latter part of this book. Serving in a different war, a different continent and a different time, Dorothea Wiens states: "In contrast to those of the Red Cross women who served in World War II, my memories are not of bombs and blackouts but more resemble the picture created by the television series *M*A*S*H.*" Unlike the Red Cross volunteers of World War II, women posted in Japan and Korea were paid a small salary. They were motivated by a sense of adventure, a thirst for meaningful work and a desire to learn about other cultures. In uncovering the different aspects of Asian culture, Jacqueline Robitaille Van Campen comments on her discovery that she is not only a Quebecker but also a Canadian, "I gained a great sense of my country which has never left me. Et voilà—a wonderful episode of my life!"

After the Korean War, the Canadian Red Cross Corps members continued their work in cities across Canada. They assisted the nurses at the Red Cross blood clinics and drove people to and from the blood clinics as well as to other health services such as cancer clinics. About fifteen years ago the Corps officially disbanded. However, several decades earlier, the Overseas Club was founded by Betty Bussell Simone, Vi Gore Parkinson, Marguerite Roberts and Nancy Laing, with the purpose of continuing the friendships that had been formed overseas and supporting the National Canadian Red Cross Society with substantial financial contributions. The first meeting was held in December 1945 in Toronto with ninety-nine members attending. Since then there has been a national reunion at a different host city each year. There are nine branches of the Overseas Club in Canada and one in England.

Betty Bussell Simone founded the Vancouver Island Branch in 1973 and became the first president. In 1974 the group began to meet regularly in Victoria where the Corps members found a closeness and pleasure in each other's company rooted in their common bond of having served overseas. Because they had been scattered all over Great Britain, the Continent and eventually Korea and Japan, many of them were meeting for the first time. Until discovering each other, they had not realized the diversity of each other's experiences. Frances Martin Day suggested that at each meeting one of the members share her overseas experience with the others. As the stories unfolded, it became clear that they should be permanently recorded as an important part of Canadian history. To this end, Frances Martin Day collected the stories and self-published them in 1989 as _Memoirs of the Vancouver Island Branch Overseas Club_ for the members of the Overseas Club and their families.

In the summer of 1995, these memoirs were brought to the attention of Phyllis Spence and Barbara Ladouceur, who quickly realized that the stories should be published in order to make them available to the general public and to preserve them for future generations. They had recently collected the oral histories of thirty-six Canadian war brides and had published them as *Blackouts to Bright Lights: Canadian War Bride Stories* (Ronsdale, 1995). The members of the Corps were enthusiastic about the new project, and it was agreed that Frances Martin Day, Phyllis Spence and Barbara Ladouceur would be the editors.

Since most of the stories in this collection were originally written for the families and friends of the members of the Overseas Club, it was necessary to refashion them for the general reading public. In order to give a more in-depth picture of the Canadian Red Cross Corps experiences, Phyllis Spence and Barbara Ladouceur interviewed members of the original Corps and integrated new information into the memoirs. Some members provided letters written home while overseas and these added important new details to their accounts. Many of the members also searched through their photo albums for pictures of their war work; these unique photos have been included wherever possible. Most of the women in this book have played an integral role in the evolution of their memoirs. Sadly, several of the women have passed away, and in these cases their families kindly agreed to participate in the editing process.

Women Overseas now proudly takes its place in the growing collection of books that are providing new insights into the important responsibilities that Canadian women took on during World War II and the Korean War. As P. H. Gordon says in *Fifty Years in the Red Cross*, "Without our women there would be no Red Cross as we know it." Certainly the memoirs in *Women Overseas* indicate that the women who served with the Canadian Red Cross Corps are heroes whose accomplishments have been overlooked for many years. Their legacy is now preserved to enlighten and inspire us, as well as future generations of Canadians.

Frances Martin Day, Phyllis Spence
and Barbara Ladouceur
August 1998

Original drawing by Frances Martin Day of the Red Cross Corps uniform hats: cap for dress uniform (top); tam for everyday use (middle); veil for VADs when nursing and for the escort officers (bottom).

Phyllis Elder Matheson

*"Rocket shells swished upwards,
tearing the night apart like a giant
hand tearing silk"*

—

Phyllis Elder Matheson was born and grew up in Montreal. Before 1939,
she worked mornings as a private secretary to a Presbyterian minister.
Afternoons and evenings she worked with the Montreal Repertory
Theatre—acting and working backstage. After the war she
focused on her family and volunteering with
the Social Services in Montreal.

Most of my war service seems to have been at the wheel of a car. In 1939, immediately after Canada declared war, there was almost no military transport, so a group of women was organized as volunteer drivers with their own cars. We reported to Military District No. 4 Headquarters in the Sun Life Building in Montreal. I was assigned to a permanent force lieutenant who oversaw the building of guard huts on all the bridges over the river and canals on the south side of the island of Montreal. The only thing that made me official was an OHMS (On His Majesty's Service) sign taped to the windshield of my car.

When that job finished I drove for the Child Welfare Association which organized the placement of evacuee children from England. The social workers visited the homes of all the people who had offered to take these evacuees, and we covered most of the Eastern Townships where many farm families had applied for children. We then drove the children to their new homes; that is until the ship *City of Benares* was sunk, and all the children aboard were lost. That put an end to the government evacuation scheme. I shall never forget the rows of empty beds that awaited the lost children in the reception centres.

At the beginning of 1941, I joined the Canadian Women's Transport Service. This group was organized by the late Evelyn Chambers who had been awarded the Military Cross while working with the FANYs (First Aid Nursing Yeomanry) during World War I. She had a FANY uniform sent from England as a model, and, apart from the nursing sisters, we were the first women in uniform in Canada during World War II. We were all volunteers who paid for our own uniforms and drove our own cars. Our nickname was "The Cocktail Crowd in the Ice Bag Hats."

At first most of our work was connected with salvage. We had an enormous vehicle which had once been a mobile library, and we struggled up and down Montreal's outside staircases with armfuls of magazines and newspapers. During the winter, the staircases were a nightmare. We also collected food hampers donated by a local grocery chain and delivered them to the needy families of some of the enlisted men.

Our training, which was to prepare us for overseas service, included first aid, home nursing, motor mechanics, poison gas courses, military map reading and army drill. The latter was conducted in the Grenadier Guards Armoury, by an NCO (non-commissioned officer), and we stamped and crashed our way around the Drill Hall with solemnity. What with the drilling and the heavy magazines it was no wonder that many of us developed back trouble. Later on, our drill sessions were moved to the Victoria Rifles Armoury, where the NCO in charge of us laughed himself sick and said that no one had marched like us since Queen Victoria had died.

When the Red Cross Society formed the Canadian Red Cross Corps, we were the nucleus of the Transport Division. We kept our uniforms, but were issued new cap and lapel badges. The other divisions of the Corps were the VADs (nursing), Food Administration and Office Administration. Each division had a distinctive uniform until we went overseas where we all wore the khaki uniforms of the Transport.

As members of the Red Cross Corps, our duties were now broadened to include the following: driving groups of men from factories to the Blood Donor Clinic and back to work again; taking the bottles of blood to the Canadian National Railway goods yards each evening; delivering samples of blood every afternoon to the Provincial Laboratory in Montreal for Wasserman tests; taking needles to the factory for sharpening and delivering; and picking up the empty blood bottles at the Royal Victoria Hospital where they were sterilized. All this was done in station wagons with removable seats, which belonged to the Red Cross.

In the autumn of 1941, five of us and our commandant, Mrs. Chambers, went to New York as guests of the American Red Cross. We led a parade of six thousand women in uniform down Fifth Avenue and were introduced to Mayor La Guardia. We were also entertained by two famous actresses, Leonora Corbett and Gertrude Lawrence. It was a memorable trip.

In order to conserve gasoline, the Red Cross acquired two motorcycles—one with a large box behind and one with a sidecar.

These were used for the transport of small items, including the Wassermann tubes, to the laboratory on Notre Dame Street East. This took place at 5 p.m. daily, right at rush hour. For motorcycle riding, we exchanged our khaki skirts for riding britches or jodhpurs. We created quite a sensation in downtown Montreal, especially when we stalled our machines in heavy traffic.

Those of us who owned cars were asked if we would volunteer to drive for the British Admiralty Technical Mission and the Allied Chemical Company. For this we were paid seven cents per mile, later increased to ten cents. Our passengers were munitions inspectors who travelled between the United Kingdom, Montreal and Washington, overseeing the production of munitions in local plants. This involved driving to Cherrier (just off the eastern end of the island of Montreal), Bouchard (just south of St. Jerome), Sherbrooke and Sorel, as well as many local factories. I saw the first tank christened at Montreal Locomotive Works and the first 25-pound gun at Sorel. I also chauffeured a British Army officer who was overseeing the shipping of tanks from the CPR Angus Shops to Russia. One group of munitions specialists set up a laboratory in the University of Montreal. I believe they were developing a new form of explosive. About that time all of us drivers were investigated by the RCMP. The conversations we overheard were probably top secret, but they were so scientific that they meant nothing to us.

In the spring of 1943, the first of our members went overseas. On the night of July 12, 1943, I boarded the _S.S. Baltrover_ along with twelve other Red Cross women. There were two other groups of passengers: some English boys who had been at Canadian schools and were being sent home to England and a party of Royal Canadian Naval Volunteer Reserve sub-lieutenants who were being sent on active service for the first time. All through the hot July night, coal continued to rumble into the ship's bunkers, making sleep impossible.

For five days the _S.S. Baltrover_ beat her way up the coast, followed closely by five or six other freighters and shepherded by two small escorts. There was a stop, at anchor off Sydney, Nova

Government of Canada Labour Exit Permit, issued to Phyllis Elder, 1943.

Scotia, and at dawn on the fifth day the thinning mist of early morning cleared just enough to reveal the narrow entrance to the harbour of St. John's, Newfoundland.

While the rumble of the anchor chain hung on the still cold air, a naval patrol boat shot out from the harbour entrance, and as the engine died, drifted smoothly close to the ship. In the bows appeared the figure of a naval officer, swathed in a heavy duffel coat and holding a megaphone, through which he addressed the bridge of the ship. "What is your name and the name of your owners? . . . What nationality? . . . Where are you bound? . . . What cargo? . . . How many passengers? . . . How many aliens?" Apparently the answers were satisfactory, for he waved his hand and called out, "We won't keep you long—I hope." The engine of the small craft leapt to life, and it passed on to the next ship in the little convoy to repeat the performance.

In about half an hour, the patrol boat returned to the head of the convoy and led the little line of ships safely through the minefield and into the harbour. Here they dispersed to their allotted places among the many and varied craft: trim destroyers holding themselves disdainfully aloof from smoke-stained coasters and corvettes, and minesweepers "whooping" happily to each other as they came and went. The grey of the ships was repeated in the shabby grey shanties clinging to the rocky cliffs which rose sheer from the waterfront.

At night this grey world was blotted out by a strict blackout into which most of the ship's crew disappeared as soon as they were off duty. Apparently there was more than just greyness to be found ashore for, some hours later, one of the crew came crawling aboard with his head split open, and several others didn't appear at all. With a worried frown, the purser went ashore the next morning to bail them out of jail, returning with the report that they had all been in a fight, but that the crew would be complete when the ship was due to sail.

In St. John's, the sub-lieutenants left the ship to report for active duty and more passengers came aboard, mostly women and children. All this time, cargo was being unloaded from the hold, then more cargo was stowed away, and four days after arrival, we were again ready to put to sea. At dawn we slipped quietly through the minefields, sailing alone to take up our place in the ocean convoy already assembling "somewhere off the coast of Newfoundland." Before we reached the rendezvous the inevitable fog had engulfed us and we were left to wallow alone in the submarine-infested waters. For twelve hours we steamed slowly along, on a course parallel with the convoy, until finally, the fog lifted and we were able to slip thankfully into line.

The English schoolboys were pressed into service to help act as lookouts and to make up gun crews. The gunnery officer was a British Army corporal and the armament consisted of one Oerlikon gun on the afterdeck, and two machine guns, one at each end of the bridge. The boys had not been properly equipped for the North Atlantic weather, but the Newfoundland Red Cross had rectified that by giving them warm woolies. Everyone had been issued a life jacket and a waterproof suit which had to be carried at all times. Each life jacket had a small red light clipped to the shoulder, activated by a battery that fitted into a special pocket in the jacket. Everyone was ordered to sleep in slacks, sweaters and socks; an officer made rounds each night, shining a flashlight into each bunk to make sure that these orders were followed. There were daily boat drills, and the girls were made responsible for the safety of some of the children of those families with more than two. There was also daily gun drill, during which the corporal directed the schoolboys, and the Oerlikon gun was fired each day at noon, with great ceremony.

There were also other passengers aboard, but they were confined to the forward part of the ship, making the lounge out of bounds to everyone else. They were a party of Distressed British Seamen. These were men whose ships had been torpedoed and who were being taken back to England—incommunicado for security reasons.

There was little to relieve the monotony of the crossing which took two weeks from St. John's to England. No one knew which port we were headed for—or if they did, they were not telling. The purser was a good friend and let us use his iron; in return, we ironed his shirts. One girl helped him with the account books and also helped the first officer in the infirmary. There being no doctor aboard, the two of them did their best with the help of a book for use on His Majesty's ships at sea. The weather was good in parts and bad in others, and in bad weather the trip to the smoking room, the only sitting room available, was hazardous. Access to it was only from the deck, with ropes being strung along in rough weather to provide a handhold.

One of the women passengers, the mother of two small children, was more interested in the crew than in the welfare of her son and daughter. One particular night when they were crying miserably, two of the Red Cross girls could stand it no longer. They went to the cabin and found the children, who complained that they were itchy. On investigation, it was found that they were covered with flea bites—the ship was far from clean. The girls undressed and bathed the children, dusted them and the bunks with Keating's Powder, and finally got the children to sleep. The powder had been bought in St. John's when it was realized that there were some unregistered passengers on board.

Two years later, when a Red Cross girl was returning to Halifax, she was recognized by an immigration officer who said, "Glad to see you made it across—we never thought you would!" Before the war, the *S.S. Baltrover* had been considered too old for the North Atlantic, but had been reinstated due to the wartime shortage of ships.

As our convoy neared the Irish coast, a storm scattered the neat lines of grey ships, and those with deck cargo had to turn and run before the towering seas. Our passenger ship forged ahead at a snail's pace, and twenty-three days after leaving Halifax, she was led through the minefields into the quiet waters of the Mersey.

On arrival in Liverpool we were met by an RTO sergeant who expected to be paid, in pounds sterling, for thirteen first-class tickets to London. The woman in charge of our party didn't have the money and the situation seemed desperate until I remembered my "mad money," a chamois bag worn around my neck which my father had filled with pound notes. Retiring behind some packing cases on the wharf, I partially undressed and produced enough pounds for the tickets—we were on our way!

It was the beginning of August 1943, and already the grass was growing among the heaps of rubble left by the German bombers, as though it could clothe the naked inner walls of buildings from which the outer walls had been torn. Beyond the port, the mellow English countryside looked much as it had in peacetime. There were fields under cultivation. The sturdy figures of the Land Army girls, the green and brown uniforms of working parties of Italian prisoners of war, coupled with the numerous airfields and army camps, were all additions to the peacetime landscape.

London is always London, but what a pitifully shabby London it was then: great gaping holes where buildings once stood, and those still standing were unbelievably dingy. Many of those which at first sight seemed to be undamaged were only empty shells. Ragged fragments of blackout curtains fluttered from what once were windows. Clouds of dust, which never seemed to have time to settle, swirled along the unwashed streets.

The people were almost as shabby as the buildings and they looked so tired. Before the war they had hurried along the streets, jumped on and off moving buses, and run up and down the escalators in the tube. Now they walked slowly and stood resignedly in queues for everything from fish to newspapers. At night many of them queued up again for a bunk in the underground tube stations. Whole families, carrying their bedding with them, went down night after night and slept there—within a few feet of the trains and almost under the feet of the passersby. Little children would run along to the canteen at the far end of the platform for a hot drink before they went to sleep. The wonder was that they could sleep in the midst of all this—these children who didn't remember sleeping anywhere else.

That autumn and winter of 1943, London—in fact, the whole of England—was packed to overflowing with troops. Every conceivable uniform was to be seen on the streets. To men on leave, London seemed a Mecca. From August 1943 to January 1944, I worked in the B.C. House canteen, open to men and women of all services, all nationalities, everyone including the police force. The food ran short regularly, but we never stopped serving meals. Looking back, I wonder what we used, but wartime England had produced endless substitutes. We made custard with powdered milk—grated on a cheese grater because it always solidified—no

Canadian Red Cross Corps House, Queen's Gate Terrace, London.

eggs and no sugar. The standard question was, "Will you have sausages or hamburger?"—"What's the difference?"—"One has skin and the other hasn't." The law said they must contain at least forty percent meat. On Saturdays and Sundays, the line of men at the counter snaked between the tables, up the stairs and out into the street, and it seemed to be never-ending. One especially gruelling Sunday, an exhausted voice from behind the serving hatch exclaimed, "The whole Canadian Army must be here today." Whereupon an equally exhausted voice from the waiting line answered, "No, only half—the other half's at the Beaver Club."

After one of those days we used to wonder whether we would ever get home, whether it was worth the effort of changing from smock to uniform and queuing for a bus. Sitting in the small stuffy dressing room, staring resignedly at our stained and roughened hands, it seemed easier to stay there until it was time to start work again. When the nights grew longer, going home meant groping through the blackout, very likely in an air raid, for at that time the Jerries were fond of short, early evening raids. Indoors, no one paid very much attention to them, but outside there was bound to be shrapnel, and it would be so stupid to be killed by one's own guns.

During the autumn and winter of 1943, there were several weddings in the Canadian Red Cross Hostel. In many cases, the bridegroom's leave was put forward suddenly, and the ceremonies took place at very short notice. My roommate, who had been engaged for two years, woke me up at seven one morning and said, "If I can get a special license, will you be my bridesmaid this afternoon?" From then on, that day will always be a rather blurred memory but, with the help of everyone who was off duty, the wedding did take place that afternoon, complete with a full service, organist, flowers, reception and wedding cake. Someone even had the groom's best uniform pressed and his buttons polished. Those weddings were always very happy affairs. Everyone worked hard but enjoyed doing it. They were often the scene of happy reunions—friends who had been stationed in different parts of the country for months would find themselves standing side-by-side in the crowded dining room of the hostel.

In January 1944, I was fortunate enough to be transferred back to my old job as a transport driver. Our vehicles were wooden-bodied station wagons, of assorted vintages, with the Canadian Red Cross emblem painted on the side. The Brits referred to them as shooting brakes! After working in the canteen underground, it was a wonderful relief to get back to a job in the fresh air—even in the English winter. The best part of the job was delivering supplies to Canadian medical units stationed outside London. The soft, faded colours of the winter sunlight were kinder to the shabby buildings than the clearer summer light. Supplies were delivered regularly to medical units stationed all through Surrey, Sussex and Hampshire, which meant driving through some of the most beautiful country in England. There were occasional trips to places farther afield. I remember the awful devastation of Coventry and the beauty of the Essex countryside after a winter storm which had left each tree and hedge clothed in a sheet of silver ice.

Earlier, when there had been a threat of invasion, all the place names and road signs had been removed, so finding one's way about the country was difficult. The only thing that didn't change was the names of the pubs, and we used them as our sign posts. One was told to go as far as the "Jolly Roger," where the left fork went to Staines and the right to Slough. To hear us giving directions to each other sounded as though our life was one big pub crawl.

The city streets were confusing, too; many of those shown on the map didn't exist anymore. They had been obliterated by the Blitz. I remember once suddenly finding myself in the middle of Billingsgate, reputedly one of the toughest districts in London. The narrow street was teeming with men hurrying back and forth with fish baskets piled high on their heads and shouting to one another in unintelligible Cockney. One of them stopped by the car and I quite expected to be told to "Get the blinkin' h—— out of here!" But instead he said, "Kin I 'elp ye, miss?" When I said that I was looking for the Customs House, he said, "Strite along, on yer right, miss." Then he bellowed at the others, "Out of the way, you up there—the lady wants to come through!" Miraculously the road ahead cleared and through I went.

The London bobbies were wonderfully helpful. One day, one of our drivers was sent to deliver a parcel to Mrs. Churchill. At the entrance to Downing Street, the policeman on duty stopped her and asked where she was going. When she told him she had a parcel for Mrs. Churchill, he said, with all seriousness, "Oh yes, miss, she lives at No. 10—just over there."

Downing Street reminds me of Buckingham Palace and the thrill I received when I first drove through those gates, taking my passenger to an audience with the Queen. On another occasion, one of our ancient vehicles nearly broke down outside the back door of the Palace. The driver had been sent to collect some honey which Princess Elizabeth and Princess Margaret donated regularly to the Red Cross Children's Nurseries. With a vague picture of a few tins of honey in her mind's eye, the driver light-heartedly set off for the Palace. About an hour later she came back looking very upset, and exclaimed, "The Princesses must have the most prolific bees in the world; they loaded honey into the station wagon until the springs almost touched the ground. I very nearly couldn't get going and had visions of being towed away. I've crawled all the way back along Piccadilly, with everyone honking at me, and if we don't get the car unloaded immediately it will fall apart in the street."

During February and March of 1944 the Germans stepped up their raids on London, and we had what was commonly known as the "Little Blitz." The raids lasted only an hour or two, but sometimes there were two or three "Alerts" in one night. On one unforgettable night, we heard a bomb whistle, and not long after, two came down at the corner of the street where we lived. The second two bombs didn't whistle like the first bomb we heard—they were too close for that. They made a noise like an express train going past at high speed. Then everything seemed to heave up, the house swayed and showers of glass and rubble came down all around.

One of the bombs was a new type of incendiary—highly efficacious. The building it hit was about six storeys high and was instantly smothered in a sheet of flame. Someone came and said that the gas main, which passed under our house, was burning and that we must be ready to leave at any moment. Apparently they got it under control, as we didn't blow up, and eventually most of the household went back to bed. Tomorrow was another day starting at 7 a.m. and sleep was the most important thing at the moment. The unfortunate girls on the fire-watch team spent what remained of the night sitting on the roof.

The next day, the repair squad appeared and asked if they might set up a temporary office in our house. In return we got our windows replaced—with cardboard—before anyone else in the street. We also found ourselves running a non-stop canteen in our kitchen, feeding sandwiches and tea to the workmen, so it was a doubtful advantage.

After that particular incident, new air-raid precautions were enforced at our hostel. When the "Alert" sounded, we all had to don tin hats, respirators and haversacks containing a change of clothing. Then we were herded down into the cellars where we stood propped against the stone walls of the passages, with the door leading to the outside area left open for easy exit. It was extremely cold and our minds went numb with tiredness, but there we had to stay until the "All Clear" sounded. One night a girl came down eating a piece of cake. When someone remarked that it seemed an odd time for a snack, the cake-eater answered, "I had been saving it for tomorrow, but decided to have it now. After all, I may not be alive to enjoy it tomorrow."

Early in 1944, our headquarters was moved from Berkeley Square to Burlington Gardens and new fire-watch teams were organized. Now we each had to do fire-watch duty twice in every nine nights—once at the hostel and once at headquarters. At the hostel, six girls were on duty each night. Two had to stay awake for two hours while the other four slept on mattresses in the next room. Very few of us were able to sleep at all under these conditions. Nevertheless, we were all on regular duty again the following day.

At headquarters there was an ARP (Air-Raid Precaution) post under one corner of the building, and this was manned each night by representatives of all the tenants in the block. In addition to the other Red Cross girls, my team consisted of an elderly man from the Red Cross shipping department, an orchestra leader who was often away on tour, a Jewish tailor who spent the evenings busily sewing decorations on American uniforms, and two hat check girls from the Bucks Club who rejoiced in the improbable names of Keene and Mustard. We all reported to the post as soon as the day's work was over and were given five shillings with which to buy dinner. Any restaurant we patronized was supposed to be not more than one hundred yards from the post, but this was stretched to allow us to go as far as Shaftesbury Avenue, there being no restaurants closer than that.

Accommodation was provided for us to sleep in the post: two small, stuffy brick cells with double-decker bunks opened off the central room. However, we were allowed to sleep upstairs in our building, provided that we immediately reported to the post when the "Alert" sounded. Sleeping on the lower floors near the shipping department was unpleasant because of the rats among the packing cases, but these never bothered us on the upper floors, where we set up canvas cots in the offices. When the "Alert" sounded, we broke all speed records getting down the stairs, out into the street and around the corner to the post. The orchestra leader used to complain that we always made it before he had time to climb into his trousers. In the morning we entertained all the fire-watch team with breakfast in the headquarters canteen where we made them toast and coffee.

By springtime, preparations for the Allied invasion of Europe had accelerated. D-Day had been talked about for so long that when it actually arrived, no one could really believe it. For months ahead of time, southern England was one great big armed camp. Troops were everywhere and the roads were a solid mass of moving convoys. Our trips to the Canadian Army hospitals would have been almost impossible, had it not been for the motorcycle dispatch riders who rode with every convoy. They would see the station wagon with the Red Cross insignia and would lead us through and past the long line of vehicles, sending us on our way with a cheery wave. The whole of southern England became a restricted area and we were issued "laissez-passers" which read: "This is to certify that Miss _____ is a driver for the Canadian Red Cross Society. Her work involves the conveyance of supplies and personnel to Canadian Military Hospitals, some of which are in the restricted area. She always returns the same day. It is requested that she be allowed to carry out these services." We particularly enjoyed the part about always returning the same day: if our lives were not very well protected, our virtue most certainly was.

On D-Day I had to deliver supplies to a hospital at Cuckfield, only about sixteen miles from the south coast. It was unbelievable: all the troop concentrations had gone, the countryside was deserted, and only the sound of birds broke the silence. I said a silent prayer for the men who had been there so recently.

With the invasion came a new visitor to London. One evening the "Alert" sounded and we all trooped down to the cellars. Distant gunfire rumbled through the warm, still air. Suddenly the heavy guns in Hyde Park took up the chorus. Next the mobile naval gun nearby opened up—something was very close. The gunfire became frenzied, the naval gun sounded like an angry watchdog barking at a prowler in the night. Rocket shells swished upwards, tearing the night apart like a giant hand tearing silk. Through all this came the sound of a strangely sputtering engine —flying very low. Would it clear the roof? Instinctively everyone crouched down as the noise went over and around and then started to fade into the distance. No one moved for a moment and then someone whispered, "What the Hell was that?"

All through that night the guns muttered and grumbled and roared at intervals. They appeared angry and baffled by this new menace which flew so low that it was beneath their range. For three days and nights they were almost never silent, and the air was full of falling shrapnel which did almost as much damage as the new bomb. The people were dazed with the noise and fear of this new weapon. It struck at anything and everything. In the daytime it could be seen flying low, like a blunt-winged plane with curved fuselage, carrying a curious-looking tube on its tail. At night its path was marked by the red flare that streaked out behind it, and always there was the unmistakable stutter of its engine. When the engine stopped, the thing went into a glide— sometimes for a few yards, sometimes for a mile or more. Usually it glided straight ahead, but sometimes it banked around like a plane about to land. These were the infamous "buzz bombs."

One never knew where the bombs would fall. Sometimes a bomb would hit a train or the tracks and cause a delay, but a re-pair gang would immediately set to work and the line would be serviceable again in a matter of hours. Other times a bomb would fly along beside a moving train; then suddenly, as if by some quirk of fate, it would turn away and hit a nearby building. The train passengers would see destruction and death receding into the dis-tance and wonder why it had been someone else's turn to die. Sometimes a busload of people would come close to oblivion and have to throw themselves under the seats. The greatest damage, apart from a direct hit, was caused by flying glass. The bombs did not penetrate very deeply into the ground but the surface blast covered a wide area. In a closely built-up East End district, one bomb damaged fifty houses.

The windows of buses and underground trains were made shat-terproof by a protective covering, making it very difficult to see out. To deter people from pulling off this covering, there were illustrated posters bearing the admonition:

> *Please pardon me*
> *For my correction,*
> *That stuff is there*
> *For your protection.*

On the edge of one of the posters someone had scrawled the retort:

> *I thank you*
> *For your information*
> *But I can't see*
> *The bloody station!*

The southern and eastern districts of London bore the brunt of the attacks. In some areas scarcely a single house was left undamaged. Repair men were everywhere, boarding up broken windows and attempting to make the damaged houses habitable. In most cases, only one room could be repaired, and the family had to live in it. The repairs never stopped because the task was gigantic. Repairmen were killed by blasts which hurled them from their ladders or scaffolding. The hospitals were filled with casualties, including women and children, slashed beyond recognition by flying glass.

The authorities gave permission to the Canadian Red Cross to donate blankets and clothing to these casualties, and we delivered packing cases to hospitals in all the hardest hit districts. These supplies enabled the less serious but homeless casualties to be evacuated to a rest centre, thus freeing beds for the new casualties which the morrow would inevitably bring.

The West End, although it did not suffer so badly, was by no means untouched. At noon one day the Annex of the Regent's Palace Hotel was hit. One night Conduit Street was smashed and the south side of Berkeley Square was damaged. On two occasions a piece was blown out of the garden of Buckingham Palace. The blast swept across Green Park, and all the buildings along Piccadilly, from Hyde Park Corner to the Park Lane Hotel, lost their windows. One Sunday the Guards' Chapel received a direct hit during morning service and one night an American barracks in Chelsea received a direct hit. The next morning, men's bodies were still being carried out and laid in rows along the pavement. Strange to think that only the night before, these silent forms were probably strolling along Piccadilly, whistling at silken ankles passing in the blackout.

All through these months the ARP (Air-Raid Precaution) Services did a magnificent job. Almost before the dust of an explosion had settled, they were at the scene and each department was doing its work quickly and quietly. Operations were directed by a central figure called the "Incident Officer." As the various services arrived at the scene, they reported to and took their orders from

A V-1 attack in London in the summer of 1944.

him. Mobile first-aid units were set up in the nearest undamaged building. Rescue squads carried out the casualties, the Incident Officer having obtained a list of the inhabitants of the building from the local air-raid warden. The ambulances transported the serious cases to hospitals and the walking cases to the nearest rest centres—and suddenly, miraculously, comparative order was restored. If the water, gas and electricity supply had been cut, mobile bath units would appear on the scene and the Ministry of Food Flying Squad Mobile Canteens would feed the people until such time as the public services were restored.

Driving back into London one day, after delivering supplies to hospitals in the country, I realized that the street I was on had been blasted since I had driven along it that morning. A neat little pile of rubble sat in the gutter opposite the front of each of the little cottages up and down the long street. The housewives had started sweeping up almost before the last of the dust had settled; they had hung the dusty curtains out on the line, tacked bits of cardboard over the broken windows and brushed the plaster dust out of their hair. Now some of them were clacking down the road in their wooden-soled shoes (leather was in short supply) to see what they could find in the shops for supper. Others were watching for their children to come home from school and wondering, no doubt, whether they should try and send them out of London.

Eventually the authorities instituted an alarm system in the city which was really quite ingenious. The "All Clear" sounded every morning at about seven o'clock, in time to get everyone up and on the go. By the time breakfast was ready the "Alert" would sound, but by that time it was too late to go back to the shelters, so people went off to work. In order to maintain peace of mind among their employees, the larger firms and shops erected flag poles on their roofs. Beside these stood "spotters" with binoculars. When they spotted a buzz bomb headed their way, they would run up a red cylinder and press a button to ring alarm bells throughout the building. The people in the streets could take cover when they saw the red cylinder go up, and those inside the building could crawl under their desks when the bells rang. We used to watch one imperturbable man in an office across the street. When the bells rang, he would peer over the top of his glasses, and yell, "Imminent danger!" and return to work, while some of his fellow workers would disappear under their desks and others would, unhappily, follow his example.

One of the most difficult places to be during these times was behind the wheel of a car. One couldn't see the cylinders go up when one was watching the traffic and one couldn't hear the alarm bells. Suddenly everyone in the street would start to run, and that was the signal to stop the car and run to the nearest cover—invariably much too late if the bomb was really close.

There was something almost hypnotic about the sound of those buzz bomb engines. I can remember standing in the street and listening to one coming nearer and nearer and not even noticing that two Air Force men were standing nearby. Suddenly the motor cut out—I found myself flying down some area steps with an Air Force man holding each of my hands, and we all crouched in a corner while the thing glided over and went off in the park, a block away.

London of 1944 was a strange place—the city of the shadow of death. In one of the railway freight sheds, I noticed a huge pile of long wooden boxes and asked what they were. "Coffins," answered the agent, "they're runnin' short 'ere so we've 'ad to ship some in from out of town." Those coffins reminded me of a day not long before. It was a bleak, grey day when I had been driving down a street in the East End and had met a funeral procession. There were four hearses carrying four coffins and one car carrying what remained of that family—such a little group of mourners who looked so unbearably tired—people, who had gone through so much and now were doing it all over again. It has been asked how they could be so brave. They weren't brave—they were just too tired to feel anything, even fear.

The tiredness was like a pall, threatening to bury one. It was hard to keep awake, especially while driving alone in the country. Night work was purgatory. Our working day started at 8:30 a.m., and the special trains taking the British war brides to embarkation ports always left Euston Station at about 1 a.m. The wives and children came into London on their own, were met at their respective stations, driven to reception centres and then driven to Euston at night. Sometimes their parents came with them, as far as the London stations. There we had to tell them that they must say goodbye, and then pretend to be interested in the posters on the walls while they cut their family ties in the dubious privacy of Victoria or Charing Cross Station. The thought of exchanging a life in Edenbridge or East Grinstead for one in northern Saskatchewan or central New Brunswick made my blood run cold.

It ran even colder on one occasion when I was driving a station wagon load of wives and children. We were just passing the front of Buckingham Palace; the wives and children were packed in like sardines, and the overnight bags, diaper bags and bottle bags were tucked around their feet. Suddenly I heard the all too familiar sound in the sky. It was obvious that no one could get out of the station wagon in a hurry, so I kept on driving and prayed. I wondered if the King and Queen were at home and if they were praying, too. The "thing" kept on going and so did we.

On the nights when the special trains left, we would drive all day, go home to supper and then start moving the wives and children to Euston. There were only five drivers so we had to keep going back and forth. We were tired, the mothers were tired and the children were exhausted. We would trudge back and forth, up and down the platform carrying babies, bags and sleeping toddlers, get them safely aboard and then go back for the next lot. Most of the women had never travelled farther than Brighton to London; they were completely disorganized, and physically and emotionally beaten. A few of them invariably lost their bags and, as these contained food, diapers and baby bottles for a twelve-hour trip, panic would ensue. The things always turned up, but only after much searching, sometimes of several cars of the train.

One trainload included several of our own girls, all of whom were pregnant and two of whom were already widows. Their husbands had been killed in action. They were being sent home to have their babies in safety. They also were cutting ties. This wartime life in which they had loved and married, and in which their friends had shared their happiness and their tragedy, was to be exchanged for the unreality of home life, where everyone would be kind and no one would understand. We put them aboard last of all, in a small carriage which we had saved just for them. The dim blackout lights shaded their misery and veiled their tears, but their hands clung to ours and we stayed with them until the last possible moment. The glass roof of the station hung menacingly over their heads, and we tried not to think about what the glass could do under the impact of a surface blast.

Bomb blasts were a constant danger, and during all that time windows were left partly open so that they wouldn't smash under pressure. In the hostel, the girls who slept on the top floors moved mattresses down to the floor of the sitting-room, and we spent the nights in neat rows, side by side. In anticipation of reinforcements arriving, the Ministry of Works had renovated a bombed house nearby, and those of us who were off duty had spent one Saturday cleaning it up for the new arrivals. By evening all was in readiness and we dragged ourselves home, tired but satisfied that it looked clean and inviting. During the night there was a loud explosion, obviously not far away, and from the floor of the sitting room a tired voice said, "What's the betting that was Onslow Gardens?" In the morning we didn't even wait to see; we just gathered up the brooms, pails and mops, and went back. Sure enough—broken windows and plaster dust. And so we worked all day Sunday.

The train carrying the reinforcements arrived at night and we met them at Euston Station. Not wanting to alarm them unduly, but feeling that they should be prepared for what might happen, I explained that if I stopped the station wagon and ran for cover—they must follow suit. As we stopped for the first, well-shielded red traffic light, I heard a commotion behind me and, looking around, realized that all the girls were poised for instant flight. Not being used to the blackout, they had not realized that we had stopped for a red light. After that, each time we had to stop for one, I sang out, "Red light—sit tight," and the girls laughed rather shakily.

One night the sleepers in the sitting room were awakened by a nearby explosion, followed by a telephone call asking that transport be sent to the Army and Navy Hotel to evacuate the walking wounded. As I rounded a corner near the hotel, a warden stepped out with his hand up and said, "I shouldn't go that way if I was you, miss. You see, there ain't no middle to the road." I could see his point and so followed his directions to make a detour.

It seemed an incredibly short time since the explosion, but already the lobby of the hotel was manned by the Women's Voluntary Services. Two perfectly groomed, middle-aged ladies were seated behind a table. One felt that they must have been ready and waiting for the "incident" to take place. How else could they have managed to look like that in such a short time? They were taking down the names of survivors and checking them off on the hotel register. They gave me my instructions and assigned me a helper, a young Canadian Army officer who was spending a week's leave at the nearby Junior Officers' Club. The first survivor he carried out was an elderly and very frail retired British Army colonel—the Outpost-of-Empire type. The colonel was very indignant at being carried in his pyjamas and wrapped in a blanket, but his feet were bare and the ground was covered with broken glass which crunched under the wheels of the car. The old gentleman had just been badly shaken up, but he was very gracious and apologized for being a nuisance. This was more than my young helper could take. As he sat back in the station wagon, after carrying the colonel into the Reception Centre, he said, "This is too much for me; I'm applying to go back into action tomorrow. A little quiet mortar fire is more in my line than this sort of thing!"

That was the night that one end of Bute Street was destroyed, including a little house which had once belonged to some friends of mine and of which I had many happy memories. Nothing was left of it; it was as though a giant knife had cut away the corner as one might cut the corner off a cake. The dust was still rising from the rubble, and halfway up a wall which was still standing, a small flame flickered from the end of a broken gas pipe.

The worst night of all was one that I spent in the home of a friend whose husband was out of town for a few days. Their handsome flat was in a fairly tall, modern building and before the night was out, she and I felt like a pair of sitting ducks. We were both tired and went to our respective rooms early—I to enjoy the luxury of smooth sheets after the rough unbleached cotton of our hostel bedding. I didn't have much time to enjoy them, for the buzz bombs came over all night long. Each time one headed our way, we ran into the corridor and crouched there as the thing passed overhead. In the morning, while we sipped our coffee, we read the paper, the headline of which screamed, "Worst night yet—83 Buzz Bombs." We smiled wanly at each other, and she said, "I hope my husband doesn't hear about this."

One day we were ordered to pack one suitcase each, with a complete change of uniform, underwear and night clothes. Being women we were much more interested in preserving our prized possessions, and some girls included their best evening dresses. I packed my fur coat and my cultured pearls along with the more necessary items. We discovered subsequently that this was part of a plan to evacuate essential services from London. It was good to know that we were now considered important enough to be included in this plan. It had been disillusioning to find, on first arriving from Canada, that there was no air-raid shelter for us.

Although the official evacuation of London never did take place, there was an unofficial move away from the city. Having sent my pearls and fur coat off into the blue had reminded me that the insurance on them would soon be due for renewal. The insurance company's office was near our headquarters, so I went down there soon after in my lunch hour. The place was deserted and a sign on the door informed me that they had moved to Scotland. "Lucky you!" I thought to myself.

The Dominion Bank in the city did not leave town, but they took some precautions. I was sent there one day and walked into a completely deserted building. It was eerie, to say the least, to find a large bank with not a living soul in sight—rather like the "Marie Celeste." On the counter was a sign saying, "This way, please." Following the arrow brought me to a circular iron staircase, which wound down into the cellar. At the bottom were the bank personnel, working away in makeshift quarters. Business, though not quite as usual, was the order of the day.

Eventually London was declared out of bounds to our troops. Driving up from the country one day, I picked up a hitchhiker, a Canadian soldier. When I asked where he was going, he begged me to take him into town where his wife and children lived. He hadn't heard from them and was sick with worry. Against my better judgment, I agreed to smuggle him in, and he crouched down on the floor of the station wagon. As he slipped out near an underground station, I prayed that he would find his family alive and well.

Many of our men had married English girls, and if these wives became pregnant, they were each entitled to a free layette from the Canadian Red Cross. So it was not at all unusual to find a big, hulking Canadian soldier hanging around the door of our headquarters, getting up his nerve to enter and ask for baby clothes. We would rescue these men, take them up to the Civilian Relief Department where the workers would welcome them and help them choose between "pink for girls" and "blue for boys." They would leave wreathed in smiles and accompanied by good wishes.

That summer of 1944, theatres, hotels and restaurants were no longer filled, and a friend, coming up from a hospital near Aldershot, was surprised to find that we could get good theatre seats and dinner without advance reservations. He was also delighted to be given a room at the Savoy overlooking the river with a magnificent view of South London. Not wanting to spoil his leave, but feeling that he should have some prior warning, I urged him to take cover if it should turn out to be a noisy night. He obviously thought that I was exaggerating the whole thing, but telephoned me the next morning to say, "Thanks for the advice—I spent most of the night under the bed."

Apart from the noise of the buzz bombs themselves, London was strangely silent. As has already been mentioned, when the buzz bombs first started coming over, the guns in Hyde Park had opened up, but it soon became apparent that this would result in more casualties from our own shrapnel than anything else. Accordingly, the guns and the barrage balloons were moved south of the city and anything which got past them came on unchallenged.

Before the move out of London took place, I was sent one day with some civilian relief cases to the Channel Islands' Relief office. This was in the basement of a house in Mayfair and was administered by two gentle, elderly ladies. The three of us were standing on the pavement, wondering how to get the great heavy wooden cases down the area steps, when the guns in Hyde Park opened up. I started to shake with fright, but the little old ladies paid not the slightest attention. They looked up and down the street, and one of them spotted a coalman unloading a lorry in the next block. In no time she was back with him, and with great good humour, he carried all the cases down into the basement.

Unloading heavy cases was never a real problem, because there was always someone offering to help. At one of the railway stations, I had to deliver a case of chocolate for shipment by rail to a hospital in the north. By careful maneuvering I managed to pull the case over the tailgate so that it fell onto a hand trolley. Feeling very pleased with myself, I then grabbed the handles of the trolley and pulled down. Nothing happened, even when I jumped on them. The case weighed more than I did. Suddenly I heard laughter behind me and turned to see a very tall British guardsman. He said, "I think you could use some help, miss," and in no time the case was in the shipping room, and my benefactor went on his way, puffing a Canadian cigarette—a token of my thanks.

Learning to drive a route in the blackout which I had never seen in daylight was a hazardous experience. On the straight stretches, I kept count of the traffic lights passed, and at turning points, I hoped for a glimpse of some landmark to pinpoint the place. In the early hours of the morning, after being on duty for sixteen hours, my brain grew tired and I sometimes lost count of traffic lights. On one of these occasions I found myself in Regent's Park and never really knew how I got back onto the right route. On revisiting London some years later, I drove from Marylebone Road to the Camden Town Underground just to see what it looked like!

In order that those of our girls attached to medical units might be billeted with the nursing sisters, we all wore small metal "pips" on our shoulders, and were given the rank of lieutenant (Red Cross). When going out with someone other than an officer, we simply removed the "pips" and put them in our pocket.

Total mobilization meant just that: everyone had some part to play, some job to do, even the older people. On a weekend leave, I went to Ashdown Forest to stay with the headmistresses of my old school. They were two very aristocratic, elderly ladies, whose war work took the form of growing vegetables, which they did wearing slacks and sunbonnets. They were also members of the local Air-Raid Precautions. Upon my arrival they announced that they were to take part in an exercise the following morning.

By nine o'clock we were ready and waiting for the alarm to be given, and it was—by a son of one of the local gentry, who pedalled past the cottage on his bicycle, blowing a Boy Scout whistle. This was the signal for us to spring into action. One of the ladies picked up a stirrup-pump and I grabbed a pail—dumping out half the water because otherwise I couldn't lift it—and we hotfooted it down the lane, followed at some distance by the other lady, whose rheumatism slowed her up and who kept calling, "Wait for me, dears."

About a hundred yards away, we came upon the "incident" where, supposedly, a stray buzz bomb had come down and set fire to the bracken. Several elderly members of the local aristocracy were gathered and I was formally introduced, after which we all went home. The thought of preventing the destruction of Ashdown Forest with stirrup-pumps seemed perfectly ludicrous to me, but the others appeared quite satisfied with the arrangements. It was this "never admit defeat" attitude and the inexhaustible sense of humour which won the war.

After the buzz bombs, came the rockets or V-2s. The first of these came down in Hammersmith, doing considerable damage. The next morning the newspapers reported that a gas main had exploded. From then on, this new weapon was known as "the flying gas main." Although these new V-2s were just as deadly as the buzz bombs, they never had the same demoralizing effect—probably because there was no defence against them. Since they gave absolutely no warning, there was no time to be afraid.

When our commissioner was about to return to Canada, I was sent to the Censorship Office to collect all the written matter which he proposed to take with him and which had to be censored before leaving the country. The clerk who handed me the documents said, "Oh yes, and don't forget to remind the General that he must not mention the flying gas mains outside this country. Officially we're not having them!"

This same commissioner had been a member of the Home Guard and had taken his turn on night duty with the guns in Hyde Park. As he was leaving to return to Canada, he found he had forgotten to hand in some of his equipment and asked me to do so for him. Off I went to the artillery post and, just as I was leaving, a sergeant came running after me. "Excuse me, miss," he asked, "But was Gunner Price a Major-General in the Canadian Army?" When I answered yes, he replied, "Then I think he would like to keep these," and handed me the General's "dog tags" which had been found in the respirator haversack.

May 8, 1945, VE-Day: trainloads of Allied prisoners of war were arriving at Waterloo Station and Red Cross girls were there, handing out chocolate, cigarettes, etc. Their supplies kept running out and Transport kept receiving calls to bring more. The crowds grew and grew in and around Piccadilly Circus. About 3 p.m., I managed to drive back to headquarters to pick up more supplies, with the amplifiers broadcasting Churchill's voice and servicemen clinging to the sides and roof of the wagon.

Eventually we had to make the return trip from headquarters to Waterloo Station via the Albert Bridge. When our work at Waterloo Station was done, I left my wagon at Corps House and walked back to the Park Lane Hotel to join two friends. After dinner we went across the park to the Palace, where the crowd continued growing until it was wall-to-wall people. The Royal Family came out on the balcony several times, and the cheering and singing continued far into the night. A memorable evening!

The full story of the people of England during these years is written in the hearts of those who shared with them the shortages, the cold winters, the tiredness and the danger. It is also written in a set of volumes containing the names of all the civilians who were killed. These volumes are housed in Westminster Abbey where one volume is always on display in a glass case and a page is turned each day. Those who would like to know the whole story can read it there.

In June of 1945, the first draft of Corps girls returned home to Canada, with myself among them. The Transport Department drove our group to Addison Road Station to catch the train for Greenock. There were thirty-four of us under the care of a junior army officer. We travelled all night and arrived early the next afternoon at the port. There we boarded a tender, and the pessimists among us pointed to the smallest ship in sight and said, "What's the betting that's ours?" For once, however, we were in luck; ours was the *Aquitania*.

We were among the last to board and our arrival was greeted by a salvo of wolf whistles from the troops who were leaning over the side of the ship. Not having eaten since the evening before, we searched for food, but were told we would get only two meals a day and nothing until that evening. There were over seven thousand men aboard and thirty-six women—our group, an Auxiliary Territorial Service girl and one stewardess. Four of us shared what would normally be a two-berth cabin. The floor space was so small, we had to take turns getting dressed.

The only time we sat on chairs was in the dining saloon; otherwise it was the floor. The tannoy system seemed to blast non-stop instructions, and daily boat drill was the only activity. The trip lasted only five days and it was here that I met my future husband, so it always seemed to me to have been a good crossing. The arrival in Halifax was memorable—bands, sirens, fireboats, waving, cheering crowds—seven thousand men and thirty-six women happy to be home!

Frances Martin Day

"I decided to go . . . there was
a war to be won"

—

Frances Martin Day was born in Craik, Saskatchewan and then
moved to Vancouver where she spent her childhood. She
was studying Art, Fashion and Drawing in Montreal
when she joined the Red Cross. Fran went on
to be an accomplished artist and is the
recipient of many awards.

Growing up in Vancouver was idyllic for a teenager, as it offered so much in the way of magnificent scenery: the mountains where I skied, the ocean where I could swim or sail, the sandy beaches where a group of my friends could dig for clams and then roast them over a bonfire. It was a happy, carefree time when I could attend school and then go out and play an energetic game of tennis or grass hockey afterwards. But suddenly it was all over. World War II began in September 1939, and immediately the carefree world became serious and sombre.

Arthur Norman Martin, my fiancé, had joined the permanent Royal Canadian Air Force in 1937 after he graduated from the University of British Columbia. We could not marry, however, since prior to the beginning of the war, flying officers were not allowed to marry till they became flight lieutenants. The war changed all that and, at the beginning of January 1940, I travelled four days across Canada by train to Toronto, where we were married at Deer Park United Church with my aunt, cousin and several of Norman's fellow officers present.

Two years later, after Norman became involved with Canada's intensive flying-training programme at Camp Borden in Ontario, we moved to Montreal where Norman was now a wing commander in charge of flying at No. 3 Training Command at headquarters. He felt deeply that he should contribute more to the war effort, and in August 1943, he got his wish and was posted overseas. His new post was with the 6th Bomber Group in Yorkshire where he was squadron commander at Skipton on Swale. At that time many members of the armed forces were flown from Dorval Airport to England in the military airplanes of the Ferry Command. Driving Norman to Dorval Airport in the dark of the early morning, and being brave, was difficult. What did we say? It was no time for words, only a long warm hug, and then I watched him walk off until he disappeared into the darkness.

At the time Norman was posted overseas, I was already involved with the Blood Donor Clinic in Montreal once a week, keeping the blood donation records. After he left, I decided to take a more active role in the Red Cross and joined the Office Administration

Section where I worked in the main office, assisting girls to complete the paperwork involved in going overseas with the Canadian Red Cross Corps. I wanted to go overseas myself, but Norman thought it was too dangerous. Still, it seemed ridiculous for me to be helping other women complete their papers to go overseas and for me to remain behind. Finally I suggested to Dorothy Mundy, who was on her way overseas, that she should talk to Norman in England and explain to him that working overseas for the Red Cross wasn't as hazardous as it might seem. She convinced him, and he promptly wrote and urged me to move heaven and earth to join him in England. We were very young and very much in love—so I did.

I was in the unique situation of having a dependant—my son Grant, a dear little three-year-old. I could not take him with me to England, and for a time I did not know what to do. Norman felt that the war would only last about another year, and he suggested leaving Grant for a short time with his grandmother (Mrs. Matie Parks) and my sister and brother-in-law (Eunice and Sandy Sanderhoff) who would all love him dearly until we returned from the war. My brother-in-law Sandy was one of the United States foreign service officers posted at Fort Pepperall, St. John's, Newfoundland. Today I cannot imagine how I even considered leaving Grant for a year. But understanding war requires understanding how it was in wartime—living from day to day and grasping at straws of happiness when you could. In war there is no certainty for tomorrow, particularly at that time when the air raids across Germany were at their peak.

My lawyer drew up papers that resolved my problems regarding guardianship of Grant while I worked overseas; they were basically temporary adoption papers for the duration of the war, until Norman and I returned to Canada. As I now had no dependant, I put my name on the waiting list for overseas duty and waited impatiently. The call came in January 1944. Ten of us, selected from across Canada, were to leave for England. I passed my physical, holding my breath because I had a heart murmur—my last hurdle. I sent a cable to Norman to say I was coming; the thought of being together again was pure elation. But Norman never received the cable as he was shot down over Magdeburg when the German night fighters were at their prime. My life seemed over. I was stunned and numb to the point I couldn't feel anything.

Quite naturally, my family urged me to relinquish my overseas posting. My commandant and adjutant pointed out, however, that I had worked hard to gain my posting: I had volunteered over two hundred hours a month at the Office Administration and the Blood Donor Clinic. They had even gone to Ottawa at one point to recommend an early posting for me. They also felt that being involved overseas would help me bridge a difficult time in my life. I decided to go, not only to be busy enough to ease my sadness, but there was a war to be won.

The ten of us arrived by train in New York where we stayed for several days while our convoy was convening. On the day of our departure, we all staggered with our heavy duffel bags onto a tugboat that was bouncing about on a wintry ocean. When the tugboat reached the Dutch ship _Curacao_ anchored in New York harbour in the freezing drizzle, we were given instructions to leap from the tugboat to a small, wet platform that was at the bottom of stairs which came down from the ship's deck. The whole idea was frightening since we knew if we didn't make the jump, we would go down like a stone with all our gear. I am happy to report that, athletically inclined or not, we all made it!

Our ship was one of 125 in our convoy surrounded by the famous and wonderful Canadian corvettes which were assigned to protect us. Besides our group, there were fifteen passengers who were escaping from Dutch colonies now threatened by the Japanese. About halfway across the Atlantic (we were at sea for ten days), the whistles blew and panic reigned. We were supposed to carry our life jackets at all times, which we did, except when we would lay them in a corner while we were eating or visiting. With sheer animal aggressiveness, the civilians grabbed our jackets because they couldn't find their own. It was my first exposure to how shallow our "civilized" behaviour can be. Apparently there were German subs nearby, but luckily there were no further incidents.

Arriving in London by train after we had disembarked from the *Curacao* in Glasgow, we soon found ourselves at Corps House at Queen's Gate Terrace, where we were given room assignments, regulations and gas masks. My room was on the top floor where I roomed with Doris Mabe and other girls who were coming or going to different posts.

One night, soon after we arrived, the sirens started up. Doris and I had not really experienced any air raids at this point, and our curiosity urged us to see what was going on. We turned out all our lights and then opened the blackout curtains. What a sight to see the searchlights combing the sky, picking out the many barrage balloons that hung over London at that time. Then a plane appeared, flying very low and with fire coming from the tail. I felt that the pilot must be injured or dead. Suddenly the plane turned and seemed to be heading straight for our window. I understand that I set some sort of record closing the curtains and running down to the main floor from the third floor. What I had seen was one of the first buzz bombs to hit London.

From then on, at the first sound of the air-raid warning, the Red Cross Corps girls on the first floor were betting who would arrive on their floor first from the third floor, Doris or me.

After our disembarkation leave we were given our assignments at headquarters in Burlington Gardens. I was assigned to wrapping layettes for babies whose fathers were Canadian. Since I had taken a refresher course in typing and shorthand in Montreal before I was posted overseas, this seemed like an odd job. However, the job with the layettes lasted only until my flat feet said "uncle" from so much standing, and eventually I was assigned to "Parcels for Prisoners of War." Because of my extensive art background, this work was more interesting for me, as I was now designing patterns for slippers, vests and regimental crests.

I worked with an enthusiastic English girl, Gina Raymond, from the British Red Cross (loaned to the Canadian Red Cross). Not only did we design patterns, but we cut out materials such as leather, wool or felt, then packaged the pieces with instructions, as well as lacing, thread or glue. The packages were sent to the dif-

Handicrafts room at Red Cross Headquarters, London, 1944.
Fran Day (l), Nan Roberts (r)

ferent Stalags in Europe where Canadian prisoners of war were held. The idea behind all this was for the men to have something to occupy their time in prison, and then be able to wear what they made.

Soon we were able to talk to the exchange prisoners of war. This was a sad and unforgettable experience, as these men had been badly wounded, usually with two or three limbs missing.

They were in dismal little rooms while waiting to be shipped back to Canada. The stench was unbelievable. From the information we received from these interviews, it was decided to close our department, since the Germans were confiscating the handicraft parcels for themselves.

After this, Gina and I were designated as handicraft officers and were sent to Colchester Hospital for training to work with occupational therapists in a military hospital. My first assignment in Colchester was to greet the rows and rows of boxcars full of wounded soldiers. This was shortly after D-Day, and trains brought them each day. We handed each soldier a ditty bag with a comb, tooth-brush, some shaving cream, a razor, etc., all the time talking to them with a lot a cheerful banter. After all they had endured, their spirits were surprisingly good.

These patients were then put in ambulances, with three men tiered up on each side of the back of the ambulance compart-ment. We went along to make certain they were safe and didn't roll out of their litters, for the drivers drove as quickly as possible. After dinner, I often felt like going to bed, as the whole day had been so emotionally and physically draining. I was exhausted. Occasionally, however, Gina would lure me to the nearby Amer-ican base to hear such bands as Glenn Miller.

When our course was finished, I was assigned to No. 18 CGH (Canadian General Hospital) in Horley, Surrey, which was amaz-ingly similar to the hospital featured in the TV series *M*A*S*H*. What special characters were those wonderful doctors and nurses at No. 18 CGH. Since many of them had been there for five years, one could understand why zany moments occurred. At the height of one of the mess parties, the CO (Commanding Officer) and a few others went out, found a gypsy caravan, and pulled it back proudly. Our CO was a dead ringer for Colonel Potter in *M*A*S*H*. The matron stood seven feet high, I'm sure, but she was kind and capable, and "Hot Lips" Houlihan was there, too—a darned good nurse. Peggy McFarren worked with me in the Occupational Therapy Hut with two occupational therapists, as well as two wel-fare officers from the Corps.

I had always had a horror of hospitals or anything medical, which was a reaction to being ill so much when I was young. At this hospital, I learned to put my feelings aside and remember why I was there, and be good at what I was doing. Peggy and I would wait until some of our patients had recovered enough to be on their feet, usually with crutches. We would then take them on a bus to a darling inn called the Wagon Shed where we would all have a wonderful dinner, washed down with ale. Some good friends

Cafeteria on the top floor of the Red Cross Headquarters, London, England.

of mine, the Spencers, owned this charming spot and also a beautiful stone home on the Thames where I visited many times.

The most outstanding time was the day before VE-Day (Victory-in-Europe Day) when we were all having a few days' leave and spending it with the hospitable Spencers. I brought a good friend of mine from Vancouver, Bob Payne. Bob was a second officer in the Merchant Navy on a ship that picked up Sherman tanks in Saint John, New Brunswick, and delivered them to Bombay, India.

We spent the day picnicking and punting on the Thames. Then, to celebrate the happy news that the war was over in Europe, we joined many jubilant people at the George and Dragon that night, and left early the next day for London to be part of the huge crowds going wild with joy.

Our work at the No. 18 Canadian General Hospital included designing regimental crests and instructing patients in rug-hooking, macramé and needlepoint, as well as all types of leatherwork.

We made our rounds in the wards after lunch where we pushed a wooden trolley loaded with a variety of handicrafts for about 150 patients in three wards. My wards had patients who had received stomach wounds or were amputees. I was impressed how gifted the soldiers were, particularly in needlepoint. We had to sell the handicrafts to the patients (at a very minimal cost) and keep all the accounts in shillings and pence.

Sometimes it took longer to balance the account books than it did to give instructions to the patients in crafts, as our head occupational therapist was a serious and dedicated stickler for detail. At one stage I pointed out that I often worked overtime or came back to the hospital on my day off to help a patient learn to draw. I also explained how long it took to make up the regimental crests. Surely that was as important as having every sixpence in its proper place. She took it to heart and after that would often have the patients in the Occupational Therapy Hut stop and look at a crest that Peggy or I had just finished.

One day when I was visiting one of my wards, the nurse stopped at the entrance and held out a three-quarter finished needlepoint of a full-sailed galleon. She had tears in her eyes. She told me that the patient who had been working on it had had another operation on his bad leg and they had given him the wrong blood type. He died within hours.

There was such a feeling of inadequacy and helplessness when the buzz bombs went over our hospital—as many as four and five a day at times. If any had stopped instead of heading for London, there was no place to run for cover. Even if I had wanted to hide, I couldn't leave my patients who were in bed and couldn't move on their own.

There seemed to be such an interest in art instruction at our hospital that I went to London to ask Mrs. Stickney about the possibility of including art, such as drawing and pastels, in the hospital format. I told her that I would be interested in going to a few hospitals, besides No. 18, to give instruction, but she turned the idea down flat. Actually, now some fifty years later, art therapy has become an important part of a hospital's schedule. I also presented Mrs. Stickney with the idea that a memorial book should be made up, printed in old English lettering, complete with illuminations and design in gold on parchment paper with all 641 names of the Canadian Red Cross Corps girls on it, and where they served. At that time I thought that I could do it all in six months alone. But Mrs. Stickney felt I should stick to whatever I was doing at the time. It is a pity, really. It would have been so "special" to have a leather-bound book like that in the War Museum in Ottawa now.

Once the war was over, I went to my CO and told him about my life at home, and within a short time he had me on the first ship returning to Canada. Now this was an experience, too. Gina was back from Londonderry where she had been posted when I went to No. 18 CGH. She met me in London to give me some of her mother's Russian raisin wine to help me on my trip. A patient gave me two books of poetry, so I was on my way with thirty Red Cross gals and seven thousand men on the good ship *Aquitania*. We were allowed only two meals a day, but fate stepped in one day while I was drawing on the deck.

The food officer wanted me to draw a portrait of him in exchange for an extra meal and the use of his suite of rooms in the daytime. There were fifteen of us girls in one large room on the ship, complete with lines of washing. He also said we could have the use of his record player with all the great tunes of the day— "Sentimental Journey," "Rum and Coca-Cola," etc. I was to invite eight girls to join me, which I did. Believe me, it made the trip pleasant, because we couldn't use the ship's lounge—it was like dropping in on a men's stag party. The food officer even sent in trays of sandwiches.

When we docked in Halifax and went ashore, it felt wonderful to be back in Canada, where one believed for a brief moment that one could continue life where one had left off before the war. What an illusion.

Grant's godfather, Air Vice-Marshal Ed Reyno, who was stationed in Halifax, arranged for me to fly over to Newfoundland, so in a very short time, I was at the gates of Fort Pepperall, Newfoundland. There, a little boy stood beside his grandmother, holding her hand. As I stepped down from the bus, he ran to me, laughing and waving, and threw himself into my arms saying, "Hi, Mommy, where's Daddy?" I had waited for this moment for over a year and now we hugged each other hard. There had been so many casualties in a war that touched many in different ways forever.

My time overseas had done little to reconcile me to my loss or to prepare me for peacetime life. However, working with patients who were often seriously wounded, coping with daily bombings, and last and least, a very Spartan diet (we were rationed the same as civilians) had matured me quickly. So I decided to rejoin the Red Cross in Halifax for a short time.

I stayed at the Sword and Anchor in Halifax with some of my Red Cross friends whose husbands were stationed at the navy base there. I was assigned to meet the troop ships that were now returning to Canada. There were several of us who served coffee to the soldiers while they were waiting to be transported west on trains. We also sent telegrams for the soldiers, so their families would know they were heading home.

My more traumatic experiences occurred when I drove new British war brides to their husband's family homes in the area. They were understandably nervous and excited. It was interesting to observe their different reactions: how disappointed a lovely war bride would be when I drove her to a tiny fisherman's house perched near the water on a rocky coastal beach, or how shy a young war bride would appear when she viewed a large impressive home with beautiful gardens.

On July 18, 1945, I was returning from swimming near Halifax on a "free day" when I experienced a tremendous blast. This was immediately followed by lesser explosions. When I returned to my Red Cross friends at the Sword and Anchor, they informed me that the Burnside Magazine east of the Bedford Basin, three miles long and a half mile wide, had caught fire and the north end of Halifax as far down as North Street had to be evacuated. Ten thousand Dartmouth citizens were being withdrawn to A-25 Military Camp located beyond the Eastern Passage Airport away from the burning magazines.

The Red Cross was now involved in caring for the people in the crowded city parks who came from the north end of the city. Rapid explosions continued night and day, with increasing violence. Ships were being moved to the outer harbour while the surrounding hills looked like a volcano crater. The fire would roar and roll and burst for an hour, and then be quiet for a time while the flames would advance to a new shell bay. Finally after several days, car horns blew to signal that civilians could return to their homes. Many veterans remarked that it had been about as bad as anything they had experienced in Europe. For myself, the months I spent in London during the buzz bombs and V-2s could not compare to the terror of experiencing four thousand tons of TNT exploding in a single blast.

When all the evacuated people had been returned to their homes and Red Cross activities slipped into a more normal routine again, I knew I was now ready for civilian life. I cabled my family at Fort Pepperall that I was safe and returning immediately.

For a time, I experienced a "lost" feeling, a feeling of inadequacy, for the tremendous responsibility of going forward with our lives together. Yet the quietness of the windswept island of Newfoundland, with its little coves and quaint villages, gave me time for walks and picnics with my little boy. We chatted and waded in streams together and got to know each other again. He said, many years later, that when I was overseas he would often ask his grandmother where his mummy and daddy were. She would point in the direction of the Atlantic Ocean. He said he would stand by the window looking at the ocean to see if he could see England in the distance.

Even as I write this, I cannot believe that it was really I, Frances Martin Day, involved in such a horrendous event as World War II. Yet one did become involved—swept up by the fervour of national duty, the excitement and one's own sense of honour.

Lois Goodwin Golding

"We sat and shivered in the
pitch dark railway station"

Lois Goodwin Golding was born in Calgary, Alberta. At the age of five
she went to live in Durban, South Africa, moving back to Canada at
the age of fifteen. She studied music and was teaching piano at
McGill University when she joined the Red Cross. After
the war, she married, raised four children and
combined a music career, concertizing and
teaching at the University of South
Florida until her retirement.

So much is embedded in the crusts of time that it really takes some digging to explain why I went overseas. Yet as one starts to dig, it is almost like opening the proverbial Pandora's box— thoughts long since forgotten come scampering out, making it difficult to put them in order. I think I would have to say my reason was twofold, the first being that my husband was shipped overseas in early 1941. At that time, I was teaching music at McGill University, which seemed far removed from the "war effort"—somewhat akin to "fiddling while Rome burns"—and once my husband left, it seemed important for me to go as well. The second reason was that the Red Cross in Montreal was asking for volunteers on Saturday mornings to help with an enrichment programme for underprivileged children, and I was attracted to working with the Red Cross.

From that small beginning, it wasn't long before I put music aside and found myself a VAD (Voluntary Aid Detachment) at the Montreal General Hospital, doing twelve-hour shifts. Twelve months later, the word got out that there was to be a "crash course" to train a few gals (twenty-five, if my memory serves me correctly), to be sent overseas to help in occupational therapy. For one who had never been "artsy crafty," it seemed sheer idiocy to apply, but the temptation was too great, and I was fortunate enough to be among the group chosen.

The emotions and experiences with the Red Cross were legion. No one could be left untouched by the suffering, tragedy, courage and pathos that are all part of war. But for this particular moment of reminiscence, humour seems to surface, so I shall relate two or three episodes that, in retrospect, seem to be particularly funny, yet typical of my experiences.

The first occurred in Montreal, shortly before going overseas. Several of us were detailed to meet and assist war brides at Windsor Railway Station. One evening, at about midnight, we were just winding down, thinking we had taken care of all the arrivals, when at the end of the station, we saw a lonely (somewhat elderly) soul wandering down the platform. A couple of us went to see what we could do to help, and in the ensuing conversation, she informed us that her final destination was a farm in Saskatchewan where her husband had been living since World War I. Apparently her "husband" had never sent for her after World War I, so she was taking advantage of the World War II war brides' transportation to come and join him! Her comment of "My, is he ever going to be surprised to see me," seemed a masterpiece of understatement. I would have loved to have been a fly on the wall of that farmhouse when she showed up. We never did hear the outcome.

Humour overseas often seemed to be linked with some form of transportation—bus, train, boat, or "à pied." The "à pied" form of mobility produced a startling, but hilarious moment when a couple of us decided to walk home to Onslow Gardens from Burlington Gardens where we had just completed a night of fire-watch duty. It was a beautiful spring night, and our only concern was that we might have to take cover from bombers—but our actual scare came from a totally different and unexpected source. As we walked briskly but happily down the darkened streets, all of a sudden a voice hissed out of a blacked-out doorway, "Get off my beat." When we regained our aplomb we had a good chuckle—the "ladies of the night" did not appreciate our infringement on their territory. We debated whether to tell them we were not the competition, but decided an exchange of words was not in order.

Travelling in the usual incredibly crowded, "sardine-can" style, a British lady and I were standing together in the corridor among the unfortunates unable to get a seat. Seated in a nearby compartment was a big, burly American sergeant, taking up enough room for two, and with the usual generous array of ribbons on his chest. Part way through the journey, "nature" called, and he had to go in search of the "loo"—crushing past everybody in the corridor. When he was out of earshot, the little English lady turned to me and said, "And I suppose he will come back with another ribbon."

We were being shipped out to Italy, so two Red Cross girls, eight nursing sisters and a full complement of army troops were put aboard a train late one night—the destination supposedly unknown, but the leak said "Glasgow." Once again I found myself sitting up all night in the corridor of a blacked-out train. (I have never figured out why I always seemed to end up in the corridors of English trains—maybe they thought only small people could fit into those areas.) It was a long night before we arrived at Glasgow Railway Station at 6 a.m., when everybody disembarked from the train, groggy and dishevelled, to be accounted for and checked off by a dour-looking captain prior to boarding the ship. All, that is, except the two Red Cross girls! Everybody's papers were in order except ours; the captain had no verification for us to board the ship. So, without a backward glance, the rest of the group all climbed aboard and the ship promptly steamed off.

What to do? Not much we could do! It was a rainy cold Glasgow day in December, so we sat and shivered in the pitch dark railway station until 8 a.m., when the kindly station master turned up, threw a few pieces of coal in the stove, and listened to our tale of woe. He got busy on the "wireless" and telephoned, and by 10 a.m., everything was straightened out. Yes! We were supposed to be on the ship, which was now sitting out in the harbour. But the problem was how to get us there. What follows stands out—without question—as one of the most awkward moments of my life.

Donning full battle gear, we were put into a little "rowboat" (which fortunately had a motor, or this tale could have been worse), and we were putt-putted out to where the ship lay at anchor—whereupon they lowered a rope ladder, and we were ordered to climb up. Even upon order of death, I don't believe I could ever do it again. With every step up, the ladder would shake and shimmy violently against the ship—the weight of my various packs threatened to pull me into the chilly waters of the Clyde— and all this to the accompaniment of cheers, whistles and clapping from the troops lining the decks above. It must have been an incongruous sight. Being only five feet tall, I was always being teased, the favourite joke being that when big pack, small pack, haversack, helmet, etc., were in place, all you could see were two feet sticking out at the bottom, somehow propelling this baggage along. I certainly didn't bargain to take it all up a rope ladder. Despite my embarrassment and all the kidding, I was most grateful for the many arms stretched out to help heave me aboard

Red Cross vehicle transporting hospital personnel to Naples en route to London.

when I made it to the top.

We arrived in Naples on Christmas Eve and, since no one was interested in helping to disembark a troop ship at that time, we had to stay on board all night, anchored in the harbour. Several enterprising young Neapolitans swam out to the ship with bottles of "hooch," allegedly "good Scotch," for sale at a fairly hefty price. Many bottles were bought to bolster the flagging spirits on that Christmas Eve in such strange surroundings, but if that was "good Scotch" I hope never to taste that brand again. It tasted and smelled dangerously close to gasoline. Some of us decided it was the better part of wisdom to pass it up. For others the "party spirit" was too enticing, and the night was spent in gay abandon.

Come morning, much moaning and groaning was heard as we rapidly dressed to disembark, but above the moaning and groaning was heard the wail of one young woman who could not find a piece of intimate apparel. When a friend said, "Oh, come on, don't worry about it, we have to get off the ship," the wail became louder as she replied in anguish, "But my name was on it!" Those beastly name tags we had spent so much time sewing on garments —this was one time someone wished they had never been invented. However, her dilemma helped to inject a little levity into our disembarking as we stepped off our ship onto the only wharf available and gazed at the prows and hulks of ships that had been bombed in the harbour—a sobering sight.

How did I adjust to civilian life upon returning to Canada? I don't remember giving it any conscious thought, for there was so much to be done. One thing stands out in my mind. With the handsome $25.00 discharge pay we received, I went out and bought a second-hand bicycle. Don't ask me why. Probably because I had never owned one as a kid (I must have felt underprivileged), and one certainly couldn't put a down payment on a car with that kind of money. Maybe it was the only thing I could buy for $25.00 that would give me a sense of ownership!

Jane Rogers

*"I had never made pastry, but I
did have my trusty cookbook"*

—

Jane Rogers was born in Toronto, Ontario. During her school years she
attended the Toronto Conservatory of Music. She was part owner of
Mary-Mac Designer Boutique in Toronto when she joined the Red
Cross. From 1983 to 1988 her husband was Lieutenant Governor
of B.C. and Jane was Chatelaine of Government House,
Victoria. Currently she is Honorary Vice-President
of British Columbia, Yukon Division of the
Canadian Red Cross Society.

1943—Hitler had overrun Europe. My husband Bob had been overseas for two years. My young brother John had been in the army for over a year and was on his way to England. I decided to do my "bit"—call it frustration or sheer loneliness, with some patriotism thrown in—but I had to get involved, so I joined the Red Cross. However, I am getting ahead of my story; let's go back to 1941.

Bob enlisted in 1941. He joined the First Hussars, a tank regiment from London, Ontario. The regiment was stationed in Barrie, north of Toronto. I used to go up and visit him on weekends for the tea dances and he would come down to Toronto to visit me. As it grew closer to the time when Bob's regiment would be going overseas, one of his friends from Montreal, who was in the same regiment and was married, kept telling Bob that he should marry me before he went overseas. So we decided that we would, and we were married at the end of June 1941. To this day I call Andy Fyfe "the marriage broker."

After our wedding we rented a cottage near Barrie on Lake Simcoe for the summer. It was a great summer. In the fall we moved into Barrie where we rented a bed-sitting room, because Bob was supposedly going overseas at any moment. Finally on Halloween morning in 1941, the First Hussars Regiment left Barrie. I had a terrible cold, and I can remember packing up the car and driving to Toronto crying and sobbing and blowing my nose all the way there. So, after four months of married life, here I was going home to live with Mother and Dad again.

After completing a typing and shorthand course, I found a job with a morning paper in Toronto, soliciting news and typing up engagements, marriages, and birth and death notices. It didn't take me long to realize that it wasn't for me, so I left and took a job with the Wartime Prices and Trade Board, doing comparative shopping; my job was to go into different grocery stores and compare prices. I think that I visited every grocery store in the Toronto area during the time I was with them. I wasn't very happy there, so when a friend offered me a partnership in a dress shop, I accepted. We had a wonderful time getting it organized, decorat-

ing and buying all the stock. We worked really hard, but it was satisfying, and we did quite a good business.

I'd been with the store nearly a year, when a friend of mine
came in to buy some clothes. She said that her husband was overseas and she had joined the Red Cross Food Administration. She
told me that she was guaranteed to go overseas before long. I really didn't believe her, but she wanted me to join and, since I was
beginning to feel the need to contribute to the war effort, I joined
the Red Cross Food Administration. We took the same three-
month cooking course given to the Army, Navy and Air Force cooks
at one of the trade schools in Toronto. We were taught large-
quantity cooking, which included how to cook with powdered
eggs and powdered milk. It was a great course. In our innocence,
we thought we would be the dieticians, plan the meals, and teach
the English cooks how to cook the Canadian way. Was I in for a
surprise!

When it was obvious that we were going overseas pretty soon, I
left the dress shop and joined the daytime Red Cross, where I
worked full-time, since I had to have a certain number of hours
before I could go overseas. We cooked the noon-day meal for the
CWACs (Canadian Women's Army Corps). Because we had to
learn to drill as well, we formed a precision squad and would
march around the armouries and universities putting on precision drill shows. When we also took a course in the use of gas
masks, things became very exciting, and it began to seem a privilege to be asked to go overseas. The Red Cross bought our uniforms and paid our passage there and back. We were given an
allowance of about one pound a month plus room and board; we
paid for all the rest.

I had to have permission from my husband to go overseas, so I
wrote Bob a long letter, telling him my plans. He wrote back that
he was over there protecting me and his country, and he didn't
want me coming. But I cabled back that I was coming anyway;
there wasn't much he could do about it. Our parents were not too
happy either, but they realized I had to go. So in January 1944,
thirteen of us Red Cross girls of the Food Administration took off

from Toronto on the train for Saint John, New Brunswick.

Our luggage was quite a problem. We were allowed only a limited amount of weight and we had to have our dunnage bags, our uniforms (we had blue smocks and white veils to wear when we were on duty) and our khaki uniforms. Then, of course, we had to have our civilian clothes for off-duty hours.

When we got off the train in Saint John, New Brunswick, it was miserably cold January weather—foggy, damp and cold. After spending the night in the only hotel, we were taken to the docks the next morning, and there was the ship on which we would spend the next eight days. It was called the *Indochinois*, a French freighter that had escaped from Brittany as the Germans moved in. The officers were all French and the crew came from every country imaginable. Among the passengers there were thirteen Red Cross girls, including Mrs. Tudball, head of the Ontario Division of the Red Cross, three Air Force pilots returning to England after training in Canada and three businessmen. Within an hour of sailing I didn't feel very well and quite a few of the other girls felt the same way. In spite of this, the first night out was very lively. We had dinner with the captain and two leading officers; afterwards we played bridge, and then off to bed. That was the only time that I went to the dining-room until the last night of the voyage. I lived on crackers, celery and fruit juice for the eight days. I lost some weight, which was good for me.

First of all, we went south and then north. We bobbed around in that ocean all by ourselves. We knew where the lifeboats were, but we had no lifeboat drill. The officers said that if their ship were spotted by the Germans, they would be captured anyway, and they were prepared to shoot themselves. The officers didn't trust the crew, and the passengers became increasingly nervous as the trip went on.

On our last night at sea, we had drinks first in the captain's quarters, and then we had dinner at the captain's table. We played games and had a singsong. The tradition is—or so we were told— that you're not supposed to go to bed the last night out at sea, so it was very late when we went to bed. As I was to be up early the next morning, after very little sleep, I was up and dressed, and with my whistle as officer of the day, I went out on deck for some fresh air. Another passenger, a Scots bomber pilot, joined me in my walk around the deck.

We watched a boat come out with the pilot who would guide us up the Mersey River to Liverpool. The next thing we heard was that the pilot could speak no French and the captain of our ship could speak no English. The only other person that could speak French on board was Mrs. Tudball, the head of our Red Cross group, so she was asked to go up on the bridge and help to translate the captain's and the pilot's orders. Suddenly the Scotsman grabbed me, threw me against the bulkhead and screamed at me, "We're going to hit that ship!" Much to my amazement, when I looked around—sure enough—there was a large ship right on top of us, and in no time at all we rammed it. I guess Mrs. Tudball's French wasn't so good, after all. Anyway, the crew were exhilarated, since they would have at least a month's leave in London while the ship was being repaired. Shortly after, the tender came out and picked up us Red Cross girls, and we were very happy to leave the *Indochinois*. We found out later that the ship we hit was a hospital ship. By some miracle, no one was hurt.

The tender took us into Liverpool, where we went through customs and then on to a hotel for lunch. Afterwards, when we walked through the downtown area, we were shocked to see the amount of bomb damage in the city. Then we boarded the train for London. By this time, it was evening and we had dinner on the train— our first meal in wartime England with all the shortages. It was probably the worst meal I have ever eaten. I can still remember the soybean sausages, the lumpy, grey mashed potatoes and the mushy Brussels sprouts. When we arrived in London early in the evening, it was pitch black—our first experience in a blackout. We got used to it later on, but to see people's ghostly figures moving around in the city and the cars with just a tiny little speck of light showing from their headlights was eerie.

We were met at Waterloo Station by Red Cross officials and the husband of one of the girls. We were all envious that this husband was able to greet his wife at the station. One of the Red Cross girls who met us came up to me and told me that my husband had been calling every day for the last week, but unfortunately he was now on maneuvers. He left a message saying that he would come to London as quickly as he could, but he might be a day or two. We were driven to Red Cross Corps House at Queen's Gate Terrace, which was actually three terraced houses made into one. It was rather good quarters when I think back on it now, and it could sleep about fifty girls. We would stay there until we were posted either to a hospital, to one of the four Red Cross Clubs in London, or to Corps headquarters for office work. We were greeted by the "veterans," the girls who had been there for one year or more.

There were four of us to a bedroom, and we had gone to bed when the air-raid siren sounded. In Canada we had been told what to do in an air raid, so we quickly got up and dressed, packed the panic bag, grabbed our gas masks and went tearing downstairs. This was much to the delight of the veterans who appeared sleepily in the front hall in their night clothes. We heard later that this was the first air raid they'd had in about three months' time and they were as confused as we were, but they were pretending that they knew the drill for such occasions.

The next morning all of us new recruits were given a week's debarkation leave by General Price of the Red Cross. It was about six that afternoon when Bob my husband finally arrived. I was upstairs when I was called to come down; I went tearing down the stairs and rushed at Bob with such excitement that when I threw my arms around him, we both fell on the floor, to the embarrassment of both of us. I guess you could say that I literally knocked him off his feet.

Bob and I spent the first night of the debarkation leave at the Mayfair Hotel. After we went to bed there was another air raid and the windows in the old hotel rattled and shook. I was quite nervous but Bob calmed me down. The next morning I was very hungry, as I hadn't been eating much since arriving in England, and had not eaten much on the trip over, either. When we asked for our breakfast to be sent up to our room, this gorgeous, big

Jane Rogers with husband Bob, Trafalgar Square, Feb. 7, 1944.

table arrived with all the silver on it you could imagine. When I lifted off the cover, there was a bowl of mushy porridge and two pieces of cold toast shivering on a rack and a grey-looking piece of fish. And tea, of course. So all I had to eat was a piece of cold toast and a couple of cups of tea.

After our disappointing breakfast, we left to catch the train from Waterloo Station down to Torquay. In peacetime this train had been a special excursion train called *The Cornish Riviera,* and the crew was proud of their dining-room. Soon after boarding the train, we went to the dining-car for lunch, which was nicely done. Actually it was the best meal I had eaten since arriving in London. The waiter came around and asked if we had enjoyed it, and I said, "Yes, very much." Then he asked if there was anything else that he could do for us. "Yes," I said, "may I have a second helping?" The whole dining-car heard me, and everybody looked at me in horror. Bob whispered to me, "Jane, please be quiet. You know there isn't very much food in England, and it is rationed." He was right, of course, but I was so happy finally to have a good meal that I had forgotten.

We arrived in Torquay where we stayed at the Imperial Hotel. It was a beautiful hotel on the coast, but unfortunately the coast was all barb-wired, so there was no access to the beach. We had a lovely stay at the hotel, however, until I had to go back to London, and Bob to his regiment. At that time, Bob's regiment was stationed on the south coast of England, about an hour and a half train ride from Waterloo Station.

Once back in London, I was posted to the Junior Officers' Club—just me. The Junior Officers' Club was again two old terraced houses joined together. You walked into the front hall, and on the left was a long room which was the reception room and lounge; on the right was the office and registry. There was a staircase which led up to the men's quarters where the junior officers stayed when they arrived on leave in London. The dining-room was in the other house, and off the dining-room was the still-room (the room from where meals were served). Down the stairs in the basement was the kitchen. The girls' quarters were upstairs, our home-away-from-home.

When I arrived, the assistant matron of the club took me in to meet Miss Duff who was the matron of the Junior Officers' Club and responsible for all the Canadian Red Cross girls in the clubs in London. Miss Duff was a tall, forbidding-looking Scotswoman who I thought was really old, although she was probably no more than forty. She took me down to the basement to the kitchen which horrified me, as it was like a cavern with its cement floor and large gas stove in the middle—with eight burners on the top and three ovens. There was also a long table for mixing food, with cupboards along the wall for storage.

In charge of the kitchen was a woman by the name of Mrs. Fernie, a Canadian from Vancouver. I liked her immediately. She was a widow and she had run the Jericho Officers' Club in Vancouver. She had joined the Red Cross as a dietician; actually she had thought she was going overseas to run the Junior Officers' Club Well, Mrs. Fernie ended up in the kitchen as a cook. At first she hadn't been happy with the job, but she had grown used to it because she was in a good position to obtain information about her son, who was missing at sea. In the kitchen there was also an old fellow by the name of Jock, who had been shell-shocked in the First World War. He cleaned the pots and pans and peeled the potatoes.

By the time I arrived it was about ten in the morning, and Mrs. Fernie was down there all by herself. Miss Duff introduced me to Mrs. Fernie and told her that I would be her new assistant. Moo, as I called her later, looked at me, and said challengingly, "So, you're a cook." I replied, "Yes, I took a course in Canada." "Well," she said, "we are making meat pies for lunch. I am going off duty in half an hour and I haven't time to make the pastry. Here is the filling." And she pointed to two huge pots of meat, gravy and vegetables on the stove. "Now you make the pastry for the meat pies and put them in the oven to cook. When they are ready send them up in the dumb waiter."

So here I was, all by myself, in this terrible kitchen. I had never made pastry, but I did have my trusty cookbook put out by the armed forces for large-quantity cooking. It said to take two pounds of flour and one pound of lard and mix together—this was to make pastry for a hundred people. So I rolled up my sleeves and rummaged around for a big tub. In my hurry, I think I dumped in five pounds of flour and two pounds of lard. Anyway, it was an awful lot of flour and an awful lot of lard. I finally mixed it into large balls of pastry and then started to roll it out. There was so much pastry that I was literally running around the big wooden block table, rolling it out. I ended up with flour all down the front of my smock and all over me. I filled the eight pans with the stew, put the pastry on the top as best I could, and popped it in the oven. At twelve o'clock, I took out the pies, put the pans on the dumb waiter, and sent them up to the still-room where the dining-room girls would cut them into servings for the dining-room.

By this time I was exhausted so I sat down in the kitchen and thought, "Oh dear! I've poisoned everybody." I was quite sure that the pastry was going to be as tough as can be.

In about fifteen minutes time, I heard a voice call down the dumb waiter, "Mrs. Rogers, are you down there?"

"Yes," I confessed reluctantly.

"Aren't you going to have any lunch?"

"No, I am not hungry."

"Did you make the pastry?"

"Yes, I did."

"Well," she said, "you are to be complimented; that is the best pastry I have ever tasted."

So from then on, I was "in" with Miss Duff. We not only did breakfast, lunch and dinner, but also "elevenses" in the mornings and tea in the afternoon. Lunch was the main meal of the day; at night we had salad and soup for supper.

One particular day I had been on duty for breakfast and lunch, and I was to make a cake for tea. I planned to make a spice cake, and pulled out my Red Cross cookbook again. I read the directions, and somehow or other I must have mixed up the sugar with the powdered eggs, since I put in too much sugar. I didn't realize this because the batter looked fine—a little loose but quite good. Then I put it in the oven to bake, and told our helper that I was going upstairs to the dining-room to talk to some of the girls. I

Red Cross Corps preparing meals, London.

Red Cross Corps serving meals, London.

Red Cross Corps Lounge, London.

Red Cross Corps Handicrafts Poster Display.

asked her to let me know when the cakes were baked.

I'd been upstairs for a while when suddenly the dumb waiter bell rang and rang and rang. I rushed over and our helper in the kitchen said, "Mrs. Rogers, are you there?"

"Yes."

"Well, I don't know what you've done, but there's an erupting Vesuvius in the oven! You'd better come quickly."

So I tore down the stairs to the kitchen and opened up the oven—sure enough, the batter was bubbling and frothing. After I had taken it out of the oven, I began to wonder: "Now what am I going to do? I can't waste all that sugar and powdered eggs." Since the batter was quite sticky, I moulded it into small balls and then rolled the balls in icing sugar, so that they tasted like Chinese Chews (which was a favourite bar I used to make at home). I sent them up for tea, and they were very popular. I was asked many times to make them again, but I never could because I didn't know what I had done to get the results in the first place.

I can remember one Sunday morning in particular. Bob had come up to London on a Saturday, and we went out that night together. We stayed at the Hotel Rembrandt, and when we went down for dinner, we found that the menu featured steak. Steak, in London, in wartime! This was just unheard of, so we had steak and it was very good. I enjoyed every bit of it, and it wasn't until I was finished that Bob said, "Now, you realize what that steak was?" When I said no, Bob informed me, "That was horsemeat that you ate." But still it was very good.

The next morning I had to be on duty at seven o'clock for breakfast. I rushed out of bed at a quarter to seven, threw on my clothes and made Bob come with me. When I began running along the street, he made me stop, and asked, "Jane what on earth is wrong with you?" I said, "Oh, I'm the only one that can get breakfast today. Nobody else is on duty, I can't disappoint them and I'm scared to death of Miss Duff." When I finally reached the club and threw off my coat, I started in immediately to prepare the breakfast of bacon and eggs. The eggs were called fresh eggs, but they came from Argentina; you can imagine how long they had been in transit and how fresh they were when they arrived in England. Well, I had a slight hangover from the night before, and you had to open these eggs on a saucer. I would say that three out of ten were bad, so you can imagine what that did for me with a hangover. But eventually I got them cooked, and the breakfast of bacon and eggs was served.

Bob had gone back to bed and left me and my mess in the kitchen. He came back for dinner at Sunday noon. On Sundays we were allowed a "joint," as the English called a roast. Everyone looked forward to Sunday dinner. It was usually pork or mutton, and we would cook at least eight huge roasts. As we had no meat slicer, we had to slice this meat ourselves. Eventually we did get two more girls to help us. This Sunday morning, Bob came in as I was mashing potatoes on top of the stove. We would cook the potatoes in a large pot, and then I would drain and mash them with a huge wooden mallet. I'd made the gravy, but I hadn't carved the meat yet, and it was nearly time for lunch. So I put Bob to work carving the meat. He said, "Do you mean to tell me that if I weren't here you would be doing this all by yourself?" When I said yes, Bob was most impressed, realizing finally that I did work hard in my job.

I can remember a very good friend of ours from Montreal coming to the club to see me. They sent him down to the kitchen where I was on duty. He came down as I was doing some menial task—perhaps peeling potatoes or something—and he said, "Jane, what have you done? Have you been naughty? Have you done something terrible and you're on KP duty down here?" I explained to him that I was the cook. I think he was quite surprised about the whole thing.

Another day at lunchtime, I had served up the lunch and I was off duty, so I went upstairs to have my lunch. Just as I was coming up the stairs, three of Bob's brother officers came into the club. I greeted them and asked if they would like to join me for lunch; they said they would be delighted. So we went into the dining-room where we sat chit-chatting back and forth, when Miss Duff came in for her lunch. Now Miss Duff was very strict with "her girls"; I guess she had to be. She could be very abrupt with us, and when she saw me at the table with the three officers, she said, "Jane, what are you doing here in the dining-room having lunch?" I said, "These are friends of my husband," and I introduced them to her. She answered, "You just get back to the kitchen—you get back to work—back to the kitchen!"

On one occasion, Bob's uncle from Cambridge came to visit me, and we had lunch in the dining-room. That day, however, I invited Miss Duff to join us. Fortunately, he was a delightful old gentleman and really charmed her. From then on she and I got on a little bit better.

I arrived in January 1944, and by May, things in England were growing tense. Everybody knew that there was going to be an invasion sooner or later, but nobody knew exactly when. All travel around England had been stopped unless you were army personnel. Civilians were not allowed to travel out of their own area. At the beginning of May, I wasn't feeling well. I had what I thought was the flu and then the flu developed into strep throat, and I ran a temperature. I'd been in bed about three days when Bob came up to London to see me. He went into the office and was told that I was ill and to go on up and visit with me. So he started up the stairs on the girls' side of the club; he was halfway up when there was Miss Duff standing at the top.

"What do you think you're doing in the girls' part of the club?" she asked Bob.

"I am going to see my wife."

"Well," said Miss Duff, "I am sorry, but there are no men allowed in this section of the club."

"Miss Duff," Bob informed her, "I am going to see my wife, so please step aside."

Well, Miss Duff did step aside. When Bob saw that I was really very sick, he talked to Miss Duff and they called a doctor. The next thing I knew, I was being taken by ambulance up to the Canadian hospital at Watford outside of London.

I had infectious mononucleosis and strep throat, which kept me in the hospital for two weeks. When I was ready to be discharged, Bob came to see me and talked to the doctor, who informed him that I had to have three weeks' convalescent leave. Since at that time Bob was stationed on the south coast of England, he asked if I could be moved there for my recovery. The doctor said that he would give me papers, but there was a problem with civilians travelling outside of their residential area. Bob told me to wear my Red Cross uniform and he would meet me at the station at Southampton. I took the train and pretended that I was a Red Cross girl bringing comforts for the troops. That was how he smuggled me into the area.

Bob's regiment was bivouacked all along the coastline near Lee-on-Solent, a little town opposite the Isle of Wight. In the sound were hospital ships and huge square docks that looked like concrete blocks floating in the water, and on the shore were the tanks. I asked Bob what those huge structures were, and he just said, "Oh, they are for target practice." Later I found out they were part of Mulberry Harbour, the floating docks that they towed across the Channel so the troops could land on the French shore.

Most of the regiment were living in and under their tanks along the coastline. The officers were billeted in the different homes around Southampton and Lee-on-Solent. Bob took me to the home where he was billeted with a delightful English girl and her two children. They had such a strong Southampton accent that I really couldn't make out a word they said. They were very kind to me, however, and I stayed overnight.

After breakfast the next day we checked into a place called the Inn By the Sea. We had a pleasant room with a big double bed and a fireplace. The proprietors of the pub were Dusty and Joe Hannah. I hadn't been there more than ten minutes when a civilian policeman came around to the pub and asked Joe Hannah, "What is this girl doing here?" He said, "She is a Canadian Red Cross girl who has been sick and her husband will be going off to France soon, so just forget she's here—have a beer and forget about her." So the policeman did. He had a beer and left.

Every night the officers of Bob's regiment would come into the pub for drinks and dinner. They would say, "Well, we've been to France and back," and, of course, I didn't believe them. One fel-

Mulberry Harbour, the artificial port created for the Normandy landings, 1944.

Unloading at Mulberry Harbour

low said, "I nearly drowned today, that was quite an experience." Later on it came out that they had been maneuvering the amphibious tanks—the tanks that later floated into the coast of France looking like little fishing boats; they really surprised the Germans.

There hadn't been any air raids around London for quite some time, but on the coast, the Germans were sending over reconnaissance planes, checking equipment and the movement of the troops. The air raids would start every night; the Germans would come over the Inn By The Sea, and Dusty and Joe would wake us to go down to their cellar. There Dusty would open a bottle of brandy, and everyone staying in the pub would have a few drinks and tell tales until the "All Clear" sounded.

I had been at the pub for about ten days when the policeman came back. He told Joe Hannah, "I'm sorry but this girl has to go." So that same day on the third of June, four of Bob's brother officers who were going up to London in a huge crummy took me with them. I still had another week's leave coming, so I went to stay with the wife of a navy officer in Purley. Her husband was also stationed on the coast where Bob's regiment was located. He was a navigator in the Navy and was to navigate the troops to the coast of France. We listened to the wireless and heard the news of D-Day on June 6th. Then on June 8th, her husband came back on a twenty-four-hour leave and filled us in on D-Day. It was a fascinating experience to sit in their living-room, hearing about how rough the weather was and how they dropped those amphibious tanks two miles out. He didn't go on shore, but he was able to see the troops disembarking from the landing craft.

I was soon back in London, back to the Junior Officers' Club, and back on duty. Moo Fernie took one look at me when I walked down into the kitchen that first morning, and said, "Jane, you're pregnant." Well I *was* pregnant and very pleased, because I had this terrible feeling that Bob could be killed, and I wanted to have his baby. I decided that I wasn't going to report that I was pregnant to the Red Cross officials, because if you did, you were told to stop work and sent home immediately. Of course in those days the girls weren't being sent home because there was no travel. But

I wanted to go on working in London, so I didn't report it. About the 10th of June, I had a telegram from Bob saying that he was safe. That was such a relief.

The news on the English wireless had been very good: the Allies had landed; they had reached their objectives; and everything was going well. Then, all of a sudden one night the buzz bombs started, and nobody knew what they were. I remember that night so well. A friend of ours from Toronto who was in the Navy had invited me out for drinks and dinner. I was really looking forward to a night out, so off we went with another Red Cross girl. We wined, dined and danced and had a great time. Then about eleven o'clock we were told not to leave the club because London was under attack. The guns were firing and they weren't sure if it was an air raid or not, so we stayed at the club until about one o'clock in the morning. Finally we decided that it wasn't really a good place to be. Moreover, I had to get home as I was on kitchen duty the next morning.

On the street, we could hear the guns and smell the gunsmoke. I will never forget that smell. London, of course, was all in darkness, but we could hear what sounded like an outboard motor putt-putt-putting along, then silence, and finally a big boom! We couldn't get a taxi, we couldn't find any transport, so we ended up walking for miles before we got back to Corps House. The guns fired all night and the next morning. Then suddenly about eleven o'clock in the morning they stopped and all was quiet. In the stillness you could hear the buzz bombs coming over. We discovered that as long as you heard the buzz bombs—the motor putt-putting along and putt-putting over your head—you were safe. But if the motor cut out before it got to you, you ran for cover and just prayed.

I can remember one night after the buzz bombs had been coming over for about a week, we were at a little pub down the street when we heard this thing coming over. It cut its motor before it got to us, so we all ducked for cover under the tables. All the windows were blown out of the pub and all the glass shattered from the bar. Everything was thrown all over the place, but no one was hurt.

Not long after that, I was down in the kitchen one day getting the evening supper, a huge pot of creamed chicken. I had cooked all these chickens—boiled them and boiled them, since they were pretty tough old birds—and I had made a cream sauce for them because that night we were having creamed chicken on toast, a big treat. It was about three o'clock in the afternoon when this buzz bomb came along. As soon as we heard it cut out, we all ran for cover. It landed in the mews across the road from us. All the windows in the club blew out, and some of the furniture was blown onto the street, but there were no casualties in the club. Across the street in the mews, there were many casualties, which were brought to our club. That night I must have fed about two hundred people and made coffee until midnight. Soon the bombing became so bad that the officers on leave who used to come to the club were too frightened to come to London, and so we had very few guests at that time. London became an unpleasant place, quiet, with few people on the streets. The English people took the air raids well, with great bravery, but by the time the buzz bombs came along, they were almost at their wits' end. It was a trying time.

After having cabled Bob to tell him that he was to be a father, he wrote to say that I should make arrangements to go home as he did not want me to have the baby in London. I began to worry that the buzz bombs were becoming too dangerous and decided it was time to report my pregnancy. Miss Harvey, the assistant matron in our club, lived with Miss Duff, and together they raised cats. It was to Miss Harvey that I had to report that I was pregnant. When she heard my news, she told me that quite a few of the married girls were reporting pregnancies. She said that she thought it might be the "bread"!

I was then sent along with four other girls to Reading to stay in a darling little pub called Nettlebed. We were sent there out of harm's way until they could get us off to Canada. I waited for news of Bob, and finally one afternoon he surprised me by walking into the pub. It was one of the most exciting moments of my life to see him there in the flesh after all we had been through. After arriving in London he had taken a taxi and asked the driver to go to 88 Queen's Gate, where the club was. The taxi driver said, "Oh, you don't want to go there, mate, that place has been blown to bits!" Not knowing what to think, Bob said, "Take me there anyway." When he arrived, the club was still standing, but the two corners on either side of it had been bombed. It was with some trepidation that he walked into the club and asked to see me. What a relief for him when one of the girls told him that I was at the Nettlebed in Reading!

We stayed at Nettlebed for a couple of days. Then we went up to London to make sure that my passage was all set, after which we went to Corps headquarters. While we were there a buzz bomb came over, and the expression on Bob's face was panic—I'll never forget it. He said, "Jane, we are not going to stay in London tonight. We are going back to Reading." So we completed our business and we went back to Reading.

The next day Bob left; he was to go home immediately on the *Queen Elizabeth*. Since I had to wait another two weeks before I was to leave for home, I went back to London a few days later to stay at Corps House until I was scheduled to board the *Aquitania* for home. There were five of us Red Cross girls going. I felt bad because I was going home to my husband, and the other four girls' husbands had been killed in the war. It was a sad situation.

We were to take the train to Greenock in Scotland to board our ship. About five minutes before the bus arrived to take us to the train station, a buzz bomb came over. We all looked at each other and listened. When we heard the buzz bomb cut out, we hid and it missed us. That was the last thing I remember of Corps House—crouching under the stairs in the front hall waiting for this buzz bomb to explode.

We finally boarded the *Aquitania* in Greenock, Scotland. All five of us Red Cross girls were in one cabin, and next to us were six English war brides with their babies. On board were also prisoners of war and wounded soldiers. The crossing to Halifax was uneventful. From Halifax I took the train to Montreal and then to Toronto. I arrived about seven in the morning in Toronto, and

A Canadian Red Cross Corps House single bedroom, London.

there was Bob with my mother and father. Bob and I were both home safe and sound.

I am glad that I made the decision to go overseas. It was a wonderfully exciting experience and I wouldn't have missed it for the world. It was also good for my marriage. My being in England meant that Bob and I didn't lose contact with each other for a long length of time. I could also understand, to some extent, what Bob had been through in the war.

Our baby was a boy and we named him John. When John was to be married in Sweden, we stopped off in England to show him where he was conceived, but many areas we had known were almost unrecognizable. I guess the story is that you can never go back to the way things were. The war brought my husband and me very close—a shared experience which has stayed with us for over fifty years.

Joan Macarthur Lindley

"Lots of laughing, some crying, but everyone pulled her weight"

Joan Macarthur Lindley was born in Winnipeg, Manitoba and raised in Calgary and Winnipeg. She graduated from high school and attended the University of Manitoba for two years before joining the Red Cross. In 1948 she joined the Blood Transfusion Service until she married in 1954. After her marriage she lived in Saskatoon where two sons were born. Two daughters followed, the first born in Calgary and the second in North Vancouver.

Finally, after six months of waiting for our orders to come through, we were on our way overseas. Four of us left Winnipeg in January 1945, amid good wishes, waving arms and 30-below-zero weather. I had wanted to go into nursing when I graduated from high school, but those were the days when they wouldn't take you before you were eighteen. I was only seventeen and, since a year seemed a long time to wait, I decided to go to university, and then signed up with the Red Cross as a volunteer, working as a nursing assistant (VAD). First we had to put in 260 hours at the General Hospital in Winnipeg. Then we went to work at the Deer Lodge Military Hospital. After that, we were on our way to England as escort officers.

Although I wanted desperately to go overseas, I confess that I felt uneasy about leaving everything familiar in Canada to cross an ocean. My only experience with boats had been a trip to Vancouver Island at age seven on a Canadian Pacific Railway ferry, and in my teens I had enjoyed canoeing at the lake.

After a stopover in Montreal where we were joined by other VADs (Voluntary Aid Detachments), we eventually arrived in Halifax. We were met by Mrs. Evans who was in charge of all the escort officers. After gathering up our luggage, we proceeded to the area alongside the *Lady Rodney* where we were given our embarkation papers. Then up the gangway and to the cabins. The cabins weren't large, and there were three triple-decker bunks which, of course, meant nine girls per cabin plus the luggage we had carried on. I took the bottom bunk and immediately wished I had a top one where there was more air. After an eternity, everyone was bedded down and quiet, and by and by I fell asleep.

When we awoke the next morning, we had already left Halifax Harbour. I was one of the first ones up, but one of the last dressed. I guess the other eight gals were better organized. Two Toronto girls and I went down to breakfast together. I lasted about five minutes. All I had to see was a plate of bacon and eggs served to a lad beside me and I took off for the deck. One of the Toronto girls joined me after her breakfast with two hard rolls for me to nibble on. We walked for miles around the deck; I ate the buns and felt much better.

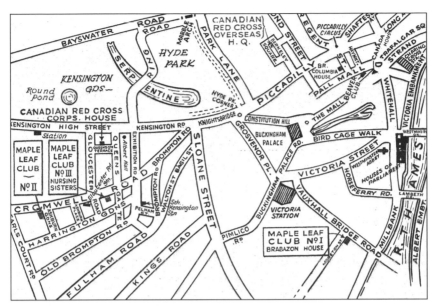

Map of London, showing Canadian Red Cross H.Q. and Clubs.

As we walked, we harmonized a song called "Some Sunday Morning" and to this day, when I see Mercia Norris (Harrison), I can hear that tune. I'm pleased to say that from then on, I ate a hearty lunch and have never felt the slightest tinge of "mal de mer" since that first morning on the *Lady Rodney*.

We were accompanied on our crossing by hundreds of troops from Debert, Nova Scotia, who were going across to relieve other occupation troops. There was always something to do on board, but it was the roughest crossing they'd ever had, so it was a bit hazardous to try to play some of the shipboard games. I might mention that in peacetime the *Lady Rodney* was used to transport bananas from South America.

On our seventh day we arrived at Southampton, and after disembarking, we found our way to the train station and hence to London. I was one of the lucky ones who hopped into the station wagon driven by Jane McGillivary. As she whisked us across London to Queen's Gate Gardens in South Kensington, she gave us a running commentary on all we passed and various other newsy tidbits, answering our questions in between.

There was a meeting of all the Red Cross girls when we arrived in London at Queen's Gate, and we were assigned to teams: five of us to a team, plus an OC (Officer Commanding) per team. My OC was Elsie Moorehouse from Halifax. We were known as escort officers and our uniforms were navy blue. We would be accompanying war brides and their children from England to Canada.

I'm a bit hazy about the length of time we stayed at Queen's Gate. I do remember six cots in the room, being really cold in bed every night, paying for a bath, not understanding the telephone system and being taken to Strollers, a pub near Queen's Gate. The next phase of my time in London that I can recall is living in the hostel for Red Cross volunteers on Brook Street and working at the South Street Hostel for war brides, which was actually a beautiful old home.

The war brides and their children were brought to a hostel in London before being escorted to their ship by escort officers at either Liverpool or Southampton. At the South Street Hostel there could be as many as two hundred war brides and children. We would work at South Street Hostel until it came our turn to escort them to Canada. We would then escort them to their ship and accompany them on their voyage to Canada.

At the hostel our responsibilities included preparing three-decker bunks for hundreds of people—back-breaking work. Then, of course, the "little" job of feeding everyone. The Army provided the cooks, but as there was not enough space for everyone to eat at once, it was a matter of serving one shift, and then clearing away and preparing for the next. Later everyone worked in the kitchen to get all the dishes washed and dried, and the tables set for the next meal.

Next came the job of settling everyone down for the night. This had its problems: those with top bunks wanted lower bunks, or they wanted to be near a window—or not near a window. Baby formulas had to be sorted out, and of course people would often be up in the night wanting an aspirin or whatever. It wasn't unusual to work a steady eighteen hours.

Brook Street was just a skip away from Claridges, an exclusive hotel. We always peered into the cars that pulled up there, although we never saw a celebrity. Naturally we had time off and really enjoyed seeing a bit of the countryside and some of the shows.

The walk to work took us through Grosvenor Square with its delightful little park, and South Street Hostel itself was interesting. It was the former home of Lord Abercrombie and had the most beautiful sweeping staircase of marble. We also had an elevator which was forever getting stuck between floors. Miss Duff, who supervised both British and Canadian Red Cross projects, paid us frequent visits and, for these, we all dashed madly about to see that things were shipshape. I think everyone was a bit nervous around Miss Duff.

One of the army cooks acquired a dear wee puppy which was promptly christened "Duffy." On one of Miss Duff's visits she spotted the pup (which we had unsuccessfully tried to keep out of the way) and, although I'm quite sure she already knew it, she asked what the pup was called. Everyone just stood dumbly around without daring to answer. Finally as she turned and walked off, we thought we heard her murmur, "Cowards!"

I made three trips across the Atlantic, bringing the war brides to Canada on various ships—*Lady Rodney, Lady Nelson, Letitia*—but the trip I enjoyed most was on the *Aquitania*. It was so luxurious. I appreciated the ship's beautiful furnishings and decor (especially the wood panelling and carvings), because I grew up surrounded by the antiques my mother collected.

On board, we escort officers didn't have our own cabins; five of us would share a cabin together. We were each assigned a group of war brides, and we were kept busy the whole trip. We did what we could to keep everyone cheery—not easy when half your group of war brides and children were seasick. Keeping up the morale of the war brides was often hard because many of them were sad about leaving home and some of them were experiencing second thoughts about leaving Britain. They came from all walks of life, and we even had the occasional war bride coming from Holland, Belgium or France. The war brides loved to ask questions about Canada and we did our best to answer them.

In Canada, we would have forty-eight-hours leave before re-

Maple Leaf Club, No. 1, London.

turning to England. That's when we would stand in line to buy a pair of nylons for someone in England who had begged you to bring nylons back for them. On one trip, I was lucky and bought one or two pairs to take back—after standing in line for five hours at Simpson's.

On one of the return trips from Halifax to England after the war ended, we took quite a large group of German prisoners on the ship with us. They had been sent during the war to a prisoner of war camp in Ontario and were going back to England, and then on to Germany. We were not allowed to fraternize, but they would wave from their deck. One of them was quite an artist. He would do little sketches of the girls who were sitting on deck, and then he would send them down to us. It was hard to imagine that only a short time before they had been the "enemy."

In May 1946, I had to give up my overseas duties because my mother was ill. At first I was a Red Cross worker at a hospital in Winnipeg. Then I became an escort officer on the trains that were taking the war brides to their different destinations across Canada. I travelled from Winnipeg to Calgary, Winnipeg to Edmonton, and did one trip from Winnipeg to Vancouver. On the trains, we looked after the war brides and tried to make them feel welcome. We also made sure that each war bride got off at the right station with all her luggage and that someone was coming to meet her. The war brides were very brave to leave home, because they didn't know when they would see their families again. They had come to a country with which they weren't familiar, and to a husband that they had probably known only briefly.

Sometimes we would stop in the middle of the prairies to let a girl off, and away in the distance you would see headlights coming. The train would slowly pull away, and the girl, who might have a child with her, would stand there with her luggage waiting for this truck coming across the prairie to pick her up. It seemed so sad. Some were picked up in horse-drawn carts, and some really didn't know where they were going. I think most of them were happy, although some certainly returned home—discouraged and disappointed. Often they had been told a wonderful tale of what they were coming to, and they were not coming to that at all.

In 1948 I joined the Red Cross Blood Tranfusion Service. I worked at the Blood Transfusion Service in Edmonton for almost a year, and then in Winnipeg when the service opened there. It was still the Red Cross, but it was now a paying job. All my work as a VAD had been voluntary. I was responsible for setting up the bottles and the needles, for washing out the bottles and tubes, and assuring that they were all autoclaved (sterilized). The Winnipeg clinic covered the whole province. The first Red Cross Blood Transfusion Clinic had opened in Vancouver in 1948. I was with the service for about five years, until I was married.

I met my husband Bill on a train from Toronto to Winnipeg when I was returning home from a holiday. Bill was working for a pharmaceutical company and had been in Canada for only a short period of time. After we were married in 1954, we came to British Columbia for a two-week holiday. Bill was from England, and once he saw the west coast, he said, "I don't care how I do it, but I am going to live on Vancouver Island one day." He also said that every Canadian should live in a log house, so we had a log house built when we moved to Vancouver Island in 1971.

I enjoyed my time with the Canadian Red Cross as an escort officer, meeting new people and making them feel welcome. We had a great bunch of girls in our group—lots of laughing, some crying, but everyone pulled her weight.

Jean Ellis Wright

*"Down the shaky rope ladder
we went"*

—

Jean Ellis Wright was born in Winnipeg, Manitoba, where she resided
until her family moved to Victoria. During the 1930s she worked
in a bookstore in Victoria and later she worked as a bank
secretary in Vancouver. She joined the Canadian
Red Cross Corps in Victoria. After the war she
wrote *Face Powder and Gunpowder,* a book
about her wartime experiences with
the Canadian Red Cross Corps.

After receiving the dreaded cable in 1942 advising that my navy husband had been killed overseas, I joined the Canadian Red Cross Corps and trained to be a VAD (Voluntary Aid Detachment) for Canadian military hospitals. A few months later, I was called to go overseas to work as a welfare officer in a Canadian military hospital. This involved doing whatever was required, other than nursing, for the patients.

In Toronto in June 1943, six of us Red Cross girls travelled by train to Halifax where we boarded the *Oregon Express,* a 3,000-ton vessel—formerly a fruit boat. To our surprise, our quarters bordered on the luxurious—staterooms with chintz curtains and meals in the officers' quarters. We all said: "Enjoy it while we can!"

Next morning we sailed out to join a convoy of eighty ships, eight abreast and ten deep, flanked by navy escort ships. It was a thrilling sight. We soon had lifeboat drill, clad in heavy greatcoats and lifebelts, which included a whistle and flashlight. Down the shaky rope ladder we went and into the lifeboats. The crew rowed us around a bit and back to the ship and then we climbed up the shaky rope ladder—thinking it all great fun.

Fourteen days later, our little ship broke convoy in the Irish Sea and sailed up the Mersey River to Liverpool on a cold, wet night in September. A Canadian Movement Control Officer came aboard; he knew all our names and where we had come from and put us on a train for London. And so, R/C Jean Ellis, OD, the 109th Red Cross girl to go overseas, set foot on English soil—glad to be there, but still a bit apprehensive. Little did we know that our *Oregon Express* would be torpedoed and sunk on her return trip to Canada; nor did we know that when we were aboard—she had carried ammunition!

We were billeted at Corps House in London, the official residence for Red Cross girls. For a few months we worked in several departments at Red Cross headquarters on Berkeley Square— doing various necessary jobs. At night, everyone had a turn at fire-watching on the roof of Corps House, searching for any damage from air raids.

In February 1944, Connie from Saint John, New Brunswick,

Marjorie from Windsor, Ontario, and myself from Victoria, British Columbia, were posted to No. 18 Canadian General Hospital in Essex for welfare training. Our patients were convalescing from active duty in North Africa or Italy. Each of us visited them daily and, for rehabilitation, we taught them occupational skills to restore muscles. As they were bed patients, we started them making string belts, embroidering cushion covers (dreadful pictures of Churchill with a cigar) and working leather articles. Getting them started was difficult, but once someone decided to try, we soon had the whole ward busy making belts for their girlfriends, vying with each other as to who could make the best. String was everywhere, different colours for each patient, and the competition was on. The cushion covers were a bit more difficult to handle, but soon we had everyone doing something.

In April 1944, we three girls were posted to No. 7 Canadian General Hospital which had six hundred beds, sixty nursing sisters and three Red Cross girls. No. 7 was slated to be the first Canadian General Hospital to cross to Normandy after D-Day. In the meantime, our hospital was in Yorkshire on hold awaiting the Big Day. We spent several weeks under canvas, going on long daily route marches—first carrying only a water bottle, but later on, carrying full packs. We moved quarters several times, learning to pack and move to another location quickly.

On the morning of June 6th, during our daily morning exercise, our matron came running out of her tent, shouting, "It's D-Day!" There was sudden silence. No doubt silent prayers were offered for the men in the landing, many of whom we knew. Ten days later, No. 7 was on its way to Eastbourne, Sussex, in a closed train with blinds drawn. Here, we waited for two weeks in hotels along the sea front, before being transferred to the marshalling area, just north of Southampton.

The area was known as the "Sausage Machine" through which all units (British, American and Canadian) had to pass before crossing the English Channel. Day and night, "The Voice" boomed out orders and instructions about who was to do what. No. 7's orders finally came one morning at 5 a.m., when the public address system barked out: "No. 7 Canadian General Hospital arise at once and be prepared to move at 7 a.m.!" After a hearty breakfast, we were driven to the dock and loaded onto a hospital ship for Normandy. Little did we deserve such luxury—real beds!

The next morning our ship anchored a hundred yards off the Normandy shore, and we transferred to water ambulances which took us to the beach. No sooner were we out of the water ambulances than slats were placed over them and stretchers loaded with wounded were placed aboard—to be taken back to English hospitals on the hospital ship. We girls were greeted on shore by Colonel Earl Wight of the Medical Services, who directed us to waiting lorries. What timing! What organization! Driving through towns, we were waved at by French people leaning out of their windows, throwing us flowers and kisses, while passing lines of cheering soldiers, shouted, "Women!" We were on the famous "Maple Leaf Up," the main highway from Normandy to Germany, the only road which had been cleared of land mines. We sang "O Canada" and "The Maple Leaf Forever" to let everyone know we Canadians had arrived to join the troops who were still forging ahead.

It was July 14, 1944. Few, if any, buildings were left standing. Dead cows and other animals were often lying upside down with legs up in the air. The fields were desolate. A motorcycle dispatch rider joined our convoy, weaving in and out along the route. In convoy, his word was law. At one time, when aircraft were approaching, he ordered us all out and on the ground under our lorries. We eventually arrived at a British hospital near Bayeux where half our girls were dropped off to stay a few days, until our tent unit was set up five miles ahead. The other half, including me, joined No. 75 British Hospital. It was a long day, and we were happy to crawl into our cots in a large tent.

The next morning, the British matron asked our girls for help, as a huge convoy of wounded was about to arrive from the front, and her staff would be hard-pressed to handle them all. As Connie and I were not nurses, the matron asked us to report to the admitting tent and do what we could for the wounded awaiting medical attention.

Soldier hitch-hiking on the Maple Leaf Up highway, France.

The Red Cross had provided us with cartons of cigarettes. Huge urns of hot coffee and tea were brought from the kitchen. This was the day Caen was taken, and casualties were so heavy that many patients had not been able to go to dressing stations or casualty clearing stations first, but were brought directly to the British hospital after having only first-aid treatment. Stretchers were lifted from ambulances into the admitting tent and gently laid on a large tarpaulin on the grass.

We gave cigarettes and hot coffee to patients who had been medically examined and given permission for such items. The permission was written on the records hung around their necks. While the lads dictated, we wrote hundreds of letters home to wives, sweethearts and "Mum." Some of the lads were too badly injured to dictate, so we found the next of kin on their dog tags and advised the relative that he was safe in a British hospital and would be transferred to England within a few days. New arrivals were undressed with the help of orderlies and put into pyjamas. One lad asked me where he was, then said: "Please—take my . . . boots off." He hadn't had them off for two weeks, and his socks were stuck to them. I washed his face in a little pan of water, then washed his feet. He gave a sigh of relief, opened his eyes and whispered, "Ahhh . . . thanks." This was a precious moment for me.

A few days later, the No. 7 nurses and Red Cross girls piled into lorries, drove five or ten miles forward on "Maple Leaf Up," then stopped at an orchard, which was to be our home for the next two months. It was like a homecoming—to join our entire No. 7 unit. The men had come directly to this site, bivouacked on the ground for five days, and set up our tent hospital for six hundred beds. We were five miles from Bayeux. Around a large compound were tents: an X-ray tent, an operating-room tent and two rows of thirty tents each for the nursing sisters' quarters. Across a hedge were the medical officers' tents and the men's quarters.

A "biffy" for the girls was at the end of our tent lines. The sanitation squad had dug deep holes and placed apple boxes over them carved into "ovals." They then hung sacking around three sides of the biffy, leaving the fourth side and top open to the elements. Very good thinking, as eventually many of us had the "trots" from the wasps invading the biffies, then getting into the kitchen. Our sleeping tents were furnished with safari beds (just seven inches off the ground), eiderdown bedrolls, dunnage bags, suitcases and—believe it or not—our trunks! They had followed us from England.

Scrounging began at once: a long piece of rope, strung from front to back of the tent, kept our clothes hanging high up from the damp ground (and later on, from the water on the ground). Trunks became tables. A great treasure we found was three long boards which were placed under our cots to keep us a bit drier, although we had to wear rubber boots as soon as we got out of our beds. Our Red Cross tent had trestle tables and folding chairs. We had packing boxes full of cigarettes, books, razors, shaving soap, washcloths, gum, chocolate bars, paper and pencils—all of which were to be distributed to incoming patients in their "battle bags." Light was from a hurricane lamp, as it was in the wards and quarters. A mobile generator provided electricity for the operating-room.

For three days, we rolled bandages and helped the nurses prepare the wards. Then No. 7 Canadian General Hospital was open for business. Our first casualties came from Caen and the Falaise Gap. Many of the men were treated first at a casualty clearing station, and some were even in pyjamas on arrival.

Our first convoy arrived at night, having advised us by phone that they were en route. Convoys consisted of long streams of ambulances, travelling slowly because of potholes, each carrying about five or six stretcher cases. One Red Cross girl was on duty each night to greet each patient. After he had been examined by a medical officer, we followed the same procedure as before: if his medical card attached to his clothing permitted it, we gave him a drink—many drinks—and cigarettes. Then came that important letter to be written home.

The stretcher-bearers were patient, gentle and seemed tireless. They carried the wounded in, laid them gently on the tarpaulin-covered grass, and later, carried them to the wards. As our location was not too far behind the front line, our patients were all moved within forty-eight hours, either to England or to hospitals farther back from the front lines; and again, the wonderful stretcher bearers moved them ever so gently. Each patient carried a complete record of any treatment he had received, what drugs he had been given, and so on. Frequently, up to three hundred wounded were admitted at a time, always travelling at night in case of observation from the air. We visited every patient each day, and our most important duty seemed to be to listen—most of them longing to talk about the battle and how they were wounded.

Water was very scarce. One water truck went out every twenty-four hours, taking four hours to make the trip, and its load had to supply all our hospital's needs until the next day. Laundry was difficult, but a nursing sister who spoke fluent French went with me on a hunt for a laundress among the neighbouring farms. Many farms had been abandoned, but a few people still clung to their homes. We found a French woman who agreed to do our personal washing each week, if we supplied the soap and gave her some extra for her own use, as soap was very scarce.

Food rations were always suspected of being horsemeat, which wouldn't have been so bad, but the thought of all the bloated dead horses we had seen in the orchards made it seem repulsive. Food was food, however, although nearly everyone in the unit developed dysentery, which was immediately termed "the Normandy Glide." We assumed it was caused by flies and wasps, and it became debilitating.

One day, our matron asked for eight volunteers to attend a party with British Engineers. These requests came rather frequently, but as we were all so tired at the end of a day, volunteers were hard to come by. However, she persuaded Connie, Marge and myself to join five nursing sisters to drive in a truck a few miles away to Arromanches. The engineers had made a wooden floor for dancing and provided a six-piece band recruited from batmen, cooks and the sanitary squad.

In front of the band, a large sign read "Mulberry," which at first we thought a bit ridiculous. However, we discovered we were on the site of the famous "Mulberry" operation. These officers had constructed the now famous prefabricated harbour built with concrete caissons hauled over from England. We had seen the caissons on the coast at Eastbourne in England and wondered what they were. The harbour was used for the landing in Normandy on D-Day. It was an engineering marvel.

We had frequent air raids and a few scary nights in our tents. As our hospital was clearly marked by a huge red cross on the ground, we were supposed to be safe from attack. Nevertheless, we had our share of nightly enemy aircraft overhead. The Allies sent up terrific barrages of anti-aircraft fire, and much of the resulting shrapnel flew around—one big piece made a hole in our tent. Some nights I wore my steel helmet on my face and other nights on my stomach, because I had no idea where the shrapnel might land.

After two months, our hospital had orders to move forward to another location. We evacuated our patients to England or to another military hospital in France. Then the nurses packed beds and hospital equipment; doctors and orderlies looked after the operating-room equipment, dispensary and X-ray equipment. We Red Cross girls packed all our equipment, nailing everything down in twelve large crates. Connie and I lost many of our treasures, such as a broken mirror, two lovely logs which made coffee tables, a dandy biscuit tin which had been a table for us—all classified as impossible to transport.

Next morning we got up at 4 a.m., packed beds and bedrolls, and had a rather dreadful breakfast of bread, jam and a sort of "fluid intake"—quite unidentifiable. An hour later, on that cold morning, all the girls were sitting on bedrolls watching for our lorries. But it was not until 7:30 a.m. that the vehicles arrived and we were on our way. A rearguard stayed behind to bury all the garbage and to cover latrines, leaving our orchard as neat as we had found it. There were twenty girls to a truck, sitting on hard board seats lining both sides, with some of us sitting on our bedrolls in the centre. Once on the road we were surprised to see ambulances joining us. They turned out to be our SIW (self-inflicted wounds) patients. They had all been assigned to our hospital and were awaiting court-martial.

It rained and rained. After three long hours the convoy stopped and the matron appeared at our lorry, advising us to use the biffy now as it might be a long time before the next stop. She led us to a vehicle in our convoy with a small stepladder at the back. In we went, two at a time, to find apple boxes and tin containers underneath. It was necessary that we carry our own "convenience" as many roads and verges had not been cleared of mines and under no condition could we go into the bushes. Cooks arrived at the lorries with huge urns of hot tea, and handed out large nameless sandwiches. The cooks consoled us by telling us they were carrying delicious beef stew for our evening meal upon arrival.

At 7:30 p.m., we drove up to an old French château. What a joy to be under a roof! We were welcomed by the owner, elderly Madame la Comtesse, who had been allowed to stay in segregated, soundproofed rooms, while the rest of the château was used as a German headquarters for years. Marble floors, crystal chandeliers and a real roof. The matron allotted rooms which housed all but twenty-four girls. The château bedrooms were beautiful—mahogany beds, chintz curtains, etc. The lucky girls put their own bedrolls on top of the mattresses upon which the German officers had slept. The other twenty-four girls, myself included, again slept in tents out on the lawn—with a "biffy" tent at the end of the lines. We each had an oil stove, very welcome as it was cold and wet outside. Never mind, there was always that delicious stew to look forward to. To our horror, the cooks announced that the SIW patients had eaten all our stew, explaining that the patients always had priority. So we had dog biscuits, jam and warmed-over tea. Oh well, so be it.

The hospital tents were put up about half a mile down the road. It wasn't possible to use the château as a hospital, since it wasn't big enough. When patients finally arrived, they included many German prisoners sent down from the huge prisoner of war camp near Dieppe. One was a major-general who wore an iron cross and brought his own medical orderly and batman to look after his interests. However, after two days of tests and diagnosis, our doctors couldn't find anything wrong with him but a cut finger, so he was promptly sent back to prison camp, protesting loudly. What a fine group—German prisoners, self-inflicted wounds, and finally we got the VDs for a while. However, we realized that every man was not cut out to be a fighting front-line soldier and some just couldn't "take" it.

The conditions now—"compo" rations combined with the rain and fog—caused a general depression among the staff. Finally the old "Normandy Glide" returned, now called the "Dieppe Dance." Nearly everyone had a touch of it, but Nursing Sister Phil McElroy and I were really ill. I was in bed for a week and very grateful to Connie and Marge who carried food to me, although not very much stayed down. Finally, the matron sent Phil and me to Deauville to a rest centre for forty-eight hours. A truck drove us there in about two hours. What a joy! It was warm and we had real beds in a bedroom with a light. There was no heat and no hot water, but that was unimportant. These cooks took regular army rations and glamorized them into delicious dishes—soufflés instead of pieces of cheese—and fresh bread. Soon we were human again, and two days later were back at work at our hospital.

One day, one of our nursing sisters came back from a party saying: "Guess what? I met an officer of the Mobile Bath and Laundry Unit." He belonged to a British unit which went around, setting up in different areas where there were army units. It had its own pipes and generators, and it piped water from a nearby stream into specially equipped trucks where the water was heated. A unit's blankets and clothing were then washed and sterilized, leaving them completely debugged. They also had equipment for taking a bath. These baths were usually reserved for themselves, but we fixed that. We invited them to a party in our mess, where we turned on the charm and wangled an invitation for us to have a bath.

The matron put up a notice that eight girls a day could go, between the hours of 3 p.m. and 5 p.m. The British men even sent cars to take us on the ten-mile drive. And away we went, equipped with soap, towels and anticipation. The tubs were enormous galvanized iron things with a ladder to climb up into them. Oh, joy! Abundant hot water! We scrubbed each other, washed our hair, put it up in curlers and kerchiefs, and then had tea in the mess. As long as the Mobile Bath and Laundry Unit was in the area, we could have a bath once a week. This marvellous unit did free laundry service, too, so we sent blankets, dressing gowns or battledress to have them beautifully cleaned. We hadn't seen such luxury since leaving home.

At this time, Antwerp and Brussels were leave centres for troops on forty-eight-hour leaves. The Canadian and British Armies were trying to keep the port of Antwerp open to sea traffic for importing supplies, so the Germans were striving to make the port useless, hitting it with V-1 and V-2 bombs. The Canadian hospitals there (No. 6 and No. 8) sent out a call for help, as the number of men on leave in Antwerp who became casualties of the bombing was tremendous. Connie and I were sent to augment the number of Red Cross girls already working in these hospitals.

As Antwerp was being V-bombed every half-hour, day and

night, the girls of No. 8 Canadian General Hospital did not live in the hospital. So the nursing staff would not be wiped out, we were posted in five different places in case one place was hit. I drew a top-floor billet in a very modern apartment building. There were already twelve girls there, and being last in, I was assigned to the living room, with its glass doors, windows, mirrors everywhere and the usual huge glass chandelier. I decided the safest place for me was under the grand piano, so there I put my safari bed. It was good news, indeed, when our matron announced that she was moving us to another billet on the second and third floor. The move proved most fortunate, since we learned the next morning that our former penthouse had received a direct hit and that the walls of my living room billet had caved in.

November 26, 1944 was a day of horror. During lunch a bomb fell which sounded pretty close. We dropped everything and rushed over to the hospital where we saw vehicles of every size and shape bringing in wounded. Handcarts, ambulances, horse-drawn wagons—all were filled with wounded civilians and soldiers. At the hospital gates, I saw eight bodies, including a British nursing sister laid out on the doorstep—the work of only one V-2 bomb which fell at an intersection in the heart of Antwerp.

At our admitting-room, the medical officer told me to do anything I could for the roomful of patients, but to start with washing out their eyes. I also served hot tea to anyone who could drink. A general call had been sent out, and every army nurse and doctor in Antwerp returned to duty. Blood was streaming down the streets; headless bodies and pieces of arms or legs were lying in the street. A few days later, another direct hit was scored. It was a sad week. I scribbled many messages to the next of kin of the dying men, as my heart ached for them. Soon afterwards, the military hospital was moved to a safer area, and early the following month, Connie and I had orders to rejoin our very own No. 7 Canadian General Hospital at Turnhout, Belgium, twenty-five miles east of Antwerp. It was good to be back with our friends.

For the first time, No. 7 was operating as a General Hospital. We were farther behind the lines and patients were kept longer, then either evacuated to England or sent back to the Front. Surgeons were busy night and day. Our hospital had formerly been a three-storey boys' school with large rooms, cement floors and large sunny windows. We had room for three operating rooms. Nobody had to sleep in tents. As before, we Red Cross girls made daily visits to every patient except those in certain contagious wards. Each man received identical Red Cross comforts—books, battle bags, cigarettes and chocolate bars. We had a sort of "tea-wagon" holding supplies, which made it much easier to distribute things. In addition to the comforts we distributed, we encouraged the men to engage in handicraft activities. We had many Polish and Belgian patients who had been on operations with the Canadians. We found our common language was French, since the Poles spoke it at least a little and the Belgians spoke it fluently.

During December, we admitted a large number of diphtheria cases. After tests given to every member of the staff showed "negative" reactions, Connie, Marge and I were allowed into their ward. We wore sterile masks, were forbidden to touch anything and were told to drop cigarettes or magazines on the beds. No letters could be written for the boys.

Most patients, however, were wound cases, and operations were performed continuously. Doctors had little time to enter details on each patient's medical record. As I knew shorthand, it became part of my job. I would report to the operating-room at night and take dictation as the surgeons operated. Then I wrote up each operation on the cards.

One night I passed a patient waiting in turn on a stretcher. He looked frightened and said, "Sister, I'm scared. Will you go in with me and hold my hand until I'm right under the anaesthetic?" When I told the surgeon that I had promised to be with him, he agreed. So gowned, capped and masked like the others, I went along with the boy. After that, I performed the same service several times. One evening, the surgeon asked me to sit on the operating table and lean forward so he could place the patient against me, also leaning forward. A piece of shrapnel was embedded in an awkward place, and he wanted his patient in that position so he could remove it.

Relative to what we had become accustomed to, the girls' quarters here were luxurious. Apparently the boys in this former school were very young, as our individual rooms were tiny. However, we had whitewashed walls, cement floors and a very small cupboard besides our own tiny wash basin. Safaris and cots went up, in went the trunks, and the rooms were furnished.

By early December, we started making Christmas decorations. Everyone saved silver paper from cigarette boxes and coloured paper from newspapers. Anything and everything was saved. We had seven hundred patients in fifteen wards and each ward was decorated. The bed patients cut out strips for light shades, paper chains, and cutouts for stars, moons and letters.

At last Christmas Eve arrived. At 7 p.m., twenty-five members of the unit gathered in our Chapel, then strolled through the corridors and into each ward, singing carols in harmony—some sang descants. Lights had been extinguished. As we entered the room, a patient turned on the Christmas tree switch (the Christmas trees were supplied by the Royal Engineers, with no questions asked about the source). As we sang, some of the patients joined in; others were in tears. Patients on crutches, some in blankets, others in plaster casts, but all sang with us. It was an experience I'll always remember.

At midnight, we Red Cross girls tiptoed into each darkened ward, stealthily moving from bed to bed, tying a pair of socks to the foot of each. Christmas morning, we rose early to see how the boys liked their new socks, oranges, chocolate bars, peanuts, cigarettes and various other articles from the Red Cross. We explained that the socks were knitted by women in all parts of Canada and that many of them had notes in the toes. That evening, nursing sisters and Red Cross girls served dinner to other ranks in the men's mess. On Boxing Day, the sergeants served dinner to us. No one was permitted "out" to any parties as the entire Canadian Army in our area was confined to barracks, owing to the threat of enemy paratroopers who had landed nearby.

Wounded Canadians in a hospital tent near the front lines.

Two months later, three Red Cross girls, including myself, were picked up in a lorry by the official driver and driven forward to three different casualty clearing stations closer to the Front. I was taken to No. 2 Casualty Clearing Station (CCS) at Meppen, having passed through the Reichswald Forest, past the famous Siegfried Line, and across the Rhine. Everywhere were large white "surrender sheets" hanging from windows, attached to verandahs or whatever.

We were a small unit in the female department—a matron, nine nursing sisters and myself. We had beautiful spring-filled mattresses in two apartments across the road from our CCS. Our patients were brought directly from the Front, placed in our admission-and-dispatch room and examined by medical officers. Those fit to travel were sent on to the general hospitals. If not, they were admitted to our Allied ward, operated on and kept for at least a week. Nearly four hundred patients a day went through our admission-and-dispatch room.

It was my job to greet every patient as he came in. Those able to chat often shouted: "Gosh, she's a Canadian!" When I had looked after all the stretcher cases, I joined the walking cases who were eager to talk. They told me what they had been through, who had been wounded, asking about Canada—many not having been home for four years or more. I wrote many letters home for them and handed out tomato juice and grapefruit juice, but above all I just listened. These patients had to be lifted when their beds were changed, fed at every meal, moved carefully when IV needles were in both arms and legs. Time passed slowly for them when they were conscious.

One night when the men were restless, an orderly sat down and quietly played the chapel organ. One head after another turned to him and said, "Please play louder." Rich notes swelled and filled the room. The nursing sister on duty suggested a singsong, and those who were able took part while the rest lay back contentedly on their pillows listening to old favourites like "Annie Laurie" and "Pack Up Your Troubles." From then on, music in the evening was a regular event.

April passed quickly. Operations went on night and day. By May 1st, bets were being placed that the war would end before the D-Day anniversary, June 6th. On May 4th, we were sitting around the radio listening as usual when at 8:15 p.m. the BBC announced the electrifying news: German surrender had taken place in Holland, Northwest Germany and Denmark. "Cease Fire" would begin at 8 a.m., May 5th.

Suddenly the mess was a madhouse. Everyone was laughing and crying and talking excitedly. We rushed to the wards to tell the good news to our boys first, then to tell the German patients and watch their sullen responses. In fact, there was no joyous outburst among our boys, just contented relief—they would not have to return to the Front to endure further horrors. The official Victory-in-Europe Day came on May 8th. By this time, No. 2 CCS had again moved forward about twenty miles to Leer, Germany. All messes held celebrations with a rum-ration handout, but there was also an undercurrent of sadness. Victory would not wipe out the memory of the horror, nor restore sight to the blind or health to shattered bodies.

Across the road was a British unit, and to an accordion accompaniment, one hundred and twenty English lads were singing like inspired choir boys. We had two pianos in our lounge, and before long the British boys had rushed across the street and carried our piano outside to the middle of the road. One of the officers sat down, ran his fingers over the keys, and drew out lovely melodies dear to us all. The British were joined by our boys, and the whole group stood around the piano singing the old favourites—"Drink To Me Only With Thine Eyes" and "White Christmas." After dark a huge bonfire was lit and the music carried on. The flames were fed by old carts, fence posts and even wheelbarrows, while our German neighbours looked on, very angry. Civilians, thousands of miles away, may have celebrated by getting drunk, but these lads were content to stand in the middle of the road in a German village as they sang around an old piano.

Although the fighting had stopped, there was still plenty of work for the hospitals. New casualties came in even after the "Cease Fire": many of them shot by snipers; others as victims of mines or accidents.

It was wonderful to awaken on the morning of May 5th and know there was a ceasefire, but our unit was too busy getting ready to move to feel much emotion. Early that morning, a convoy formed, complete with our treasured spring-filled mattresses, and bumped along the frightful road filled with potholes. Our new building had formerly been a German Marine Hospital. When the enemy fled, they left behind a deplorable mess: Marine uniforms on the floor and in cupboards, filth and dirt everywhere, and an awful smell. The minute we arrived, our matron, the nursing sisters and I rolled up our sleeves and started scrubbing. We sterilized all the beds, furniture and walls, rearranged beds into wards for surgical or medical cases, and within twenty-four hours we were ready to admit patients.

On June 3rd, from our building, we saw the first great trek of German prisoners from Holland. Three times a day for five days, these columns of men and vehicles passed our door. Thousands of Germans were marching from an area around The Hague, Rotterdam and Amsterdam, across the famous twenty-mile Causeway over the Zuiderzee, into Germany, where they would be placed in camps. There, they would be sorted into work parties to repair the damage in countries they had pillaged and destroyed. It was a five-day trek through blazing sun or pouring rain.

Leading the parade were Canadian gun carriers manned by well-armed troops. Behind them were cars carrying German officers and men who were physically unfit, followed by column after column of men on foot. Next came a huge column with horses pulling every kind of wagon and car fitted up as portable kitchens or supply carriers. One kitchen, formerly a hay wagon, was now covered with plywood and canvas sides and had a roof with a chimney poking through the top. First-aid cars were covered with canvas with red crosses on their sides. Behind all this confusion came soldiers on bicycles, or pushing wheelbarrows and even old baby carriages containing more supplies. There were no happy expressions anywhere, as the men knew they were going to prisoner of war camps, and we couldn't feel smug over victory.

For the next five months, our CCS operated as a small general hospital, treating cases of all descriptions—serious fractures, sore throats, and many jeep-accident injuries—apparently the result of carefree drivers after the war was over. We also had patients injured by the many undetected mines in the area. What a waste to have casualties after the war was over.

My duties returned to handicrafts—a Godsend for the patients, as most of them were not wounded, just sick or convalescing, and time hung heavily. Large amounts of handicraft supplies arrived from good old Red Cross headquarters in Brussels, which never failed us. The doctors and nurses were kept busy dodging the confusion, but all agreed that the therapy was definitely speeding up recovery. Again the wards looked like textile mills, but the patients now had activities to keep them busy. We had a recreation hall which became more cheerful after a can of red paint was used here and there. Here, the boys could play cards, do handicrafts or just sit around discussing their futures. We also had an auditorium, and movies were brought in by Auxiliary Services, with many patients being carried in or moved in their beds.

Returning home was on everyone's mind. This was based entirely on the point system—so many points for length of service, length of service overseas, marital status, etc. Some were eager to get home; others almost reluctant, since many marriages had broken down during the war. We had all led a very unnatural existence for years in which privacy was unknown. We had eaten food cooked in great quantities, all tasting alike or having no taste at all. Many hesitated now to share their deepest thoughts with anyone, fearing ridicule. They all hoped they could go home to experience a normal life, knowing that this privilege would be denied to many. Much could never be forgotten, but much, too, would be a basis for a fuller, richer life in the future.

Farewell parties started during the summer. How do you say goodbye? One night after a farewell party, a returning officer was sitting in a darkened room with the glow from a lamp shining on the grand piano. He was playing again the songs we had sung together during the evening—loath to leave it all. When my turn came to go home in October, I knew then how he had felt. I could feel myself looking back over my shoulder, silently saying goodbye to a never-to-be-forgotten experience.

I sailed home on the *Ile-de-France,* along with seven thousand others. My stateroom, built to accommodate four, was occupied by twenty-three girls in double-decker bunks. In the adjoining room were twenty-five girls, a six-week-old baby and a small black spaniel, smuggled aboard. Between the two staterooms were four biffies, four tin wash basins and very little floor space. Five of the girls in my stateroom were pregnant and had "morning sickness." We sailed at dawn to the stirring strains of "The Maple Leaf Forever" and "O Canada" played by an army band.

On board, life became a series of orders and directions. The PA system went on day and night, the speaker always calling for someone to report to so-and-so. When the announcer ran out of names, he started listing lost articles which must be returned AT ONCE to the Orderly Room. Water was turned off between 8 a.m. and 4 p.m. We had to queue for meals—and so it went, relentlessly.

The Officers' Lounge was located by various signs along the way, and once inside the door you were greeted by hot air mixed with a haze of blue smoke. The few chairs had been filled hours before, and most of the floor space was occupied by bodies, sitting or sprawling. A chair was never vacant, as groups of passengers would stare at it, waiting greedily in the hope it might be free before long. A general rental system had sprung up with no vacancies.

The main entertainment was provided by the series of queues. If you saw three or four passengers in a group, even remotely suggesting a single file, you joined them. It must be for something! The door of the wicket opened and the guessing began: would it be chocolate bars, gum or Coca-Cola?

After five days we neared Halifax. I didn't know what lay ahead of me. It had been three years since my husband had been killed, and I had gradually come to terms with my loss. I was ready to begin again with many precious memories.

Aircraft circled overhead bidding us welcome. The PA again belched out directions: Don't get in the lifeboats. Don't do this or that. Closer and closer we sailed. Necks craned for a glimpse of Halifax. Tears flowed down many cheeks. Fireboats sent up sprays of water in welcome. The band played "O Canada." Yet it was a day and a half before we Canadians set foot on solid ground. When at last we came down the gangplank, we were stopped short by a huge sign that said it all: "Maple Leaf—Home!"

Eileen (Biddie) Wilkins

*"The whole side of
my ambulance came off"*

—

Eileen (Biddie) Wilkins was born and raised in Victoria. She attended
Queen Margarets School in Duncan, a small town north of
Victoria. She married and resided in Halifax and
Kingston before returning to Victoria where
she joined the Red Cross. After the war
she focused her time on her family
of three children and her
volunteer work.

There were many reasons for wanting to join the Red Cross—to help in the war effort and to see Europe—but I confess that the main reason was to follow my husband overseas. And my mission was accomplished, eventually. We'd been married in April 1941, but it was July 1944 when I finally left Canada. I travelled over on a British freighter, the *Glenstrae*—a terrible old ship. The engines kept conking out, and we even had to sleep in our clothes in case of an emergency. She was the slowest boat in the biggest convoy that had ever gone overseas at this time (and incidentally she was sunk shortly after in the Mediterranean Sea).

There were about twenty Red Cross girls on this trip. There were also many Fairbridge Farm boys being returned to England. These were children from Britain who had been sent out to Fairbridge Farm in Duncan, where they learned about farming, but the original idea had been to get them away from the war. These boys must have come to Canada when they were about twelve years old, and now they were returning to England as fifteen- or sixteen-year-olds. I think they were going back because they were now old enough to help on the English farms.

I went over to England to work as a Red Cross ambulance driver. When we arrived in Liverpool, we were told that all the Canadian Red Cross drivers were seconded to the British Red Cross and that the job would involve a certain amount of danger. I don't remember being nervous at all—only excited, because I was going to see my husband. However, the very day I landed in Liverpool, he left for Algiers from Southampton. I would not see him until the war was over. I must have been upset for a time, but we were so busy that I didn't really have time to think about it. Once we received our assignments, we were just pushed into work right away.

We spent several months based in Chester, from where we'd drive to Liverpool to pick up patients—either from a hospital ship or a railhead when they came in by train. Chester was very close, part of Liverpool really. The patients we picked up were usually British Army soldiers. Occasionally these would include Canadians and Australians, but mostly they were British. We usually drove by ourselves. When we arrived at the hospital ship, an orderly put the patient into our ambulance. Then when we reached the hospital or wherever we were taking him, another orderly arranged to take him out.

I vividly remember one particularly gruelling assignment. I was carrying a prisoner of war who had been critically injured, but when I arrived at the hospital with him, I was told, "We're not taking him—he's dead." I drove him to other hospitals, but they wouldn't take him either. That night I drove to hospital after hospital until I finally found one that would take him—somewhere on the outskirts of London. All through that night there was bombing going on, but I was more scared of the dead man than I was of the bombing. I'd never had anything to do with a dead person before. I was twenty-three years old.

Although quite a few hospitals were situated in remote places, there was no time for training or learning the routes we would have to drive. Nor was there any time for learning how to drive the British vehicles. In fact, I had never driven a large ambulance in all my life until I had gone to Toronto for a brief stint of training, which fortunately also included maintenance of the ambulance.

We were always given a pretty good idea of where we going, but driving an ambulance in England in wartime was not easy. Everything was blacked out, and with our little slits for headlights on the ambulance, we could barely see the road, far less any landmarks or signs. I lost my way many times. What was worse, we had to fill out a report when we returned as to where we'd been and account for all those miles. Driving on the opposite side of the road was not difficult, but it seemed whenever we went round the block in England, we never came out where we started.

After several months in Chester, we were stationed at a Royal Air Force Station at Broadwell. One occasion was particularly memorable. I had been out on the job, and I was coming home alone, when I met an ammunition convoy coming towards me. It stopped, and the lieutenant in charge slipped out and told me to "come forward, come forward, come forward," so I could pass. Then, while I was coming forward, there was the most godawful crunch, and the whole side of my ambulance came off. Lucky the whole thing didn't explode. Imagine if I'd been carrying a patient! I said, "You've got to come back with me to my headquarters and tell my sergeant about this, because she'll never believe that it wasn't my fault." We had a bad-tempered, red-headed British woman in charge at headquarters, and I thought, "I'm not going to tell her!" The lieutenant agreed to come with me and confessed that it was his fault, so all was well. My supervisor was tough, but she was also fair.

At the Royal Air Force Station in Broadwell, we lived right in the C huts. It was awful—cold, cold, cold. We slept with all our clothes on, trying to keep warm. We had three "mattresses" that I'm sure were made of straw. I can't remember what these mattresses were called, but we used to have to pile them up in the morning. In order to wash, we went into another Nissen hut with all the basins down the middle. I'd been to boarding school, but I wasn't used to undressing in public. There was no privacy at all. A friend and I used to get up in the middle of the night and do our ablutions when there was no one else around.

Although I didn't manage to see my husband until the war was over, I had a sister living in London. I often spent time with her. In fact, I didn't often go to the Red Cross headquarters, but usually went up to my family in London. I had much of my social life through them, because my sister was married to a British officer and knew many people. I also had a grandmother in Bournemouth whom I used to visit sometimes. Since this was my first time in England, it was all very exciting.

In some of the places we worked, we had a roster of names in which each of our names would gradually work its way to the top of the list, at which point the top name would be assigned a job and then drop to the bottom of the list. In places where the driving was particularly difficult, I would sometimes wake in the middle of the night and pray to God that I wouldn't be called. But despite my prayers there were many nights I had to drive, and there were times when I really didn't know where I was going. Occasionally there were two of us, but most of the time I was by

Red Cross ambulance convoy at Stifford Lodge, April 13, 1945.

myself. I wasn't scared of the bombs—I don't know what I was scared of—perhaps just driving in the dark in the middle of the night, not knowing where I was going. I'm still scared of the dark.

I often talked to the soldiers I was transporting in the ambulance. The first time one of them asked for the bottle, I didn't know what he was talking about. We hadn't been given any instructions about those sorts of things. They often assumed that I was a nurse, and I couldn't really say I wasn't, because they'd feel very insecure. Certainly, I grew up very quickly in the Red Cross; I was quite innocent when I went over, even though I was already married. The ambulance driving also made me feel that I was a part of what was going on—not just sitting at home wondering what was happening. I really felt I was in the belly of the beast that was war.

Since the hospitals were often located twenty-five to forty miles from where we picked up patients, we usually drove just one shift a night or a day, depending upon when we were called. However, there were often as many as four men to pick up at one time. And then sometimes we'd have the walking wounded who could sit up, so on those trips we might have ten at a time. Some of the men were very lively. I remember an extremely ardent colonel who sat next to me in the ambulance. I thought the drive would never end. I could deal with him only by joking and not taking him seriously, and by getting him to his destination as quickly as possible.

Once at Broadwell I was sealed out of the camp. I had gone out to lunch with somebody when I was off duty, and when I came back, they wouldn't let me in. It was sealed because the planes were taking off for Arnhem in Holland. This was in 1944 after D-Day. When they let me back in a day later, I still didn't know what was going on. I'd had lunch with my brother-in-law who was going to Arnhem, but he never told me. Then when the Arnhem landings were finally reported, we started picking up casualties that were flown into Broadwell. Of course I heard something of the battle from the wounded.

As I've mentioned, I had never before driven anything as big as the ambulances we drove in England. I had to gear down when I

Tilbury Ambulance Unit, 1944. Biddie Wilkins, 2nd row, far right.

came to roundabouts, and I used to have to hold the wheel with my knees so that I could use both hands on the gear shift. I remember when we were in Essex, near Tilbury, the head of the Red Cross was British. He used to call me by my last name, Wilkins, which I didn't appreciate at all. One day he asked me to drive him to London in a Rover, one of those sporty little cars. When we entered Piccadilly Circus, I went round and round about twenty-five times—and could not get out. Here I was having difficulty driving this teeny-weeny little car when by this time I could drive a big ambulance with no trouble at all. I had landed myself in the inner lane, and with the huge double-decker buses around me, I couldn't seem to get by them to the exit lane. My passenger became very annoyed, but he was not nearly as frustrated as I was. I felt like a perfect idiot. I'd never been in that sort of traffic before. When I finally escaped Piccadilly, I headed straight for the British headquarters to drop the old boy off. I don't know which of us was happier when we finally arrived at our destination.

Biddie Wilkins painting her ambulance.

Another memorable character was a treasure of a British sergeant who somewhat resembled the "Hulk"—he was so enormous and had an unusually large head. He was also not quite all there. One day I was lying on the concrete under my ambulance doing some repairs. This was all part of the job. The sergeant looked under my ambulance and said, "Hey Wilkins under there, you're gonna get them bleedin' whatnots lyin' on the cold concrete." Since that day, piles have always been called "bleedin' whatnots" in our family.

Yes, we had many good laughs in the midst of the seriousness of the work we were doing back then. We had to treasure the funny parts, because it would have been too painful to have dwelt on the bad parts. It's just like today: we have to have a sense of humour about what happens; otherwise we wouldn't survive.

Shortly after Victory-in-Europe Day, the driving pretty well came to an end. I was posted to No. 1 Red Cross Club in London, and that was a bit of shock—waitressing and making beds and generally being a "joe boy," or a "joe girl"—as we might say now. Finally in March 1946, my husband returned to England, and in due time we both came home to Canada on the *Ile-de-France,* along with 22,000 returning soldiers. Mission accomplished—and I was pregnant.

Catherine MacDonald Waters

*"My God, what are you doing
here, Porky?"*

Catherine MacDonald Waters was born in Victoria, B.C. She was living
and working on the family farm near Sidney, B.C., a few miles outside
of Victoria, when she joined the Red Cross. After the war,
she married and raised two sons. She was a volunteer
for Meals on Wheels, The Red Cross Society
and The Heart Fund.

In 1943 I was working on the family farm near Sidney on Vancouver Island when I decided to join the Red Cross Corps to help in the war effort. After applying by mail to the Red Cross in Vancouver, my friend Biddy Wilkins and I went over to be interviewed. Soon after that the Red Cross called to say I must return to Vancouver for a medical examination and then I would be leaving for Toronto a week later. That gave me barely enough time to buy warm clothes and various other necessities. Another friend Mary Senay also joined the Red Cross, and we spent Remembrance Day of 1943 thinking about the war as we travelled by train to Toronto. We were met in Toronto by a Red Cross driver and taken to a large brick boarding house in Rosedale for breakfast (juice, toast and coffee cost only fifteen cents back then). Another girl had arrived a few days before, so the three of us shared a room and a hotplate.

When we first arrived in Toronto it was below-zero weather, and we were assigned to changing the oil and tires of Red Cross cars. It was not easy in that cold, but my years on the farm had given me quite a bit of practice in working with vehicles. Since we were working as volunteers, and I had little money to support myself, I thought I would be sent home. My parents did not approve of my going overseas, and I was too proud to ask for help. But somehow I survived until the big day finally arrived in the first week of January, 1944.

We sailed from New York on the *Rangitiki,* which we soon called the *Rangisicki* due to the rough weather and the very sick children on board. It was our job to help look after the children whose mothers were going to England to join their Royal Air Force husbands who had already returned home after training in Canada. Nell Tinker and I turned our cabin into a sick bay so that the mothers could get some sleep. I can't remember when we got to sleep ourselves.

We each had to look after a child during life boat drill and also whenever there was a real emergency—and there were several on our trip across. Many of the ships on these crossings were hit, and it wasn't always the ships on our side. One day we were surprised to see a crew of Germans floating by in their rubber raft. They waved to us, hoping to be picked up by a ship that had so many females on board, but that was the Navy's job. A few days later one of our tankers in the convoy received a direct hit. I will never forget seeing the sudden burst of flames; it was a horrible sight.

After our eventful crossing we arrived at Liverpool where we saw our first barrage balloon. It was quite a sight—those big balloons hanging in the sky. We went by train to London where we were again met by a Red Cross driver and taken to Corps House at Queen's Gate Terrace. Some of our group went to Maple Leaf Clubs to work, but Mary Liz Wright and I were to be welfare officers in a hospital. While waiting for our posting, we rode our bikes to headquarters at Burlington Gardens and did various jobs there. Finally we were sent to a hospital near Colchester where we sold leather and other handicraft material to the patients. One of the more taxing jobs was learning how to use English money—making change with twelve pence to a shilling and twenty shillings to a pound is not easy when you are trying to hurry. And then the men would sometimes tease us by mentioning guineas (twenty-one shillings). While we were there we heard that Captain Walker of the *Rangitiki*, who had done such a great job in bringing us safely to England, had died from exhaustion from spending long hours on the bridge. Apparently he had simply spent too much of the war at sea without rest.

After a few weeks at Colchester we were sent to Yorkshire, where we joined No. 8 Canadian General Hospital and were billeted in a lovely old house a few miles outside Richmond. Our room was in the servants' quarters, and luckily had a fireplace, which helped us keep warm. A third welfare officer, Dotty Mundy, joined Mary Liz and myself at our posting. A few days later we were sent to live in tents and were taught army procedures for handling camp stretchers, water buckets and canvas baths. We also practised route marches, carrying fifteen- to twenty-pound packs on our backs. I loved our tramps over the moors. In the evenings some of us would walk about three miles along a pretty country road to an old pub where we could order a ham-and-egg sandwich and good Yorkshire beer. To cap it all, Mary Liz would play the piano while we all sang.

We were finally sent south to Hove where we waited to go to the Continent. At last the exciting day came, and we were driven in army trucks to Southsea where we boarded our infantry landing craft. Our dinner that evening was hardtack and sweet thick army tea; breakfast was the same. In the middle of the night one of the ships in our convoy bumped us. A nurse sleeping in the bottom bunk screamed, "Oh God, we're sinking!"—she had stuck her hand in the water of the fire bucket beside her bunk. When we landed in Normandy, we drove up the Mulberry Harbour, the same Mulberry which had been used in the invasion on D-Day. It was a great thrill. As we drove through Bayeux, the people waved to us and clapped. We felt like royalty.

We set up tents in a lovely orchard which was very close to No. 7 Canadian General Hospital. One night Mary Liz and I were awakened by a thud. A five-inch cone-shaped object that turned out to be a dud bomb had come through the roof of our tent, landing between our stretchers. After that we folded up our stretchers and were given hospital beds to sleep under or on—whichever we preferred—and we kept our tin hats on our heads, or tummies, whichever we wanted to save.

After a month or so there, we moved to another area outside Rouen. On our approach, we went over a Bailey bridge which had been bombed and was twisted, with soldiers' clothing and poor dead horses tangled in the structure. We drove through Rouen and were very impressed to see the beautiful cathedral standing in all its glory, untouched amid the rubble. We went a number of miles further through the devastated area to reach the improvised hospital, which once again had been set up in an orchard. There we were in charge of a Red Cross tent which had books and writing paper. Mary Liz received a donation of a gramophone and some records, and we set up a dart board outside on a tree. Shooting darts became very popular with the patients who were able to walk. Dotty, Mary Liz and I took turns at supervising.

Once again we worked very long hours, from 6 a.m. until some-

Rouen, with bombed German transport in foreground.

times 3 a.m. When a convoy was coming in, we would work late, for we knew the lads would love a hot drink, cigarettes, a tooth brush and a razor. We really didn't have to work such long hours, but we loved what we were doing, and we took turns at staying up late.

Since our hospital was in an apple orchard and it was autumn, there were many fallen apples on the ground. We were not sup posed to collect these because the farmers needed them to make cider, but since the lads were longing for the taste of an apple, one day I went out into the orchard with two water buckets, intending to gather a few. Suddenly I came face to face with the colonel accompanied by a beautiful lady. He called me over, so I quickly dropped the buckets and went over to them. He introduced me to Lady Mountbatten, who was head of the British Red Cross. I think I looked rather sheepish, but I never heard a word from them about breaking the rules.

When we first arrived, the ground was so muddy that we had to wear our gum boots at all times. When we went to bed, we placed them beside the bed so we wouldn't have to step into the mud when getting up in the morning. Later the mud turned to ice. But by then, we were on the move again, this time to Antwerp, which was very pretty—despite the shelling at the time. Most of the houses had lovely chandeliers which we could see through the large windows. This time our hospital took over the town's hospital, which had a large swimming pool in the centre. While there we worked very hard even though buzz bombs came over every two minutes, it seemed, and we had a number of civilians to treat for shock and minor wounds. Some German prisoners of war worked as stretcher bearers to help our lads. Curiously enough, they were not at all bitter, but worked well for us. I guess they had decided the Nazi times had been a disaster. In their attitudes you caught a glimpse of the new Germany that was about to be born.

During this time the three of us were invited to the Belgian Liberation dinner and concert which began at 6 p.m. On our way there we passed some Belgians who had been collaborators; they had been put into monkey cages as punishment. The dinner went on until nearly 5 a.m. with skits performed by various Allied troops. We were driven back to the hospital by ambulance, and at that hour we went right back to work. No time for sleep.

Near the hospital there were some lovely little cafés, and occasionally a local lad would take me there. Once when walking home there were so many buzz bombs that we made up a song: "The buzz bombs will get you if you don't watch out, and when they do you'll scream and shout." Unfortunately, our little song proved prophetic when the bombs hit the station, a theatre and many large buildings. It was tragic.

Just before Christmas of 1944 we moved up to 's-Hertogenbosch in Holland, and the hospital was set up a few miles outside the town of St. Michiels Gestel in an old seminary. The emergency ward was in the chapel. As it was the Christmas season, the Red Cross gals made a super big "snowman" in the entrance hall. We commandeered wool packing from the lab to make the body and found a pipe and a tall hat in a drawer. It looked splendid. On

Christmas Eve we served turkey and pudding and sang carols. After our merry meal we were shocked to hear the colonel announce, "I want you all to pack warm clothes and anything important in your knapsack because we are surrounded, and the Germans might come at any time. If they do, don't behave in an arrogant manner, be calm."

That evening I was alone, as my roommates were away for Christmas. The next morning I awoke to hear the tramp, tramp, tramp of many boots outside my window. I thought of my Christmas liquor ration and the large box of Rogers chocolates I had received from home. In my distress I wondered what to devour first, the chocolates or the booze! Then I heard church bells chime and realized it was the Dutch people going to church in their wooden shoes. The Germans didn't march in on that morning, but I saw a German plane fly past the window. It was so close that I could see the pilot's face, and he could see mine.

I remember travelling to Nijmegen in the Netherlands for a New Year's party at the Hamilton Regiment's mess. It was announced that a colonel or general (I can't remember what rank he had at that time) was coming. Then in walked Johnny Rockingham whom I had known for years, since we both came from Victoria, British Columbia. He gave me one look and said, "My God, what are you doing here, Porky?" (At home I had acquired the nickname "Porky" because I had been such a chubby baby.) Then Johnny Rockingham lifted me up and whirled me around. "Rocky" was always an unconventional person, and you could see that the men loved and respected him. "Rocky" was later asked to lead Canada's troops in Korea.

The lad I was with that evening was duty officer, which meant that he had to inspect the last post and see that all was well. I accompanied him and noticed that our lads were tapping out tunes on their machine guns. I can recall that the password was "hangover," and how it sounded like an ominous German command as the duty officer called it out into the night. It was the most beautiful moonlit night with lovely white snow, not like city snow. There was a small church on a little hill, which added to the beauty.

Shortly after, I was invited to dinner at 's-Hertogenbosch for the Dutch Liberation Day celebration, where we all danced in a big square and were given yellow flowers.

I left the hospital in April and was sent to Brussels to help with the Allied prisoners of war. The lads were from many different countries, and several had been in prisons in Austria where they said they had been well treated. When I went on leave, I attended a party for the Air Force lads who had also been prisoners of war, and from there I went with Betty Mais and Mary Liz to Paris for two nights. It was wonderful to be in a liberated Paris.

Once the war in Europe was officially over, I returned to London where I was posted to the Junior Officers' Club. I didn't see my good friend Dotty Mundy again until my return to Canada, but I often thought of her. She was a superb letter writer for the soldiers, and when she visited the ward she looked wonderfully cheery in her blue smock and lovely red hair.

I loved working in London after the war. It was certainly not the same city I had left with its air raids and rubble in the streets. Now there were only memories of the Red Cross girls wearing curlers in our hair and tin hats on our heads as we hurried down to shelter in the dark basement. Some of the nervous ones would smoke, and we could see the shaky glows in the dark.

I left London in March 1946 when my mother wrote to say that Dad was ill with cancer. He lived another year and half after my return, and I felt fortunate to have had the time with him. Now as I look back, I once again feel fortunate to have such good memories of all the fine people I worked with and all the brave soldiers I met during my time with the Canadian Red Cross Corps.

Audrey Stewart Copping

*"I wondered if I would ever see
him alive again"*

—

Audrey Stewart Copping, a fifth-generation Montrealer, was born and
raised there. Soon after WW II began, she interrupted her education
to take a job in Pathology at McGill University. After serving with
the Red Cross Corps, she returned to university to take a
degree in History and the Philosophy of Science. She
has done volunteer work with the University
Women's Club, the Victoria Natural
History Society and the Victoria
Telecommunications Network.

W hen Britain, and eventually Canada, declared a state of war existed with Germany in September, 1939, my great hope was that it would last long enough for me to "get into it" in some capacity, and that it would not peter-out as the pundits said it would. (They didn't know as much about Hitler as they thought they did.) We'd learned patriotism at school, and as well, my family, although five generations in Canada, was very conscious of having been born British Subjects and had great respect for both countries. My Dad had served in an artillery battery (3rd Siege) of the Canadian Army some four years in the Great War of 1914–18, having joined-up on his twenty-first birthday. I had grown up listening to my father and one of his wartime buddies rehashing Passchendaele, Ypres and Vimy, the three battles in which the Canadian Army acquitted themselves so brilliantly. An uncle had been killed at Ypres. It is said that "Canada came of age" in that war.

There were not many opportunities for women in the forces at the outbreak of war. The Women's Auxiliaries of the forces had not yet been thought of; in fact it was some time before nurses were even admitted. The best I could do was interrupt my education and take over a job in pathology at McGill University which had been vacated by a man who had joined the 9th Field Ambulance and was about to proceed overseas. And I joined the Canadian Red Cross Corps.

We started with drill nights in an inner city school and St. John's Ambulance courses. I well remember the class where the instructor announced we were about to learn to put on a bandage for "a hand or a phutt." What, I asked, in all innocence, was a "phutt"? It was then I learned the Scot was about to teach us how to bandage a foot.

Next came a course in nursing which was given at the Royal Victoria Hospital. As the course was given directly across the street from the McGill Pathology building it was easy for me to attend my classes regularly, but when I had qualified for some vacation, I devoted it all to the nursing course which included most of the useful things I know today. That summer I left my job and worked full time at the Montreal Neurological Institute on 12-hour daily "floor-duty" to gain my necessary hours for the Red Cross. It was while I was working at the "Neuro" that I received a letter from my fiancé who was sitting in a Canadian General Hospital in England waiting for some action to begin. He had recently seen Mrs. Tommy Gilmore, Director-General of the Canadian Branch of the St. John's Ambulance Association who was on a tour of inspection in Britain to see what was wanted in the way of volunteers. She told him, "I am as sure as I am that the sun will rise tomorrow that I can get your fiancée over here immediately, but first she will have to resign from the Red Cross. I cannot steal one of their volunteers." With this letter in hand, I went to see Miss Eileen Flanagan, the director of nursing at the "Neuro," to ask her for a letter of recomendation as it was my intention to resign from the Red Cross in order to proceed Overseas with the St. John's Ambulance Association

To my surprise I learned that Miss Flanagan was the Director of Nursing for the Canadian Red Cross Society, and that she was having none of this "resigning stuff." She telephoned Millie Hutchison, Nursing Commandant of the Canadian Red Cross Corps, made an appointment, and sent me scurrying down to see her. When I arrived at Millie's office wearing a new summer dress, she said, "Take off that dress and give it to me. I like it and you won't be needing it—you'll be in uniform." She then telephoned Huntley Drummond and buttered him up, with the result that when she hung up the phone she said, "You are to proceed Overseas immediately to run a sick bay in the basement of British Columbia House. I was there during the First War." One had to know Millie and her unusual personality to appreciate this turn of events.

Last year while sifting through some old letters in a chest, I came across an unopened one addressed to me with a postmark dated 1943. When I opened it I found it was from Tommy Gilmore confirming my job in England. I suppose it must have come after I left Canada. She must be dead by now, and I blush to think how ungrateful she would have thought me not to have acknowledged her letter.

We met for the first time that evening in June at Central Station: eleven volunteers from Ontario and Quebec. Later, in Halifax, we were joined by another from Glace Bay in Nova Scotia. At the station, in addition to the parents of the Montrealers, was Colonel "Bob" Leggat who had been my father's captain, and later major, during WWI and now, as Red Cross Commissioner for the Province of Quebec, shook hands with us all, wished us bon voyage, and said, "You are darn good sports." It is just as well we were, for we were to spend the next month en route, including ten days in Halifax, five in St. John's Newfoundland, and another twenty-three at sea in a dreadful old tub of a ship.

After arrival in Liverpool and a train ride which carried us through the awful devastation of Coventry, we were met in London by the Commandant, Margaret Lee, and her driver, Eileen Harris, who was also in charge of the Transport Section, and whisked off to Corps House, which at that time consisted of numbers 18 and 20 Queen's Gate Terrace; number 16 was added later. The next morning we were briefed as to what we could and could not do: when we were to wear our hats, belts etc.; the married girls were not to get pregnant; the unmarried were not to get married unless it was certain their husbands-to-be were on immediate draft overseas; we were really civilians but could put up one pip and were to be treated like officers for the purpose of entering army messes; the Royal Canadian Medical Corps would look after us when ill; the Canadian Dental Corps would look after any dental emergencies; we were to be issued keys for the front door— there was no closing hour, as we were supposed to be old enough to know when to come in at night, and we were to have a week's debarkation leave provided we registered in "the book" just where we were going and where we could be reached.

Following the week's leave, with the exception of one of us who was taken to headquarters and endowed with the regalia of a lieutenant-colonel, we were taken to B.C. House in whose basement was lodged B.C. Canteen. Here, below street level we were to work at washing dishes, peeling potatoes, serving unspeakably bad food

to "other ranks only," and occasionally when we had proven ourselves really trustworthy, we might be allowed to stir the enormous
basin of Bird's custard which constantly occupied a large part of
the stove. I couldn't believe this was for me and enquired about
the sick bay only to be told there had not been one there since the
First World War! Well, there we were, twelve unhappy and disillu-
sioned Red Cross volunteers doomed to work in this cavern on
two shifts, either 7 a.m. to 2 p.m. or 2 p.m. to 9 p.m. The other
workers were English women who worked part time but had been
holding the fort until the imported "Can-eye-dians" arrived. Many
of the women were very nice to us and tried to protect us from the
nasty woman who ran the canteen. One woman in particular
whose husband had been in the Foreign Office and had, until the
war, lived in Rome, invited six of us to her home in Golder's
Green for dinner. She had a beautiful and well-kept home but, of
course, due to the war, no servants. She had cooked dinner, and
after warmly welcoming us to her drawing-room, descended to
the basement kitchen (reminiscent of *Upstairs, Downstairs?*) where
she loaded the first course on the dumb waiter, ran up the stairs,
pulled up the dumb waiter and served us an excellent dinner at a
beautifully appointed table. I remember the meal ended with the
best gooseberry fool I ever ate. I don't remember any of us assisting her and I doubt if anyone was thoughtful enough to write her
a note, though we would certainly have expressed our thanks
when next she came to the canteen.

When I worked on the afternoon shift, my fiancé would meet
me after nine o'clock and we would walk back to Corps House
through the blackout, never of course forgetting to carry our
torches. There were a lot of strange things seen in the blackout
along Piccadilly, strange looking women with men from all the
Allied countries, some wearing large berets which drooped down
to their shoulders and fancy lanyards of every hue. Walking on
the north side of Piccadilly Street along by Hyde Park, one would
be hard-pressed not to notice the "Hyde Park sheep." On one
occasion, being of a curious turn of mind, I turned my torch on
something moving in the grass to discover a couple in *flagrante*

delicto and a very annoyed sailor raising his head and shouting "Get that *&#!#*@ thing out!"

After enduring B.C. Canteen for about three months, I learned while having dinner with my fiancé and his Colonel that No. 14 Canadian General Hospital was soon to leave England for the Continent. Of course it was not known exactly where it was to go, but as my fiancé had been pursuing advanced courses at the School of Tropical Medicine at London University, it was assumed the unit might be slated for North Africa where the German Army under Rommel had recently been driven out. At any rate Colonel Johnston said No. 14 was moving very soon, and if we were thinking of getting married we had better do so immediately.

The next morning I obtained an appointment with General Price, the Commissioner of the Canadian Red Cross Overseas, and on going to see him with my news that No. 14 CGH was soon to embark for the Continent, he replied that No. 14 was a base hospital and as such would remain in England. When I insisted that my news had come from the Colonel, the General responded that sometimes the Red Cross knew more about the Army than the Army did! Still, my permission to be married was again denied.

A few days later General Price returned to Canada on Red Cross business. Two days later when my fiancé came up to London he informed me that they had embarkation orders and were to be confined to barracks from midnight. We bade a tearful goodbye at Victoria Station that evening and I wondered if I would ever see him alive again. Early the next morning I was wakened by the Red Cross Corps commandant, with the news that my permission to marry had been granted by the the assistant commissioner. Well, that was all very well, but the groom-to-be was confined to barracks in Horley, Surrey. However, the following morning a telephone call brought the news that with the aid of a faithful batman the packing had been completed, and "if you can make the arrangements with the Church I can be up in London by four o'clock."

The Church of England is the State Church in England, and it is considered the right thing to do to have the banns of an impending marriage called on three successive Sundays to give opportunities for objections. I visited the Dean's Yard at Westminster Abbey, explained the reason for haste, paid over the sum of twelve pounds sterling (at that time worth about sixty dollars) and was granted a special licence, with the comment that it was customary to hold a marriage licence for at least twenty-four hours.

I had anticipated being married by the Reverend Brian Green who was the incumbent of Holy Trinity Brompton Road Church and who had acted as the padre to Corps House. Much to my amazement I learned that I could not be married in his church because I lived on the wrong side of the road, and that Corps House was in the parish of St. Mary Abbott Kensington Road. A trip to the Church of St. Mary Abbott revealed that we could, indeed, be married at 4:30 that afternoon. Although the rector was out of town and the curate was off on a course, one Prebendary Smith would perform the ceremony. I was then presented with a bill for the use of the church and the verger's fee for opening the church door. The verger also wore a fancy robe and a top hat and directed the guests into the church. The bill was paid and I went off to see what could be done about making myself presentable for the ceremony.

My roommate had been pressed into service as my maid-of-honour, and having taken to England with her a long magenta dinner dress was suitably attired for the occasion. She and the other Red Cross "girls" pressed my groom's dress uniform which had been put away in my trunk for the duration, polished his buttons, and had it ready on his arrival at Corps House. My mother had insisted that I take a wedding dress overseas with me, and I had borrowed a headdress and veil from a friend. As there was no time to have my hair done, the veil was a great help. The commandant and the staff arranged a creditable reception complete with a wedding cake which had been iced with fondant sent from Canada among the Red Cross "comforts." And so we were married at 4:30 in the afternoon and my husband left for Italy at 8 a.m. the next morning.

A short time after my marriage the commandant said that due

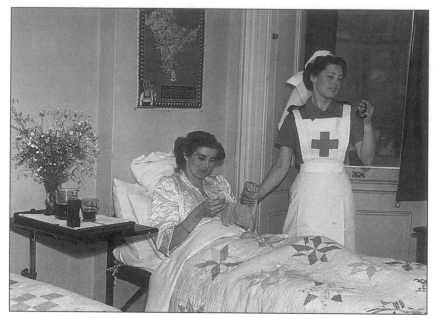

Grace Cassils and Audrey Copping in Corps House Infirmary, 1944.

to the number of colds and bouts of flu among the girls, she was finding it difficult to look after them all and required me to organize and run a sick bay at Corps House. I thought she'd never ask! I was, of course, delighted but felt badly for my roommate and the other girls who were still condemned to work in the canteen. In fact some of them spent their entire time overseas in that awful place.

It was now the end of October. On November 7, 1943 word was received that my husband's unit, No. 14 Canadian General Hospital, had been sunk in the Mediterranean en route to Italy by an aerial torpedo attack. The Luftwaffe had come out from Marseille about 6 p.m., the setting sun blinding the convoy's gunners. Much has been written of this event in the magazine *Ships* and in subsequent books about the war so I do not intend to labour the subject here except to say that it was not a happy time, especially as the Montreal papers reported my husband as "missing." Colonel "Monty" Montgomery, the Canadian Consultant in Medicine telephoned and asked me to go down to Canadian Military headquarters where he introduced me to Colonel "Brownie" Brown who, as MD No. 4 had just returned from a tour of inspection in the Mediterranean and had seen my husband the previous day in North Africa, where he and the nursing sisters in the lifeboat had been taken following their rescue by the *Monterey*. (Incidentally, imagine my amazement at learning that the ship I circumnavigated South America in last autumn was the old *Monterey* refitted and renamed! The rescue is recorded in her logbook.)

About this time the Nazis renewed their air attacks on London and we were frequently wakened, if not by the sirens then by our fellows, and made to go down to the cellar for safety's sake. I have always required a lot of sleep and certainly missed it when so disturbed. I finally coaxed my roommate not to wake me in the event of a raid, especially as we were on the first floor anyway. She finally agreed but, being more sensible, packed off to the basement at the first hoot of the siren. One night I was rudely awakened by the sound of breaking glass and a thud as a piece of shrapnel landed on my bed near my feet. After that I moved for sirens; I still have that piece of shrapnel.

Early in 1944 as the frequency of the nightly air raids increased we were told to pack a suitcase with a complete set of clothes and kit. This was, apparently, transported to Foxley Green for use in the event that we were bombed out and lost our belongings. It seems the Germans had got word that Eisenhower's headquarters was in South Kensington, hence our increased attention from the Luftwaffe. About this time we took to carrying in our haversacks a complete change of clothing except for a tunic. For me this proved to be a good thing.

In February I was asked if I would go to the home of the chairman of St. Dunstan's, the world-famous organization for rehabilitation of war-blinded, for two weeks as a replacement for a British Red Cross Society volunteer nurse who was on vacation. I was pleased but apprehensive that, never having been around blind people, I might spend my days in tears of sympathy. The chairman, Sir Ian Fraser and Lady Fraser lived in a lovely house in the centre of Queen Mary's Rose Garden in Regent's Park not far from Bedford Ladies' College. The house had been demolished during the Blitz and had just been rebuilt, no doubt due to the fact that Ian Fraser was a Member of Parliament. I can't think how else he would have been able to obtain building materials and labour during the war. The one-storey house was built around three sides of a square, and in addition to the main building there was a garage and a self-contained cottage with two bedrooms, no doubt in peacetime intended for a chauffeur. I occupied one of the bedrooms and, when she returned, the other VAD, a very pleasant Scottish girl from Stirling, the other. The cook, two servants and three blind officers occupied one of the wings of the main house; the Frasers the other wing. The lounge, dining-room and library were in the centre of the house facing the garden in which there was an air-raid shelter. Lady Fraser had requested that I bring along a silk dress to wear for dinner at night, for, while she wore a British Red Cross Society uniform in the daytime, they preferred mufti for dinner. The three officers for whom I was to be responsible were a Canadian Army lieutenant, a Royal Air Force engineer, and a British Infantry captain, a solicitor who had been wounded in Tripoli.

St. Dunstan's specialized in rehabilitating war blinded, teaching them to be independent, to learn a trade or profession, and getting them back to work as soon as possible. Michael had already returned to his pre-war legal firm. My job was to drive Michael to work each morning, and then take Charles either to a massage clinic or to the physiotherapy department of one of the teaching hospitals where he was being trained as a physiotherapist. Bill went to job interviews. Up until this time I had not driven in London, so that first day driving Michael down to the Strand was my first experience of driving on the "wrong side." However, after the first five minutes I don't recall having any difficulty. The car was an Austin Ten with license plate E L A, so of course she was known as "Ella," and Ella was mine to drive as long as I was in London.

The first night at dinner I was placed on Ian Fraser's right and I

*Eleanor Johnson and Helena Campbell Davis working with blind soldiers
at St. Dunstan's (Red Cross Archives C88492).*

certainly didn't feel sorry for this tall, good-looking, well-tailored
man who had lost both eyes when wounded the first morning of
the Battle of the Somme in 1916, who had studied law, passed his
Bar examination and successfully stood for election and won a
seat on the London County Council by age twenty-two! No, I felt
sorry for myself as I underwent what to me seemed to be a sort of
third-degree interrogation as Ian tried to find out all about me
and also about my husband. It was some time before I regained
my composure and reasoned that the only way a person who cannot see could possibly know much about one was to ask questions.
Ian Fraser was on the board of directors of several London com-
panies and the Frasers entertained out-of-town visitors frequently.
Usually there were other sightless men at dinner, such as the Lord
Mayor of Hull, or a physiotherapist from Exeter, both of whom
had been blinded in World War I. It was not unusual for eleven of
us to sit down to dinner with Lady Fraser and myself the only two

sighted people. I was always on Sir Ian's right and Lady Fraser at the other end of the table. Ian liked nothing better than to get two or three arguments going around the table and seemed to be able to keep them all going at once. It was certainly very stimulating conversation.

At the end of my two weeks I prepared to return to Red Cross Corps House, but Ian said, "We would like you to stay and be Lady Fraser's assistant and help her with the other officers at Stretton and elsewhere." I said I understood that I was to return to the Red Cross, but he announced that he would telephone the commissioner and fix things up. I've no idea what sort of argument he used, but the upshot was that I was seconded to St. Dunstan's for the duration. Sometimes in the evenings we would play bridge with the other three officers (Braille cards, of course). I have frequently commented that the best "job" I ever had was the result of being able to drive a car and play bridge, for how else would I have lunched at the House of Lords as the guest of Lord Fraser of Lonsdale, as he became, and Lady Fraser, together with Lord Amery who was at that time the Governor of the Hudson's Bay Company.

Quite often Ian's secretary, Miss Gould, affectionately known as "Goolie," would come back with him for dinner so that he could continue working and dictating to her after dinner. Sad to relate, more often than not we would all end up in the air-raid shelter with Goolie reading aloud until the "All Clear" sounded. One night that spring there was a particularly vicious raid on, and when we finally emerged from the shelter we found the house pretty well completely destroyed, with the exception of a small part of one wing—the one the Frasers occupied. Nothing daunted, Ian insisted on climbing in the window to see if he could rescue some of Lady Fraser's clothes. He threw out several shoes but, alas, none matched! We then stood around and listened to Ian's entire cellar of wine pop as it exploded from the heat. It was 2 a.m. but because of the oil bombs which had set the city on fire the sky was light enough to read by.

The Frasers asked me to take the three officers to the Welbeck-

Palace Hotel on Welbeck Street where we would be given rooms, while they remained to see what could be salvaged, and would join us later. And so with two blind men on one arm and one on the other I set out to find a place I had never been to. As I have said, there were so many fires blazing it was almost as light as day so that I could easily read the street names. We would stop at each corner and Michael, with the aid of his cane, would draw a sort of diagram on the sidewalk for me. And so we arrived at the Welbeck about 4 a.m. I had taken my haversack into the shelter so I was fortunate to have other clothes to wear in the morning. The next day I learned the Church of St. Mary Abbott where I had been married had been badly damaged by fire.

We all stayed on at the Welbeck-Palace for some weeks, but it was a mildly dull time; we had none of the comforts or conveniences we'd enjoyed at St. John's Lodge, the Fraser's house. We didn't even have a radio to hear the BBC news broadcasts by which we kept informed about the war, although each day when he returned from the House of Commons Ian would bring us some tidbit about recent happenings.

One day we learned that the matron at the Massage Hostel in Portland Place had a radio she was prepared to lend us. In "Ella" Bill and I undertook to pick up the radio and take it to the hotel. At 6 p.m. we all huddled around the wireless to hear the news. Alas! It didn't work, and no matter what Lady Fraser or I tried, it still wouldn't work. Lady Fraser said there was no more time to be spent and that we must hurry down to the dining room. The others having headed for the lift, Bill persuaded me to stay behind with him and try once more to get the thing to work. I read out the various bits of writing on the back of the radio and Bill told me what to do about the plugs. Now most people who had been in London at that period knew that there was nothing homogeneous about the London electrical system: some streets had 110 volt service on one side, and 220 on the other; in some areas the current was direct and some alternating. Well, I guess that side of Welbeck Street must have been on DC because when we got the radio hooked up it produced great clouds of very black smoke!

V-1 in flight towards London.

We quickly unhooked it and joined the others for dinner. The next day we returned the matron's radio.

Keeping us all at the Welbeck-Palace must have been quite an expense for St. Dunstan's, so after a time it was decided that the Frasers would return to their property and live in the cottage. The cook and servants had been dispersed; the officers and I would live at the Massage Hostel. I persuaded Lady Fraser that, never having been to the training establishment at Church Stretton, I felt somewhat at a disadvantage in my knowledge of St. Dunstan's. She sent me up to Church Stretton for two weeks where I lived in Brockhurst Residence. The first morning I found myself de-boning kippers for thirty-eight sightless men: I've never liked the smell of kippers and that nearly finished me off. I did learn something of the training methods at Church Stretton which stood me in good stead later on.

I returned to London and lived at the Massage Hostel where there were about twenty blind other ranks being trained to be physiotherapists, some of whom were South Africans and other Commonwealth troops, most of whom had been wounded in the North African campaign. At that time there were no Canadians.

One night, shortly after D-Day (actually it was June 13, 1944) as we sat in the lounge after dinner, the air-raid siren sounded, and after taking the usual precautions of seeing that the blackout curtains were well drawn with windows slightly open to avoid the danger of implosion, seeing that everyone was down on the ground floor—but not in the basement—we sat about either reading to the men or playing the gramophone while waiting for the "All Clear" to sound. We waited all night until 8 a.m. (Apparently the RAF did not feel the skies were "All Clear.") The morning papers added to the mystery of what had happened during the night. It wasn't until we saw the Frasers at lunch that Ian told us that "Winston" (Churchill) had been very annoyed when questioned by the Opposition in the House and that the PM was due to address the public that afternoon. The recent BBC newscasts had made frequent reference to the Allied bombing raids on the Pas de Calais, but at the time we had not understood their target had been the launching sites for the V-1 flying bombs or "Doodlebugs" to which we had been introduced that night. The fighters, as always, did an admirable job of keeping bombers and flying bombs away from London, but by the middle of June, 1944, the "Doodlebugs" came thick and fast into London, chiefly in the daytime. My room was on the fifth floor of the hostel, and one morning I was in the bathtub when I heard a V-1 motor cut out just about over my head. It was believed the motor cut out just before the bomb was about to fall and that there were about 30 seconds for the bomb to find its target. Without any thought and only by instinct I found myself down five flights of stairs and in the street clad only in a bathtowel and dressing gown—just as the thing landed in the next block with the usual roar and sound of shattering glass.

One day Lady Fraser asked me if I would like to accompany her and Sir Ian to a back-to-work exhibition at which the Queen (now the Queen Mother) would be "inspecting" some of the blinded men who had been retrained and were now working in factories. Lady Fraser explained that she would not be able to present me as no prior arrangement had been made to do so, but that in addition to Her Majesty and equerry there would only be the president of the National Institute for the Blind and ourselves. The exhibition was held in a large hall not far from Portland Place where, around the periphery, were men engaged in using various tools, including fret saws and die-making equipment. As the "Queen-Mum" approached each man, she looked into his face and smiled. Asking questions about his work, the pieces being made for the building of "Spitfire" aircraft, etc., she drew him out so that he would talk to her as to a friend. I doubt if I have ever seen such interest displayed: it was certainly a lesson in royal graciousness.

The hospital at Church Stretton had been moved to a four-ward unit in the EMS (Emergency Medical Services) hospital at Stoke Mandeville, Bucks. This allowed for the accommodation of the increased numbers of casualties, while making available Tiger Hall, the former hospital at Church Stretton, for more trainees. As the V-1 raids were now increasing in frequency, the Frasers decided it would be better for me to go out to the hospital unit where I was to escort three new officers about, visit the men in the four wards and alert the Frasers to new arrivals. The Frasers, who had gone to live in their cottage at Sunningdale, near Epsom, would come out to the hospital whenever a new contingent of casualties arrived. Ian would visit each man. Sitting on his bed he would talk to him for about twenty minutes. He would then present him with a Braille watch and instruct him in its use. These visits from a man who had himself been blinded in the First World War did immeasurable good to the morale of a recently blinded soldier, sailor or airman.

As well as service personnel, we were now admitting civilians who had been blinded from flying glass during the V-1 attacks. There were also a few women, blinded and with such badly cut faces that one knew the scars would never go away. And one pathetic little boy of twelve who had picked up a German anti-personnel, or "butter-fly" bomb, and lost not only his sight but a hand as well. In spite of much publicity, it was extremely difficult to prevent children from touching those devilish devices.

Three of the wards contained thirty-two beds for other ranks. The officers were in another wing of the hospital. The fourth ward was fitted out as a lounge for the use of the "up patients." St. Dunstan's had their own nursing staff and orderlies, as well as a house surgeon, and their own admitting and discharge facilities. The latter was presided over by the secretary. Our "fleet" consisted of a Hillman sedan and a Chevrolet ambulance, the latter a gift from some kind American friends of the Frasers, so there was always one vehicle for me.

Many of the men were up patients and would frequently be found sitting in the lounge holding their heads in their hands if we didn't keep them busy. These I would scoop up into the ambulance in the afternoon, usually about twenty in all, and drive off into the countryside in search of a pub where beer was available. There was a shortage of beer and most pubs did not open before 8 p.m., the hour by which the men had to be back in hospital or rated as "absent without leave." I found by parking the "boys" in the front and approaching the rear door and explaining my "cargo" the publican and his wife would happily open up for us. The boys would have their fill of beer (and it was usually "on the house"), the owner's wife would make Spam sandwiches (a treat instead of hospital food) and either she, the publican, or someone would play the piano and they would sing. The patients would be returned to the hospital, still singing and, I hoped, tired enough to sleep. Most blind people do not sleep well. Perhaps this was not the purpose for which the ambulance had been sent, but given the circumstances it seemed the right thing to do. Many of these lads were not yet twenty-one. I especially remember one lad from Saskatchewan who had been wounded, losing his sight, while debarking from the landing craft on D-Day: it was his nineteenth birthday.

Mornings were taken up with the usual hospital routine: wounds were dressed; rounds were made by the ophthalmologist or plastic surgeon and house surgeon; some of the up patients would go down to the Occupational Therapy Department where the OT would set up a loom and teach some to weave. We had an OT who came up to our lounge or went to the patient's bedside; as well, we had a Braille teacher, Killy. He was a private who had lost an arm and his sight in the 1914-18 war and had spent a great deal of time at Ovingdean, the St. Dunstan's home in Brighton, until it was moved to Church Stretton at the beginning of the 1939 war. Killy taught at the men's bedside almost from the moment they were admitted to us, with the result that even before going to Stretton they became quite proficient.

Somehow, it was decided that I should become the typing teacher in the mornings. A closet-sized room was found for me into which a desk, two chairs and a typewriter were placed. Teaching touch typing is not difficult. One covers the letters "G" and "H" with adhesive and then teaches the keyboard according to the Pitman typing book, it being a matter of practice whether one is sighted or not. The men took to typing extremely well and were prepared to practise all day long. In fact it was difficult to persuade them to give up the typewriter after an hour's lesson. As a result, a second machine was found and placed in the lounge where it was in use from dawn till dusk.

A real challenge presented itself when a large and brave sergeant of the Special Battalion, Aegean, who had been wounded when parachuting into Yugoslavia to join Tito's partisans, learned that typing lessons were to be had and demanded to be taught. The sergeant was not only sightless and deaf, but had lost both hands well above the wrists. The hospital engineers were pressed into service and presently Sgt. P. was fitted with metal cuffs around his arm stumps, from which protruded eight-inch strips of firm metal which ended in round, flat, discs fitted with rubber ends. He was a very bright and intelligent man and, as a result of his great determination, concentration, and willingness to practise long hours at a time, he was able to tap out letters to his girlfriend and family.

Our facilities were not nearly large enough, of course, and as soon as the less badly wounded men were discharged from hospital, they were sent to St. Dunstan's Training Centre at Church Stretton near the Welsh border, and their beds were immediately filled. The new patients came from the Oxford Head Hospital, the Canadian General Hospitals, the British Military Hospitals, and by ship and by air from Southeast Asia and Europe. The numbers increased at the time of the tragedy at Arnhem in the Netherlands, when three British Airborne Divisions were all but wiped out. When the war was winding down we also received the prisoners of war from the German Stalags. Some of the latter had been shunted all over Germany by rail in boxcars as the Germans tried in vain to move them away from the Allied advance.

It was about this time that I met Dr. Ludwig Gutman who persuaded me to visit his four-ward paraplegic unit in our hospital. As I was shown around the unit and had some of Dr. Gutman's theories and methods of dealing with paraplegics explained, I became friendly with a dispatch rider who had had his spinal cord severed quite low down so that he was able to be up in a wheel chair for several hours each day. He would wheel himself down the corridor to our unit and chat with the St. Dunstan's men. Eventually I taught him to touch-type. When the war was finally over and I left Stoke-Mandeville to return to London, he was coming down to teach some of the sightless men to type. This achievement is one of my happiest recollections.

Before I was posted back to London to work at Canadian Red Cross Society headquarters, Lady Fraser said to me, "Audrey, St. Dunstan's has received two medals for distribution to worthy members of our staff and we have decided they will go to the two teachers. They are an MBE (Member of the British Empire) and an OBE (Order of the British Empire). As the MBE is for "other ranks" we will give it to Killy, our Braille teacher, and the OBE will be given to you, but you must put up a 'pip' as it is an officer's award." What had happened to my "pip"? The British Red Cross matron whom I had known at the Massage Hostel in Portland Place wore on her shoulder only one pip—the insignia worn by all junior officers of the Commonwealth Army. Because of this, when I was seconded to St. Dunstan's the commandant of the CRCC said I must remove my one pip. As we were really civilians this had no effect on me at the time. However, on reporting Lady Fraser's conversation to the commandant, I was told that I couldn't put up my pip. Since the matron only wore one, I could not wear any. The Canadian Red Cross Society was probably no worse to women at that time than other organizations, but I do not think this

Red Cross Corps members "at the office," London, 1945.

would happen in the '90s. I've no idea who got the St. Dunstan's OBE, but on reflection I am sorry I didn't put up a fight for it.

At the end of 1945 and the beginning of 1946, both my husband and I returned to Canada. Was a readjustment to Canadian civilian life difficult? Due to the war many things were still in short supply, and it was impossible to buy much in the way of furniture. One had to shop around for a chair here and a table there. For example, Eaton's could provide a dining-room table but no chairs. I was fortunate to acquire a pair of beds from my family. The only thing which really bothered me was the quantity of food that seemed to be everywhere, although people were complaining of the shortage of sugar. The British people had had so little food for so many years, the Europeans even less as any Netherlander will tell you, that it bothered me at first to see so little hardship in Canada. When an English family invited one for dinner, a roast the size of a man's fist would be put on the table and one knew the family had gone without all week in order to save their food coupons for that piece of meat so they could invite a guest to share it. I recall being entertained at a hotel for dinner with a group who had spent the war in Canada and was appalled at the huge slab of beef which reached right across the dinner plate being placed before me.

I thought then, and still do, that we Canadians are most fortunate.

Dorothy Falkner Burgoyne Doolittle

"Sunny Italy wasn't warm
or sunny"

—

Dorothy Falkner Burgoyne Doolittle was born and grew up in St.
Catharines, Ontario. After graduating from high school she
earned a B.A. at McGill University in Montreal. In 1943
when she returned to St. Catharines, the commandant
of the Red Cross Food Administration asked
her to sign up to work overseas. After the
war she focused on her family and
volunteer activities as well as
working for the *St. Catharines
Standard* for 25 years.

My excitement at being asked to go overseas knew no bounds. With each trip to Red Cross headquarters in Toronto and with each purchase of clothes for overseas, it seemed that I could picture myself in Europe a little more clearly. At last, six of us met under the clock at Union Station one August day in 1943, and we were off on the first leg of our journey. Little did we know what lay ahead of us. Our instructions were to uphold the name of the Red Cross and see to the welfare of the troops.

When we arrived in Halifax and were taken to the docks, we were at first dismayed to see the size of the Norwegian fruit boat that was to take us across the Atlantic. She could carry six passengers only, but the officers assured us she was fast and safe. Moreover, she would be crossing in convoy for the first time and that would make the trip even safer. The crew even took us sailing in Halifax harbour, lowering a life boat for the occasion and teaching us to use the scramble net—foresight perhaps on the part of the Captain. They really did their utmost to make us comfortable, even serving lunch on deck if the weather held fair. Because our ship was small, her destination was Manchester, and we had our first sight of English villages and countryside as we sailed up the canal.

Maple Leaf Club No. 2 became my London home until I was assigned to a hospital. During this time my friend Sydney Thomson and I were posted to the layette department at headquarters in Berkeley Square. Our first "exciting" job was to untie knots in string. We were given an enormous carton of string, and for days we picked at those knots watching the "jumble" slowly disappear, only to have another full carton arrive. And for this we came overseas? Yet it was an essential service, for string in wartime was expensive and almost impossible to find, and everyone at Red Cross headquarters saved it. The string was cut off parcels and thrown into the cartons that came to Sydney and me. We became experts on the various types of "string"—twine, cord, heavy strong string and string that frayed. This operation was hard on the fingernails and required little brain power, but was necessary in the layette department, because all parcels had to be packaged and tied for delivery.

Our next chore was sorting quilts. The Red Cross had crates and more crates of them, and Syd and I unpacked, sorted and re-packed the quilts for days on end. The pretty ones were labelled for nursing sisters, the darker ones for officers, and the flannel-backed ones for the soldiers. Had we only done a little research then, we would be quilt experts now.

Finally we were packing layettes. This was a step up the ladder, and we had many a laugh reading the requests for layettes that came from soldiers' wives and "friends." Their letters would request either a complete layette or certain items, most of which required ration coupons. Needless to say, the funniest letters often produced the choicest layette. Some of the letters were straight-forward: "My husband is a member of "x" regiment, "x" rank, and I am expecting in "x" months. I need "x" items (or a complete layette), and the coupons are enclosed." Others went something like this: "I was at a party and met a Canadian soldier called "x" who I think was with "x" regiment, but now he is gone and I'm pregnant. May I have a layette?" Or "I met a lonely soldier and he was so nice and we saw one another, and now I'm pregnant but I don't know where to find him. May I have a layette?"

At long last, in November 1943, a posting to No. 8 Canadian General Hospital took me to Farnborough where I trained and worked. I was elated because rumour had it that No. 8 would be one of the first hospital units to go in with the second front, and as my fiancé was with an artillery regiment, supposedly heading in the same direction, nothing could be better.

New Year's Eve brought an unexpected message to report to London in the morning. There I found five other girls all in the same state of nervous excitement as myself. We were outfitted with battle dress, helmet, gas masks and water bottles, and sent off to Bramshott to join No. 3 Canadian General Hospital. Those days at Bramshott were ghastly. Each day we joined the nursing sisters for a route march, carrying all our gear up the highway to Hind Head or Liphook, where we'd stop at the pub and march back again. We discovered new games of solitaire; we polished boots and buttons, and we wondered.

After almost two weeks at Bramshott, we were told one evening to be ready to move in an hour. We were loaded into the backs of army transports, laden with kit bag, helmet, gas mask and water bottles and taken to a railway station in the English countryside where we met up with the rest of the unit. An all-night trip brought us to the Liverpool docks where the whole unit marched aboard a troop ship.

For the voyage, we six Red Cross girls were attached to No. 3 Canadian General Hospital, and because we marched onto the ship behind the nursing sisters, the soldiers waiting to board ship weren't sure who we were, but amid the laughs and whistles, we heard them call us the nursing sisters' batmen—and this phrase stuck with us. "Batman" is a British military term that means "attendant serving an officer."

Rumours were rampant that we were going to Italy. Since the last hospital unit sent to the Mediterranean had been bombed with the loss of all equipment and clothes, our matron was determined that we would not go through such a devastating experience of being without "our lipstick and smalls." "Smalls" is an English expression referring to underwear (vest, bra, underpants and stockings). We were checked continually for this, and she also felt we should sleep with our boots on. What a horror.

The rumour about Italy proved correct, and upon arrival in early January, we were taken to No. 14 Canadian General Hospital in Caserta, about twenty-five miles north of Naples (I was to await the arrival of No. 5 Canadian General Hospital from Catania). We were greeted with open arms by the women of No. 14 who had been in the convoy that was bombed in the Mediterranean. No lives had been lost, but they had lost all their possessions, and word had got back to London that the Red Cross girls at No. 14 needed anything and everything. What they missed most was lipstick! We had brought as much extra lipstick and smalls as we could carry. Each new Red Cross girl had an extra uniform, so if one of ours fit a Red Cross gal without a uniform, she was in luck. We had a fashion show by the gals of No. 14 when they tried on our spare clothes to replace the ones lost when they were bombed.

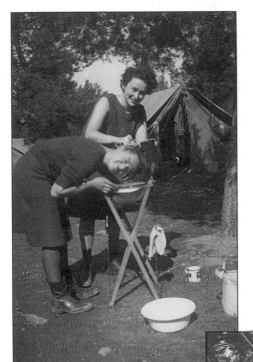

No 5 Canadian General Hospital, Andria. Washing hair at the tent lines, Spring 1944.
◀

Barb Ross Davies cutting Dorothy Falkner's hair, Andria.
▶

In Caserta the heavy guns of our troops could be heard not far away, and the battle-weary boys and the casualties in the surgical wards all brought into focus why we were needed. Sunny Italy wasn't warm or sunny that winter. Upon arrival from Sicily, No. 5 Canadian General Hospital, which had six hundred beds, was set up in a "Sportiva," a walled sports field on the outskirts of Andria, a town about six miles inland from Barletta on the Adriatic coast. The unit's officers and personnel lived under canvas outside the walls, surrounded by almond and olive groves, a gorgeous sight in spring with their pink and white blossoms.

As the hospital was completely under canvas, we didn't take the seriously wounded or desperately ill, but we did make daily rounds with our baskets of cigarettes, tooth brushes, toothpaste, combs, shaving gear and books. Since our Red Cross tent was small, it was unsuitable as a drop-in centre for walking patients, but adequate for our supplies, a few books and a gramophone with some good records—the most popular being Nat King Cole. We had a couple of straight chairs, but it was no lounge. Nevertheless, the patients enjoyed the music and a bit of chatting.

We lived in tents, two girls in each, and there were several "biffys" at the end of the lines of tents. Our biffy was a "three-holer," and I remember a night when one of the girls inadvertently put on a good show for us. A nursing sister had gone in late one night, and before putting the top down, she had dropped her flashlight down the hole, with the light blazing and pointing upward. Not too long after, another nursing sister went down to the biffy and when she lifted the top, the light blazed up. She didn't know what was in there and fled in terror, screaming all the way back to her tent. We had many good laughs over this episode.

It is curious how small things often seem important in the field. One of the highlights of my life at No. 5 was a Saturday night leave in Bari. Marion Kerr, Barbara Ross and I received permission from the matron to spend the night at the newly opened YWCA hostel in Bari. The object of this special request was to have a bath, and we did. It was nothing fancy, just lots of hot running water and steam, but after the lukewarm bird baths in our canvas basins, which was all we'd had since our arrival in Italy six weeks ago, it was sheer heaven.

Just before the battle for Cassino in May 1944, No. 5 Canadian General Hospital moved to a wheat field near Caserta, and again we were under canvas. This was to be a short stop-over until Rome fell when the unit would move into more permanent quarters. The camp in the wheat field was primitive. We heated our water in old, liberated petrol cans sitting in the sun outside our tent. Our biffy this time was a friendly meeting spot—a six-holer (three back to back), open to the heavens, and with canvas sides about four feet high supported by rough poles. Occasionally an airman would take a pass over us and drop a magazine or two from his plane (obviously a friend of one of the gals).

Because our location was temporary, only the walking wounded were admitted. Soon it was apparent that three Red Cross girls were superfluous, and I was sent back to No. 14 Canadian General Hospital, where another working body was welcome. During the battle for Cassino, in which the Canadian soldiers took a major role, the ambulances never seemed to stop bringing in the casualties. Our days were long and full in Admitting and Discharge, the Central Supply Room, and on our regular daily visits with goodies for the patients. At the same time, we took our turns at the Ambulance Control Depot in Capua. Two British and one Canadian Red Cross girl were on eight-hour shifts at this stop between the Field Dressing Stations and the hospitals where the wounded were directed.

Some of the boys had literally come directly from the field. We were allowed to give them sweets, tea or cigarettes, depending on their injuries, and tried to make them comfortable on their stretchers while they were awaiting transport. In contrast to today's modern hospitals where each person's role is highly specialized, we filled in when and where we could. Sometimes we would hold a cigarette for an injured soldier while he smoked it or bring a cup of tea to his mouth so he could drink it. Other days there was time to play cribbage with the patients or write letters for them. The prisoners of war came through, too, and what ap-

Cassino, Italy, May 1944 (Public Archives Canada 32995).

palled us was the age of these young boys. Many of them were arrogant, frightened and full of hate, and they didn't seem to know what to do when offered a comfort. This double duty for us continued until the Allies had taken the monastery.

Later on that summer, while the unit was staging in the same old wheatfield, I spent some weeks at No. 15 Canadian General Hospital before rejoining No. 14 at Perugia, a lovely old city in the Tuscan Hills. This was elegant living. We were billeted in an apartment building with a kitchenette, a bathroom with hot running water and a maid named "Fresia." She thought she could teach us to make spaghetti from scratch, but it was not a successful operation. The dining mess was across the street in a former restaurant, and the hospital itself, a former tobacco factory, was about a mile away in the valley.

One poignant sight I shall never forget was of a little Italian boy, perhaps ten or eleven years old, who was brought into our Admitting and Discharge with both legs badly damaged by a mine. He really should not have been brought into our unit, but he had been found just outside our hospital. Blood was spurting every which way, but he wasn't crying and all he wanted was a cigarette. After being attended by our staff, he was taken to an Italian hospital. Those of us who looked into that little boy's eyes were haunted by his courage for days.

My memories of Italy are not reflected in today's tourist brochures. I remember cold marble and plaster residences; tent lines that were either hot and dusty or wet, cold and muddy. I also recall the small heater in our tent smoking and covering everything, including ourselves, with soot. Then there was the air-raid alert one night in Andria, when we didn't know which part of the anatomy to protect with our helmets. Our leaves at Amalfi, Sorrento, Rome and Florence were more exotic, but the cathedrals seemed sombre and bare. I can also recall dancing at the Orange Grove overlooking the Bay of Naples, where we invariably met someone from home. Then there was the time we borrowed Major Legate's vehicle in Rome to visit seven churches on Maundy Thursday. Finally there was the wonderful trip we made hitchhiking across Italy from Andria to Naples and back. These are the things I recall while much of the sadness fades away.

I was thrilled when, on our return to London in May 1945, my fiancé, Captain Bill Burgoyne of the 23rd Field Regiment, Royal Canadian Artillery, was there to greet me. At first, thoughts of marriage were put aside, so that I could join a Casualty Clearing Station in Europe, but when this fell through, Bill and I were married at Holy Trinity Brompton later in June. The marriage was quite an operation. I had to obtain a special license at Westminster Abbey, as there was not time for wedding banns to be read. The wedding was planned for a Saturday afternoon, but in case Bill wasn't able to travel up to London, it could be postponed until Monday—same time, same place, same flowers!

As the Red Cross wedding gown was being used at a country wedding, Paunie Matthews, my old friend in the layette department, loaned me a white dinner dress; someone in the department had a court veil and tiara, and silver shoes were found. Sheila Birks had a long dress that Mary Elizabeth Wright, my bridesmaid, could wear. In the event, Bill was unable to make it to London for the Saturday, and the wedding was Monday. Mary and I, in our borrowed finery, with bouquets from Constance Spry, paraded down the aisle in reverse order to that of Canadian weddings. Ruth Adams scrounged the makings of a wedding cake, and somehow Mary and I produced four bottles of rye to add to our rations for a punch. Ibby Pepall managed to gather up a number of friends and family, and we had a magnificent reception at Corps House. Not long after we were married, we both returned to Canada—within a week of each other.

I was in Italy from January 1944 until April 1945. I seem to have been the "floater" filling in at the different hospitals, but it was always interesting, and I met many wonderful people, some of whom I still see. There are many more memories, all becoming fuzzier as the years go by, but of one thing I'm sure—while we went over to give our services to the Red Cross, we gained much more in return.

Sheila Moffat

*"We forged a bond that you
can't break"*

Sheila's mother was a nurse in World War I and her father was wounded
in action. After returning from overseas, they settled in Regina where
Sheila was born. Later, Sheila's father was posted to Work Point
Barracks in Victoria, and Sheila grew up in Oak Bay, a suburb
of Victoria. It was there she met her future husband and
joined the Red Cross. After the war Sheila
raised her two sons and pursued
her interest in sports.

I was married on May 18, 1940, and just over a month later, my husband Bob went overseas. I had already joined the Red Cross in Victoria, because I wanted to contribute to the war effort at home, but I also hoped to be posted overseas so that I could be closer to Bob. As time passed, however, this seemed more and more unlikely. While waiting for my overseas posting, I spent a great deal of time marching up and down the Memorial Hall in my snappy grey ensemble.

I soon became a Red Cross VAD (Voluntary Aid Detachment) and worked hard at St. Joseph's Hospital in the chronic care wing, assisting in the care of older people who were bedridden. But still, I often wondered how working there—gratis, of course—would facilitate my going overseas. Nevertheless we did fill a large gap as nurses left to join the forces overseas. Then the rumour went out that VADs were no longer being recruited by the Red Cross Corps for overseas service. This was a bitter blow, to say the least.

Still working on how to get overseas, I heard that the Canadian Army Medical Corps was recruiting VADs, and the prospects for being sent overseas were excellent. I promptly submitted my application and was duly accepted for duty at the Nanaimo Military Hospital.

I enjoyed the varied tasks of a VAD there and found the work rewarding. But instead of being posted overseas, the VADs were asked to take over the duties of the army nurses when they finished their training and went overseas. We were mainly caring for army patients who were stationed in Nanaimo and became ill or hurt themselves in training. I was attached to the Royal Canadian Army Medical Corps and resided with the other nurse's aides in a hut on the grounds of the hospital. It was a large hospital and very well run, even though it was only constructed because of the war and not meant to be a permanent fixture. It is interesting how quickly things are put together when it is urgent.

At the end of the three-month probationary period, just as I was about to sign up with the Army for the duration of the war, word came from Vancouver that the Red Cross was again recruiting VADs for overseas. I spoke with the matron at the Nanaimo

Military Hospital, and she kindly released me with a strong recommendation. Armed with this, I finally signed up for overseas duty in June of 1943.

I was literally rushed to Toronto as they needed me *now*, if not sooner. I arrived in Toronto in the middle of a heat wave and was whisked to Eaton's for fittings of khaki and sturdy brogues, etc. It was hot, hot, hot! We were finally given permission to wear civvies because of the heat, but I was to spend a long hot summer in Toronto. Luckily I had relatives who could put me up. No one at headquarters seemed to know what to do with several of us who were wandering in the wilds of Toronto, waiting for a call at any moment to head out.

During this "holding period," I received word that a Mrs. Tudball wished to see me. Mrs. Tudball was in charge of the Red Cross in Canada. She was a tall, elegant woman who was just like the Queen in our eyes—a very fine woman, but you wanted to keep out of her way, because you never knew what would happen when you were called into her office. "Oh Lord," I thought, "I'm being shipped back to Victoria!" However, she asked me to become a Red Cross welfare officer in North Africa—a most exciting prospect. During this interview, Mrs. Tudball also told me that she had received word that two friends of mine, Pauline Griffith and Jean Ellis, were also regarded as suitable candidates for welfare officers. I heartily agreed.

I finally left Toronto with quite a gang, and we headed for Halifax and the Atlantic crossing. When we arrived, we saw the *Queen Mary* riding majestically at anchor, and we were sure that she was our ship. Instead we were slated for the *Covina*—what a blow. Forty of us, who came to be known as the "roaring forty," sailed on the little tub. She proved a friendly little ship—for we had Royal Air Force types aboard on leave after years in the Mediterranean area and English families and businessmen. We soon drank the bar dry.

Our accommodation was crowded but adequate. Everything was neat and tidy until a storm hit and violent seasickness unravelled most of us. In fact, one of the girls was seasick as soon as she saw the *Covina* and stayed that way until she was carried off two weeks later at Liverpool.

We were part of an enormous convoy—one hundred ships. One of the Corps girls had a brother on a corvette shepherding us across the Atlantic. His ship and the *Covina* exchanged signals between brother and sister, which was exciting for the rest of us.

Docking by tender in Liverpool Harbour on September 3, 1943 proved an interesting exercise, as people and luggage were flung with joyous abandon from ship to tender. A tender is a small motor boat that is used to take people and luggage into an area that a large ship cannot enter, in this case because of all the damage done by bombing. Watching our huge duffel bags being flung from ship to tender proved a harrowing experience. One duffel bag missed the tender and landed in Davy Jones' locker. Forty of us sweated it out until we were ashore to see who was the unlucky one.

Pauline and I soon found out that life amongst the sand dunes and scorpions in North Africa was not to be. Our husbands heartily disagreed with our going to North Africa; they were stationed in London at that time. Finally, the Canadian Army came to the rescue when they sent out a directive that no married woman was to be sent to Africa. It seems that married women were meeting up with their husbands, which quite often led to pregnancies.

My husband Bob worked in London as the assistant to Brigadier Beaumont, but he was not attached to any division at that time. Because of this, they didn't have any accommodation for him, so he had his own flat. Luckily, I was allowed to "live out" with Bob, and we were able to go to work together on the underground. My job at the Red Cross headquarters was not far from where Bob worked. We had it made, really.

Bob's flat was a funny little place with a Mrs. Fortiglow and a Miss Popplet as landladies. They were absolutely delightful. They always called my husband "Robert" and treated him like their one and only son. He was spoiled rotten because they thought he was just the cat's meow. But after D-Day, Bob was posted to headquarters in Belgium, and then I had to go into the Corps House which was at 20 Queen's Gate Terrace.

I worked in the Red Cross Hospital Supplies Department and it was good—there were no problems. I had an interesting lady as my supervisor, a Miss Harvey, who made sure that we underlings toed the line. She was a good woman who had been a famous golfer in Canada before the war. But I will always remember her as a wonderful old fuddy duddy who tried to be terribly military in the organization of our work. We had orders that would come in for all kinds of items that were required for the wounded at the various hospitals. Materials such as clothing, bedding and medical supplies came over from Canada, and we would have to count them to match them up with the orders for supplies from the hospitals. Unfortunately for us, Miss Harvey had a real thing about counting.

I can see myself now. Each incoming parcel listed two dozen of this and five dozen of that, but according to Miss Harvey, we still had to count the items to make sure the listing was correct. Bureaucracy can be so maddening. I would think, "If I count this bundle one more time . . . " Finally I would ask Miss Harvey, "Does it really matter, if there's twelve or fourteen of these bloody things?" She was a purist, however. In fact, she was terribly serious about everything. But I found her concern very funny. So there were twelve instead of fourteen? It really didn't matter. Were you going to get on the phone and say, "Ottawa, what are you going to do about this? We are short two shirts here!"

The supplies came from all over Canada. Everything was placed into categories: there were categories for clothing, medical supplies and special ones for prisoners of war. Canadian women's groups made all kinds of things—mittens, socks, scarves, layettes. Layettes would include nighties, blankets, sweaters, bonnets, booties and diapers. We packed parcels for prisoners of war that included gloves, socks, shaving gear, chocolate bars, cigarettes and anything else we thought they would be short of.

We worked in a lovely part of London, but we were in a flimsy old building—one bomb and it would have been finished. There were several huge rooms, and they were all laid out so that you could find everything. When you received an order for some of these supplies to go to a hospital, you knew where the items were and you shipped them out. We worked hard, but it was okay.

Shipping supplies out to hospitals and first-aid posts in various areas was an important job. The Red Cross transport system was first-class. The drivers had a tough time, but in spite of all the bureaucracy, they got the materials to where they were needed. The materials were brought in from Liverpool, and 90 percent of the drivers were women. I never drove and I'm glad I never did—it was very dangerous.

The items we received and distributed also included clothing for bombed-out families. Again, this was an important service, because so many people's homes were blown up, especially in London. They often had nothing left—the bombs destroyed everything. People who lost their homes often had to leave London, and were sometimes relocated as far away as Wales. The number of homeless people who stayed in London was dreadful—I'd see them out on the streets. A lot of them slept in the underground tube at night, which stunk, because the air was not fresh. But you got used to it. That was the way it was.

This is one of my saddest pictures: going down to the underground and seeing layers and layers of people. They would go down at night, and they each had a sleeping bag, which was pretty "grotty" compared to what sleeping bags are now. There'd be three layers of people, because they had set up bunkbeds at three levels. I saw this when I was caught in the bombing and had to go down to the underground for shelter. For these people, it just became a way of life. What could you do about it?

I worked from Monday to Friday or even Saturday—all day, every day. For fun, there was a pub across the way and that was very handy. The pubs were wonderful. There was music, you could talk to everybody, and you could enjoy an English beer along with some food. The "roaring forty" had split somewhat, but there were still a fair number of us in London. We had a great time. In fact the pub across the street did so well, I'm sure we kept them in business.

There was the bombing, but you became numb to it. I can see myself outside watching the night fighters over Hyde Park—the Germans and British fighting in the air. It was more strange than scary. As I think back, some people were very, very upset, but some of them like me became part of it. And I can see us now standing outside watching the night-fighting and cheering for the "good guys." It may seem dumb, but what else could you do? After the fighting would finish, it was, "Let's go to the pub and have a beer."

Yet I don't want to underestimate the seriousness of the bombing. It was bad. And I hated going down to the air-raid shelters. Because they were so small, you felt trapped. I had a dear friend, Pauline Griffith, and the two of us would say to each other, "We're supposed to go down to that G——damn place, but we'd rather stay up here." In order to reach the shelter, we had to go outside and then down. We hated it, but now I realize what an idiot I was to think I'd rather not go to the air-raid shelter, considering what could have happened to me if I didn't.

We Canadians felt terribly sorry for the Brits. They had only English rations and very few of them, whereas we had a comfortable arrangement at the Corps House, with good cooks and a good supply of food. Moreover, the Brits had been suffering for a long time before we arrived.

Yet when I was living out with my husband Bob, we shared the flat with those dear old British ladies who were absolutely delightful. Although they had to put up with the rationing, they enjoyed our company and would always try to give us an extra portion. Part of it was that they were so happy to have the Canadians over there helping them with the war.

After he went overseas, my husband was able to come back to London from time to time because he was working for CMHQ (Canadian Military Headquarters) and he would be sent back from Belgium on business. I remember receiving word through friends that Bob would be returning to London, but he arrived at midnight and there was no place for him to stay. Without my knowing about it, he came right to Corps House and slept in the living room. The next morning, everyone was saying, "Hi, Bob!"

before I realized what was going on. I found out that his supervisor had sent Bob because he knew I was in London, which was generous. But we only had a little time together, and then he had to go back.

I ended up spending all my time from September 1943 to July 1945 working at the Red Cross Hospital Supplies Department. At one point the powers-that-be tried to make me a recreational therapist, and I went to Kingston for a course in handicrafts. When I made two right-handed sheep's wool mittens, I was soon back at Hospital Supplies moving crates and counting dressing gowns.

One of the most important things that kept us going during this time was the camaraderie among us Red Cross girls. We were all in it together—we all had boyfriends or husbands. It made you realize that it doesn't matter who you are or where you come from, when you go through hard times, you all end up very much the same. When we enlisted, we thought it was a great adventure until we actually experienced the war. After D-Day there were so many tragedies—the Canadian First and Second Divisions lost a lot of men, a lot of husbands and boyfriends. It was after the invasion that the immensity of the losses really hit us.

Now when I look back, I think how stupid all that shooting was, and how terrible the loss of lives. But to be honest, I also have wonderful memories of great, great friends. There were many laughs, many sad times, but always the marvellous camaraderie of the girls in the Corps overseas. We forged a bond that you can't break, and we are still a part of each other's lives through our clubs here in Canada.

Rosamund Follis Miskolczi

"Everyone on those war bride
trains was 'precious cargo'"

Rosamund Follis Miskolczi was born in Lacombe, Alberta, and grew up
in Vancouver, Winnipeg and Montreal. Before joining the Red Cross
Corps she was a nursing assistant with the Canadian Army. After the
war she set up a Red Cross Blood Clinic in Whitehorse, Yukon
and stayed to work for the Territorial Government. On
her retirement she moved to Nanoose Bay,
B.C. on Vancouver Island.

The old adage, "the harder you work, the greater the reward," was certainly true in my case. It was wartime, and I was living with my parents and married sister, working for the Inspection Board of the United Kingdom in Canada during the day—7:15 a.m. to 5 p.m. But because I wanted to go overseas, I was also working at various other projects so as to improve my chances. The first involved studying for my St. John's Ambulance certficate. Quite unexpectedly they sprang the exam on me, but I still managed to achieve 98% and a commendation. At the same time, I was travelling across town to the Montreal Neurological Institute to build up my nursing hours.

At the Institute I worked from 6 p.m. to 10:30 p.m. or even later. Sometimes I would observe neuro-surgery, and once I was fortunate enough to watch the world-famous Wilder Penfield. I had a good friend, Lorraine Rolland Mills, who worked for the Bell Telephone Company during the day, and joined forces with me at the hospital every night and all day Saturdays and Sundays. Together we survived embarrassing experiences such as rubbing a patient's back with mouthwash (mistaken for alcohol) and moving a male patient to an all-women's ward.

When our required hours were finished, we continued our nursing work to gain more experience and also because we could see how much we were needed as a result of the staff shortages. One day the Red Cross Corps commandant, with whom we had formed a precision-marching squad, phoned to ask if we were interested in going into active service with the Canadian Army. The Red Cross Corps was just beginning its overseas duty, but movement in that direction was slow. We felt we would get overseas faster with the Canadian Army because we were advised we might not even have a three-month wait. So it was off to Debert, Nova Scotia, as VADs with the Royal Canadian Army Medical Corps. We were loaded to the gills with uniforms, hospital dresses and aprons, dozens of nursing sisters' brown stockings, underwear and of course a "good" nightie and bed jacket in case of illness and a doctor's call.

Our rules and regulations were those of all nursing sisters. We were considered "Commissioned Rank," and as such there was to be no fraternization with other ranks, but even though we were attested into the Canadian Army, we received $30.00 a month pay as VADs, instead of the $5.00 a day the nursing sisters received.

Our life in Debert was really wonderful—forty women and fifteen hundred officers. You never went out, or seldom anyway, with the same man twice in one week. That would be taking him too seriously, and for me, that was just fine as I was engaged to an Australian airman. So I had a marvellous time, drinking and dancing with my "buddies."

Our work was enjoyable as there were several orderlies per ward, and all we had to do were medications, dressings of a minor nature, temperatures, respirations and pulses. Bed pans were unknown to us and the respect was great. I was fortunate to have friends in every sector, noncoms included. On Christmas leave, I spent a whole day shopping for "my boys" and their wives and sweethearts.

Doomsday came six months later when I was transferred from Debert to Sydney, Nova Scotia, and had to leave my Debert friends behind. In Sydney we had no nursing sisters' mess. Therefore I had to live out, although we had a dining-room with the medical officers in the hospital. I experienced real homesickness in Sydney, the first and only time in my life. I was considerably younger than the other girls; the only other VAD was Peggy Forbes, but she lived at home with her sisters. With my Don overseas, my room was blue, the hospital was blue, and I was blue.

In Sydney I was fortunate enough to be given greater responsibility owing to the shortage of nursing sisters, who were at that time proceeding overseas in greater numbers. For one month I was in charge of the hospital night duty with three orderlies. Sydney was a 100-bed hospital but all serious cases were taken to the big Naval Hospital at Protector.

After we had worked as VADs with the Army for some time, it was brought to our attention one day that the Army had made a mistake when they told us we would be going overseas with the Canadian Forces. The Army calculated that one nursing sister equalled two VADs, and they wanted as few mouths as possible to feed overseas. Logical, but greatly disappointing to all the VADs now stuck with the Army. Brigadier-General Letson, a man of great understanding, issued orders stating that all VADs in the Army could obtain their honourable release, providing they requested their release to go overseas with the Red Cross. Naturally I applied.

I was sent back to Montreal for my release, followed by a long six-week wait for our overseas draft. When it finally arrived, we once again sat on our trunks to close them, only this time they were lined to the hilt, not only with uniforms but civilian items for special occasions. With much excitement, apprehension and emotional farewells, we left Montreal on the "Refugee Special" bound for New York. We were certain we would be sailing on either the *Queen Mary* or the *Queen Elizabeth*. As the American Red Cross driver drove us to the New York dockside, we kept looking up—to find only sky. Finally, lowering our sights to what seemed to be about tug size, we saw the *Rangitiki*, our home for twenty-two days.

I was seasick even before we sailed because the dock pilings kept going "up and down." But once underway, all was well with my health but not with that of the ship. We sailed past the Statue of Liberty and watched as the convoy took shape with land still in sight. However, by late afternoon and out of sight of land (we knew we were over the three-mile limit because we had all purchased boxes of tax-free chocolate bars), we noticed our ship had no wake, and therefore was not proceeding forward. We then watched ship after ship pass us until we were alone—with the sun about to set. We were too naive to know that we were alone at a time when the Atlantic was experiencing one of the last bad U-Boat attacks, with German U-Boats coming up the St. Lawrence and very close to the coastline. There were British anti-aircraft gunners and guns aboard the *Rangitiki,* and the guns were now uncovered and manned. In the distance, we saw a ship approaching, which turned out to be one of the American destroyers back from the convoy—it circled us all night because otherwise *Rangitiki* was a sitting duck.

In the morning we were told over the loudspeaker that we would be returning to New York. It took us two days, with the destroyer escorting us and circling us constantly. The night before we were to tie up in New York, we were told that all passengers with relatives or homes in and around New York would be allowed off the ship for five days and nights. There were twenty-eight Red Cross girls in our draft and I think twenty of us had "uncles" in New York! Thinking back, I am amazed that we were not asked for a permanent address in case the required repairs were completed sooner, and the ship sailed prior to the planned day. Had this happened, we would have been stranded.

For our stay in New York, we were each given $20.00 in U.S. funds, but by the time we left the ship most of us had only about $10.00 left, since we had purchased Hershey bars and cigarettes with the other $10.00. We took only our haversacks but, thank goodness, we stuck cigarettes and a carton of chocolate bars in at the last minute. These proved essential.

We went to the USO and the American Red Cross, thinking they had a hostel where we could stay. But they could only take Army, Navy, Air Force and Marines, not Red Cross. There were eight in our group and we were offered a suite in the Waldorf at exceptional discounts—only $100.00 a night. This would indeed have been a terrific discount, but as I have mentioned, we each had only about $10.00 for five nights.

We had been given a security briefing before leaving the ship, and we were very conscious that talking about our situation would jeopardize our own skins. So I finally took one of the USO women aside and didn't tell all, but made mysterious innuendoes and told her we only had $10.00 each. She understood our plight and found us a Sally Ann Hostel for fifty cents a night; we paid for the five nights in advance so we would know where we stood.

Our first mistake was supper at the Automat. It may have been inexpensive, but by the time the nickels and dimes were added up, it came to a horrifying $1.50! We couldn't afford that! This was why our chocolate bars became so important. The USO was truly marvellous: they gave us tickets to everything, from the magnificent Metropolitan Opera—one box above the dress circle—to a Frank Sinatra broadcast where teenagers a block from the studio begged for our tickets. The last night we all put twenty-five cents away for a cab to the dock and spent the remaining small change on bus fare, the underground, street car and taxi to see the rest of New York.

Our second start from New York was successful, and we were soon spending our days on deck in our shirt sleeves as it was really warm for November. We later learned we were down around the Azores. During the crossing, we lost two ships on the outer perimeters of the convoy, a soldier went overboard from the ship immediately in front of us, and we ran out of our "torpedo" ration of rye by the nineteenth day. There was a great flurry of excitement one day when all the ack-ack guns were hurriedly uncovered, with great activity amongst the gunnery crew. However, it turned out to be only a lifeboat drill that was long overdue. We also became quite tense when we spotted a dot in the sky—knowing it to be a plane—but whose? When it disappeared, we assumed it must have been ours.

When the crew called out "Sunderland," and the convoy split into two sections—some ships to Cherbourg, and some up the west coast of Ireland—a great sigh of relief went up as it became clear we were to go through the southern passage between Ireland and England on the Irish Sea. Ours was the first convoy to do so in years, and best of all we were protected all the way.

We arrived in Liverpool two nights later and duly sent off our "arrival" cables to family. No matter how I tried, I could not get one of my pair of shoes inside my suitcase, so I struggled off the boat with a pair of shoes tied through the handle of my suitcase. I'd been up all night, so perhaps my energy was lacking. A sweet, old longshoreman took my suitcase to the train inside the dock building.

After an overnight trip on the train to London, we were billeted at the Baker Street YWCA. I was never so cold as that night. As my first assignment, I was sent to the hospital in Leatherhead, where I quickly realized that hospital life in England was altogether different from what we had known in the Army in Canada. We were not popular with the English nursing staff at first, partly because our uniforms were smart and new. This I could understand, but they never tried to understand how we had scrimped and saved and wheeled and dealed to go overseas. Our brown rayon nursing-sister stockings may have looked smart, but all the same we were volunteers. However, we bit our tongues to be diplomatic and finally succeeded in forming great friendships with the English girls.

One of my responsibilities on night duty in casualty was to get food from the kitchen and cook it for the night supervisor and the nurse in the next ward. On the night I made scalloped potatoes, there was no malice intended when I substituted an Ajax-like cleaning powder for a dusting of flour. I really thought it was flour. The night supervisor, a senior conscripted because of the war, and seventy if she was a day, seemed not to have noticed, since she pronounced it was delicious.

Our year overseas was one of hard work, long hours, depression and lots of humour of the black variety, such as having your veil catch fire and having to complete the shift wearing a half-burned cap, or having a deceased woman twitch long after you had bathed her and put her in a shroud. Then there was Aileen, the VAD who was always trying to break the record for the number of bed pans she could carry, dashing out of the women's ward with thirteen bed pans, all full, precariously balanced, mind you, and bumping right into the "love of her life," whom she later married. He had rushed into the hospital to propose to her. When she screamed at him to get out, he was so shocked and embarrassed, he left, leaving Aileen weeping, sure she had lost him.

Aileen and I celebrated Victory-in-Europe Day and Victory-in-Japan Day while we were at Leatherhead. I had been accepted by the British Ministry of Health and Red Cross to go to India at the end of my year in the British Hospital. But Victory-in-Japan Day put an end to these aspirations.

I spent my New Year's leave in Edinburgh and then returned to London for an interview with Dr. Stuart Stansbury. He was about to return to Canada to open the peacetime Blood Transfusion

Red Cross Escort Officer with two war brides, London.

Service and become the commissioner of the Red Cross. I was a successful applicant for a special course in blood transfusion work in Leeds, Yorkshire. I don't think I'll every forget stepping off the train in Leeds with six or so other girls, and being handed the keys to a station wagon parked at the station in downtown Leeds, with the casual instructions, "Follow me." I was too scared to refuse, although I had never driven a right-hand car on the left side of the street.

We stayed in a beautiful old house which had been turned into a convalescent home for WACs, and it meant a drive over the Yorkshire moors twice a day. After two months, we returned to London. While waiting for a draft home, I did various jobs that included cooking at the Gloucester Road Hostel. I also went to

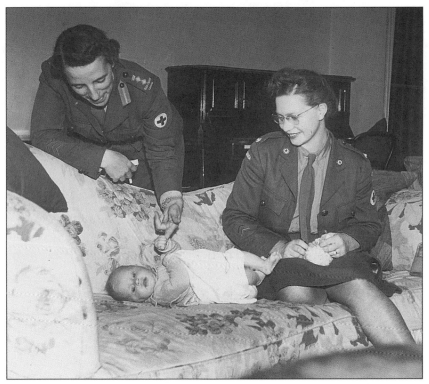

*Mrs. Lee, Corps Commandant, with new mother and baby awaiting
repatriation, at Corps House, London.*

Belgium and onto France on my own—against Red Cross wishes—
but I had a great time, especially when I ran into some old Debert
buddies who entertained me.

I returned home in April, and while waiting to join the Canadian Red Cross Blood Transfusion Organizational Team, I made
twenty train trips from Montreal to Winnipeg in twenty-two weeks,
escorting war brides and their children. It was quite an experience. I had two babies die on one trip—one with pneumonia and
one with spinal meningitis. To say these deaths nearly broke my
heart would be putting it mildly. Everyone on those war bride
trains was "precious cargo" as far as I was concerned. Some of the
mothers had little sense of nutrition and I had to chastise them
gently for giving Coca-Cola to their three- or four-month-old

babies and unlimited junk food to year-old tots. They had come so far, leaving everything they knew. But for what?—sometimes a tragic life, often a good one. Somehow it seemed that you knew what each war bride's life would be simply by watching how she was greeted at her destination.

Finally, all was in readiness for the start of the Red Cross Transfusion Service for which I had trained in Leeds, England, and we left Toronto in a special compartment car for Vancouver. We were billeted at the Gifford Hotel on Robson Street, which became my home for over six months. All the equipment was new, with suction now being replaced by the gravity method. It was months of preparation before the first clinic was opened in the basement of the old Vancouver Hotel, with the workshop in a hut at Shaughnessy Hospital. After the clinic was running smoothly, we moved on to Edmonton where I lived for over a year—the first three months in a frat house. After working at a Calgary sub-station, I finally returned to Montreal, where I worked for another eight months with the Blood Transfusion Service. The training over and promises fulfilled, I decided to return to the west which was my preference as home.

As I write this and look back on what is still a vivid picture, I can't help thinking how much good can arise out of chaos during a time of terrible struggle and strife. It can seem a cliché, but under what other circumstances would we have worked so hard for no money and no tangible reward at the time, but without complaint? What we didn't realize then was that in giving, we gained much: lifelong friendships with people we would otherwise never have met, and an invaluable understanding of life and people— far greater then most people in ordinary walks of life will ever have a chance to experience.

Audrey C. Kitching

*"I felt sure we were climbing
Mount Everest"*

—

Born and raised in Toronto, Ontario, Audrey C. Kitching worked as a
secretary before joining the Red Cross. After World War II, she
accompanied her husband to ten different Canadian Army
postings, including Washington, London and Paris. She
was a volunteer art teacher at the Royal Ontario
Museum in Toronto and the
Victoria Art Gallery.

B y the winter of 1943 it seemed as though the war would never end. Almost every family we knew was losing their younger members to the services. Certainly people felt a great desire to be part of the war effort in a really meaningful way. It no longer seemed enough to be just helping to man milkshake bars at Exhibition Park or at the Royal Canadian Air Force Depot in Toronto, or to be serving tea and cakes Sunday afternoons at the YMCA to boys in uniform, or even to be working evenings in downtown offices typing army files. Although all those jobs were undoubtedly necessary, they had come to seem monotonous and somehow peripheral. Even harder to bear were the humiliating drills for the Red Cross Corps in the University Street Armories one evening a week. Thus, when the call came for welfare officers to work in Canadian military hospitals abroad, I immediately responded and was thrilled to find I had been among those chosen. After a short training period, we would be sent to help in a military hospital overseas.

In July 1944, I sailed from Montreal on the *S.S. Manchester* with thirteen other girls. It took almost a week to reach the Atlantic after leaving Montreal, because of a long delay while taking on cargo in the St. Lawrence. We did not realize the cargo was TNT until our captain, Captain Strauss, told us. At the same time, he said, "Boat drill will not be necessary because if our ship is hit, we will all go straight up." After the crossing, we landed in Liverpool and were amazed at the excitement about buzz bombs. We had never heard of them and didn't know how they functioned until we arrived in London and found ourselves in an area of the city which seemed to be one of their targets.

My stay at the Canadian Red Cross Corps House in London was brief, but I had time to visit with my younger sister Beverley, who was with the Royal Canadian Air Force working at Lincoln's Inn Fields and quartered near Regent's Park. Any leave I received I spent with her there.

Soon five of us girls were sent to the Canadian Military Hospital (CMH) in Colchester, and there we had our welfare training. We were billeted in civilian homes near the hospital, but had all our meals in the sisters' mess. Towards the end of the course, I was given a half-day off to go into town and see the Roman ruins and other points of interest. It was not hard to find my way about, but when it came time to return to the hospital, I seemed to have lost my sense of direction. In the centre of the town, three main roads met, and at the intersection a policeman was directing traffic. When it was not too busy I crossed over to where he stood and asked, "Which road leads to the CMH?" "It's the same road you live on," he answered with a big grin, and pointed to one of the roads.

Seeing my surprise that he should know which road I lived on, he laughed heartily and said, "You live in my house." I had never seen the owners. I had a key to my room which I entered from the garden. As I left early in the morning on my bike to get breakfast in the mess before going to the Red Cross room, and as I walked home pushing my bike in the dark, completely exhausted after having an evening meal in the mess, I had never met my host.

On completion of our course, we returned to London, and I worked in Burlington Gardens packing Christmas stockings and doing other odd jobs, awaiting a posting to a hospital unit. There was considerable bombing of London during this period—those fiendish "buzz bombs." The buzz bombs were motorized rocket bombs that the Nazis sent over from France. As soon as the motor of a buzz bomb shut down, we knew it was about to drop, but we had no idea where it would land.

Finally I was posted to Helmsley in Yorkshire to join No. 20 Canadian General Hospital. It was early September and becoming cooler. We lived in Nissen huts with ninety-odd nursing sisters and other female staff members. We were a hospital unit training to live in the field. We had outdoor latrines, sensibly placed in circles with canvas surrounding them. They were shoulder-high and located at the bottom of a hill that was muddy and slippery when it rained (which was often).

We ate out of our mess tins and wore khaki slacks with large zippered openings down the front (not terribly flattering to the figure!) and army boots and gaiters. No one could ever have mis-

Canadian Red Cross Corps Church Parade, London, England.

taken us for the "ballet corps" come to town, but we had lots of laughs and great camaraderie. The greatest challenge of all, for me, was a route march with full pack, at the end of which we donned our gas masks and, on the double, climbed a hill. Probably it was a slight incline, but I felt sure we were climbing Mount Everest, and I never expected to get to the top.

In October, we were still waiting for our posting to the Continent when the "powers that be" decided to move the whole hospital unit to an empty hotel at Scotch Corner. This was the meeting place of two main roads not far from Durham and York.

Then, early in December, we left in trucks as a complete unit for Dover. On the same ship with us crossing the Channel were many Polish soldiers who serenaded us with Christmas carols—such beautiful voices. We landed at Ostende in Belgium and then moved on to Antwerp, Belgium, where we had hoped to set up as a hospital. However, the bombing of the port was intensive at this time, and many civilians were being wounded and were dying. It was not the place for a military hospital, so our hospital unit and the Red Cross group were divided and sent to other hospitals to reinforce their present staffs.

Sylvia Smellie and I were sent to No. 12 CMH in Brugge to help the Red Cross girls already there. Canadian troops were now fighting hard in Holland and the hospitals were moving forward behind them. I was moved on to No. 8 CMH at 's-Hertogenbosch, Netherlands. I had not been there many weeks when a call went out one evening for girls to go to a party in an officers' mess. It was difficult to gather a group. The nurses were exhausted, as were the Red Cross girls. However, after much persuasion and emphasis on "if you are from Toronto, you are sure to know some of the Hamilton boys," I went. Unfortunately the young driver of the HUP, an army vehicle like a station wagon, was unaware of an ammunition convoy on the road ahead of us. He was not allowed to use his lights, and in the dark he ran into the end truck. We were lucky there was no explosion, but we went into a ditch and turned over.

It was a nasty accident, and caused me to reflect on how many people were injured and killed in the war from what were actually non-combative accidents. Two nursing sisters received cuts on their heads. As I had been sitting up front with the driver and was the last one in the vehicle, I became caught under the truck. When freed, I also had a large cut on my head and a gash over one eyebrow. The nurses were driven back to our hospital, but I was put into a different vehicle and was taken forward to a casualty clearing station in Nijmegen for stitches.

The next morning I was transferred, with some wounded soldiers, back to No. 8 where I was put, first, into the corner bed in a large ward with screens around the bed and later into the nurses' sick bay. There they discovered I had an injured left elbow, a broken finger and a fairly serious back injury, which would mean a body cast for four long months. After the cast was on, I was flown back to England and eventually ended up at Bramshott Military Hospital where I was put into a ward for female patients, maternity cases, a child awaiting a tonsillectomy and various other problems. I was a walking patient having daily physiotherapy, and I helped in the Red Cross library.

When the cast was removed, I joined the other Red Cross girls on staff. Another girl and I were billeted in a small private hotel, walking distance from the hospital. This was a very amusing place to live. One of the very elderly ladies was the sister of Lytton Strachey, an English historian, and she tried to teach me to play chess in the evenings.

I stayed on staff in Bramshott and celebrated there the ending of hostilities in both Europe and Japan. After that, I was posted home to Toronto in mid-September. With a large group of Red Cross Corps on the *Isle-de-France,* we sailed for Canada and I was happy to find myself once more with Mary Macdonald. It was a very crowded troopship. We had two meals a day and, as one sitting changed with the next, we exchanged our reading material. Most people were reading *Forever Amber.* Mary and I met several young handsome officers from the Loyal Edmonton Regiment. The two who were most helpful to us in finding spots to sit were John Duggan and Alan Johnson. Both have retired to Victoria with their wives and I see them often—it is a small world.

It was great to be back in Toronto, which was still a lovely place —just as nice as I had tried to convince so many patients I had met in the hospital, who would ask, "Where are you from, Sister?" and when I would say Toronto, a great howl would go up—"awful Toronto." Not so!

The comforts of home were also very welcome. When I went overseas I left a secretarial job with an English firm in Toronto, Johnson Matthey & Co. (Canada), and they wanted me back on my return. The English branch in London had kindly sent an employee to the hospital in Bramshott to see how I was after my accident. The firm in Toronto was about to amalgamate with an American firm called Mallory, so I worked on the amalgamation until the autumn of 1946, when I left to be married.

On October 4, 1946, George Kitching and I were married in St. Andrews Presbyterian Church. This amalgamation has been a great success, and I have often thought the angels had a hand in it. Kate joined us in Kingston in 1952 and young George was born in Vancouver in 1955. We retired to Victoria with never a monotonous moment.

E. R. (Betty) Wightman

"We were all proud of being Canadian"

—

Betty Wightman was born in Inverness, Scotland. She was three years old when she came to B.C., where her father was a banker. Betty worked for the Bank of Montreal before going overseas with the Red Cross. After the war Betty and her husband settled in Prince Rupert and then Terrace, B.C. Betty focused on raising her three children, volunteering with the United Church Women's group and the Kinette Club, and playing golf.

At about the time when World War II was declared in 1939, my family moved to Powell River, B.C., while I stayed in Chilliwack to start my first job with the Bank of Montreal. A great many Canadian bank employees had immigrated from Britain and had immediately "joined up," an exodus which created new jobs for women in the banking field.

With my British background, I was devastated by the outbreak of the war. My father had served with the 54th Kootenay Battalion from Nelson, B.C., in the First World War, and we had been taught to think that it was the war to end all wars. My brother and I were both young adults, and the future looked bleak with another war. My brother Alastair was only seventeen when war was declared; he signed up a year later. He became a squadron leader and a bomber pilot who was awarded the Distinguished Flying Cross.

By 1941 I was engaged. Morris was a banker whom I had met while I was working as a secretary for the Bank of Montreal. We were married in 1943, just before Morris left for England as a bomber pilot with the RCAF 419 Squadron. I had already joined the Red Cross in Chilliwack, but when my husband left to go overseas, I went to Powell River to stay with my family. I joined the Red Cross there—my father was already a very active member. The commandant of the Red Cross in Vancouver organized the Red Cross Corps in Powell River, and I was soon promoted to sergeant major.

Thinking that I might become a nurse's aide, I spent some time in the Powell River Hospital as a volunteer, but I soon discovered that I was not nurse material. As I was still anxious to go overseas, I said I would go in any capacity. We took some organizational training and we had endless hours of drill. Eventually they recognized my clerical skills, so I was able to sign up for general duties. Finally in 1944, I was notified of my posting overseas.

I flew from Vancouver to Toronto on a North Star aircraft in late September 1944. It was my first flight. In those days, oxygen masks were used for going over the Rockies, and I remember that the plane was cold. I was fitted out for my Red Cross uniform at

Eaton's in Toronto. We had a special uniform when we were in Canada; it was a grey tailored dress with a grey cap. Then when we went overseas, we wore a khaki uniform with a beret. Our group of six Red Cross girls left a week later for Halifax.

Our South American banana boat, the *Araguanna*, took eighteen days in stormy weather to reach Liverpool. We were actually on the Atlantic a week before we saw signs of our convoy. The long voyage was quite an ordeal for most of us Red Cross girls who were violently seasick. It had been expected that we would assist the Royal Air Force wives with their children, but needless to say we were not much use to anyone. The Royal Air Force wives were Canadian women who had married Royal Air Force personnel sent to Canada for training in the Commonwealth Air Training Program. The *Araguanna* carried a maximum of eighty-seven passengers, and ours was her last voyage before she was scrapped.

As we approached land, we all felt a tremendous excitement about arriving in wartime Britain. Having been born in Scotland, I was thrilled that I would be able to see my grandmothers and aunts for the first time. But when we actually docked in Liverpool we were shocked by the bombed-out areas and blackouts. We boarded a train to London right away, and there we were met in the dark and transported in vehicles with only little slits in the headlights to show the road ahead. In daylight we visited some of the bombed-out areas and could see that in many cases they were little more than rubble. We quickly learned as well that the Germans were still attacking London with their deadly V-1 and V-2 bombs.

After arriving in London, I was given a short leave and decided to travel to Inverness, Scotland to visit my two grandmothers and enjoy a vacation with my husband. My husband, who was by this time a "Lancaster" bomber pilot stationed in northern England, had also managed a few days leave. When I returned to London a few days later, I was moved from Corps House to Onslow Gardens, where I stayed permanently.

Onslow Gardens was a four-storey house, with the unusual feature that there was a bathroom on the top floor. Sometimes in the midst of having a bath (you were allowed four inches), you could hear the "doodle bugs" coming. You could only have a bath once a week, so it was a temptation to stay in the water. The girls that were there prior to 1944 would have jumped out right away, but by 1944 everyone was getting much more accustomed to the bombs. I can remember that several times I simply stayed in the tub. It was actually quite dangerous because the "doodle bugs" often destroyed the top floors of buildings.

I was posted to B.C. House where I assisted in the canteen and in the officers' lounge. It was a very old building on Lower Regent Street, which was two blocks from Piccadilly Circus. We had bikes which we bought for only about ten Canadian dollars, and we would ride them to work. We served complete meals in the canteen in the basement. The servicemen from all the forces would come in and they ate at rows and rows of tables. A Mrs. Anderson from Victoria ran the canteen with superb efficiency.

Besides serving the food, we did all kinds of things, from operating the till to peeling potatoes and vegetables. Quite a few of the girls complained that the canteen was drab, and actually it was, but it was wartime and we felt safe from the bombs down there. After work we would walk up the street and see the many bombed-out buildings. Often all that was left was just a huge hole.

The meals at the B.C. House canteen had the reputation of being the best canteen meals in London. Tremendous roasts were cooked each day and served with vegetables and gravy. Our desserts always consisted of white cake with a choice of vanilla, strawberry or chocolate custard pudding poured over the top. The custards, which needed to be stirred by hand for an hour to keep them smooth, were made in huge pans from which we would serve hundreds of servicemen. The Red Cross girls who worked there were cheerful and did much to brighten many lives. We also worked with many fine British women, some of whom were volunteers while others received a salary. The canteen served breakfast and dinners, along with coffee and tea at the breaks. It was always full.

Each day two different girls took turns picking up slabs of cake at a local bakeshop. We used a large brown suitcase for the job. On one day when I was picking up the cake with another girl, the snap on the suitcase broke, and the slabs of white cake emptied onto the sidewalk—unlikely contents for a suitcase. There were the two of us in our Red Cross uniforms, not knowing whether to laugh or cry! Instead, we did neither, but quickly scraped up the cake to the great amusement of passersby who laughed as we worked to rescue our precious cargo. Never mind the condition, the cake was duly served for the two dinners that day.

In the lounge on the main floor, we served coffee, tea and light lunches. There were small-town newspapers from British Columbia, and the servicemen and servicewomen enjoyed catching up on the news from home. Mail and free cigarettes were also available. As I had lived in several B.C. interior towns, I was fortunate enough to know a great many service people coming in and out of B.C. House, so there were many happy reunions.

I spent most of my leaves near the Royal Canadian Air Force bases where my husband and brother were stationed. Most of our fun was centred in London and at the canteen—tea dances, shows, visits with friends—but we also attempted to see as much of Britain as we could.

The most exciting and gratifying time was the arrival of British Columbia's prisoners of war en route home. In 1945, there were many Canadian prisoners of war arriving in London after being liberated from their internment. B.C.'s prisoners of war came to B.C. House to make contact and arrangements for their return home. They picked up mail and cigarettes, read the hometown newspapers and got in touch with their families in B.C. They could have light lunches in the upstairs lounge, where we made them feel welcome.

Often when the prisoners of war came to the canteen, they would ask us out, and we would go with them to the tea dances, which were great fun. There was a dance floor and an orchestra, and we would have tea, little sandwiches and cakes. The tea dances were held in the afternoons in hotels such as the Piccadilly and the Cumberland. In the evenings we would also sometimes go pubbing. We all had Canada flashes on our uniforms, which gained us tremendous respect from all the services and the people of Britain. People seemed to go out of their way when they saw you were from Canada. I think a lot of it was the camaraderie of being in the war effort together.

There were also quite a few Canadian Chinese servicemen who would come into B.C. House, and we would always make up a party and go out with them. There was no racial feeling at all—as there had sometimes been in Canada before the war. They were wonderful men and we really enjoyed their company. The lads we met were very fine young men from Vancouver, and as a group we attended shows or big-band dances.

I shall never forget being in London on Victory-in-Europe Day, for the excitement was unbelievable. We were working at B.C. House on the shift from 6:30 a.m. until 2:30 p.m. When the afternoon shift came on at 2:30, four of us Red Cross volunteers joined the people in the streets around B.C. House; the lower part of St. James's Park and around the Palace was just a mass of people. There were great crowds, and I remember worming my way around the people in the streets. Four of us made our way down to Buckingham Palace where we found a place on a ledge by the large monument in front. At one point we were separated when the crowd pulled us apart. Being so small, I had to put my elbows up and out to make sure that I was not squashed. When the Queen and King came out on the balcony, there were uniforms in front of the Palace from all over the world. It was a wonderful feeling to know the war was over and servicemen could now rejoin their wives to start a family and begin living a normal life again.

My husband suffered a collapsed lung en route to base from a raid in Germany. Subsequently, he spent two months in hospital and was then sent back to Canada before me. For several months he was sending me parcels from Canada, and the shoe was on the other foot. The Canadian Red Cross Corps eventually released me before my term was up, which I appreciated. I had signed up for the duration of the war plus six months; I was overseas for a year and two months.

Certificate of Service

We left from Southampton on the *Isle-de-France,* a transatlantic liner that had been converted into a troopship, and we were only four days crossing an Atlantic that was as smooth as a mill pond. There were about ten of us Red Cross girls returning, and we were able to socialize with the servicemen. It was a joyous ship. Lining up for meals was quite a production, but we would wait to be called in groups and then took our turns. There seemed to be thousands of service people on the ship.

I shall never forget arriving back in Halifax in September 1945 with service people who had not seen Canada for five years. The joyous welcome that Halifax extended to all of us was beyond words. The bands were playing, the flags were flying, and people were carrying balloons and streamers. We were all proud of being Canadian.

I caught the train right away after arriving in Halifax and, after checking in with the Red Cross in Toronto, gradually made my way to Victoria, where my husband was stationed at Pat Bay with the Air Force.

One of my treasured possessions is a framed scroll from the British Columbia Government to all who worked in B.C. House during the war—in grateful recognition of service rendered on behalf of the men and women of the province of British Columbia.

Nancy Lang Tyrwhitt-Drake

*"You know this is the
end of the line"*

—

Nancy Lang Tyrwhitt-Drake was born and raised in Toronto, Ontario.
After graduating from Trinity College at the University of Toronto
in 1943, she joined the Red Cross Corps. She married in
1946 and settled in Victoria, B.C. Nancy focused
her time on her home and family and her
volunteer work, in particular with the
Art Gallery of Greater Victoria.

My loving parents kept the box containing all the letters I wrote to them from overseas during World War II, and it has remained intact all these years. Only recently have I dared to dip into that life that I once knew, but there it all was, even more precious because I had forgotten so much: funny things like the Dalmatian puppy we had at Christleton Bank who was in no way housebroken and we were expected to keep the place neat and tidy; or, our first pay parade that entitled us to the grand sum of sixteen shillings and one penny (approximately $2.00 by today's evaluation). But I am getting ahead of myself; let me start when war broke out.

My parents had taken my brother and me down to the New York World Fair. We had driven from Toronto to the Maritimes, then down to New York, and war was declared while we were there. I remember it because of my parents' great concern, for I confess that neither my brother nor I appreciated the significance of the news. I was seventeen at the time and just finishing school.

Later I went to the University of Toronto, Trinity College, where we were required to do volunteer war work along with our studies. I signed up to do first aid and home nursing, and was assigned to the Toronto General Hospital. I had never been in a hospital in my life, and those were the days when the wards were large, with twenty to thirty patients. It was an illuminating experience for me. The hospitals were so short-staffed that I had to do things for which I was quite unprepared. Doctors and nurses would say things like "change that dressing," which really alarmed me when I really wasn't certain what was to be done. Nevertheless, the hospital work was good experience and proved useful when I went overseas with the Red Cross Corps Transport Section.

I didn't join the Red Cross until I had received my degree in Liberal Arts in 1943. I asked to work in Transport, because I enjoyed driving. The reason I joined was to help in the war effort. In particular I wanted to go overseas. My mother and father were stunned when I told them I had signed up to go overseas. This was after my training, and to calm their fears, I said, "Don't worry, no one in Transport has gone overseas for two years." However, I had no sooner signed my name on the dotted line, when ambulance drivers were urgently needed by the British Red Cross to help transport the casualties from D-Day. When my mother heard that I was soon to sail, she said, "If I were your age, I would want to be doing the same thing"—so that sent me off in good spirits.

I went over to England in late July 1944 on the *Lochmonar*. It was a Royal Mail Line ship and not very large, but we were in one of the largest convoys that had been assembled off Sydney, Nova Scotia. It stretched as far as the eye could see. I had never been away from home before, but I don't remember feeling fearful; it was all just terribly interesting. When you're young, you have no fear, you just go into things. We docked at Liverpool, a sad looking place at the time—after all the bombing. We had lunch at a hotel (the famous Liver), and then we were put on the train to London.

When we arrived, I was billeted at the Red Cross Officers' Club, Maple Leaf No. 4. I went on leave almost immediately and stayed with my brother for five days on the Devon coast. He was with a motor torpedo boat flotilla which went after the German E-boats (motorized torpedo boats) and protected the coast of England. At first my brother had been horrified when he heard I was coming overseas, and he had written to say that I must not come, but when I actually arrived, I think he was pleased, and certainly our time together helped close the age gap between us. Returning to London on the train, I sat like a lump until the train stopped at Exeter, and someone finally said, "You know, this is the end of the line. You have to leave this train and get on the one over there." That was when I learned you don't just get on a train thinking it will automatically take you where you want to go, as most trains do in Canada!

When I returned from my leave, I found out that Mary McCrimmon, with whom I was sharing a room, had come back from her leave to be told that her brother Ian had been killed in action. I hadn't known Mary in Canada but we did our initial training at Christleton Bank near Chester and were posted together from then on, becoming great friends.

It was there at Christleton Bank that we were taught the care and maintenance of the wonderfully reliable Austin Ambulance—complete with exams. We started off with an experienced driver going to the hospital ships which docked at Liverpool, transporting wounded prisoners of war to hospitals in the area. We did our vehicle maintenance during the day and drove at night. I think our work on the ambulances—changing the oil, greasing the nipples and changing tires—was mainly to keep us occupied when we weren't driving.

While stationed outside Chester, my name, along with five other Canadian and British Red Cross Society drivers, was drawn to go to Scotland to pick up new ambulances. We travelled by train to London, with an overnight stop at Finchley Park, complete with buzz bombs, and then to Ayr, Scotland. The next day we were driven through beautiful countryside to a vehicle park to pick up our ambulances. In the midst of nowhere, we found acres and acres of transport of every kind imaginable. Then, all together in one large convoy, we headed south: a memorable drive with a whipping sensation, positioned as I was towards the end of a long line of "ams," as we came to call the ambulances. The overnight at Dumfries was delightful in the Old Globe Hotel where Robbie Burns had been a habitué, and where the kind proprietess, Mrs. Brown, fed two of us at one in the morning while an off-duty policeman drank a pint of mild and bitter.

From Chester we were posted to Lydiard Millicent near Swindon in Wiltshire and I was in that area for about five months. The base camp was at Lydiard Millicent. All our names were placed on a board in the headquarters' hut, and when our name rotated to the top, we would move on to Latton, the forward camp. At Latton we knew that the next call would take us to the airfield at Down Ampney. The call would usually come around six o'clock at night, since the planes would only bring in soldiers when it was dark. This was the new way (after D-Day) of bringing the seriously wounded out of the front lines and directly back to England. Our ambulances would be backed up to the doors of the Dakotas where we would receive our patients and instructions where to

*Unusual photo of a transferral of patients from aeroplane to ambulances.
Transfers were usually at night. Down Ampney, England.*

Transferring patients to a hospital ship, Ostende docks, 1945.

take them. Sometimes we spent the night at the airfield if the planes were delayed.

Often we transported the wounded to the "railhead," where the patients would then be transported to hospitals by train. At other times we would fan out around the country taking the patients to specific hospitals that specialized in the type of injury the men had. For example, head injuries almost always went to Oxford. This of course was all done in the blackouts, but everything ran smoothly despite there being no orderly to help us look after the patient. We would keep the door open between the cab and the back of the ambulance, so we could hear when a patient was in distress and stop if necessary.

At Lydiard Millicent, Tubby Grant was our British Red Cross sergeant. She was very good to us Canadians. Once when I was on a date in Swindon, and there was a fog so thick it felt as though you could cut it, she did me the greatest kindness. Realizing I was stranded and could not get back to camp, I phoned Tubby Grant. All she said was, "Stay where you are." I was absolutely terrified because I should have returned by eleven o'clock and it was much later. I thought the bottom had dropped out of my life. But Sergeant Grant picked me up without saying a word about how late it was. Normally we didn't have much opportunity to go out for pleasure in the evenings because we worked most nights.

As I have mentioned, our driving was done at night. Since there were no signposts to guide us, our travels were gauged by landmarks of choice. Some twenty-odd years later, my husband and I were driving through that area to find the important places in my overseas life, and I could not find them. This resulted in my husband asking me, "Are you sure you were really stationed here?" A bit embarrassing, but trees and hedgerows had changed, and everything looked quite different years later in broad daylight. We did, however, eventually find the camps and a now abandoned airfield.

Life certainly had its hardships at Lydiard Millicent. For some months we had no bed to call our own. Wherever we ended up on the "circuit," we were assigned a bed in a Nissen hut and there we slept; in the morning we took everything back to our ambulances, which were our veritable homes. In time, we were assigned a permanent place, and our lives took on a happy spirit of camaraderie.

We shared digs with the British Red Cross drivers and the FANYs (First Aid Nursing Yeomanry), who looked askance at us at first, but in short order found us not wanting, and we became good friends indeed. Since the winter was bitterly cold, we had to dress very warmly and keep our fires going overnight. But we were young, so we didn't really notice it—the cold was the least of our worries. I truly felt I was doing my small part in this war, and it was a good time in my life to be carrying out a job I liked doing.

After Lydiard, there was a posting to Paris which never came to pass. Instead, Mary McCrimmon and I were sent to Charlton Park, which was a holding place for anyone going over to the Continent. Living in one small quarter of the estate was the Earl of Suffolk and his young family; the rest of it was occupied by the likes of us who tended to household maintenance and our ambulances. I was assigned to logging duty which entailed sawing up large pieces of wood for the huge, long gallery fireplace which was in our recreation room. Just after VE-Day, May 8, 1945, Mary McCrimmon and I were sent to join No. 2 Motor Ambulance Convoy in Belgium, at DeHaan, just outside of Ostende.

We went over on an American LST (Landing Ship Transport), a very large barge that carried many types of vehicles. On our arrival at the other side, two long planks were put down from the LST to the beach, and over these we were to drive our ambulance to shore. Quite daunting, as it was a fair distance and the planks were narrow. We had watched one British Army vehicle ahead of us actually fall off, so we were quite pleased with ourselves on reaching the beach successfully.

I was in Belgium from June to December of 1945. There we lived in the lap of luxury: in a house, with maids to clean the rooms and wash the dishes. Our duties were many and varied. We met hospital ships carrying prisoners of war being repatriated to Germany; we returned psychiatric patients to their hospitals in Holland (they had been discharged during the worst fighting);

we did ambulance duty at British military hospitals; occasionally we did standby duty at a heavy ack-ack firing range in case of an accident. Once my ears had become accustomed to the bursting of shells, I was able to enjoy what you might call "the shoot." The target was a sleeve being pulled by a plane.

In August 1945, I met my future husband, Monty, who was from Victoria, B.C. He was a Canloan officer who had gone in on D-Day with a British regiment. Later I went up to Germany to visit Monty. I hitchhiked with a friend—one of the things my mother did not know about until later. But one could safely hitchhike in uniform then. Our plan was to meet in Nijmegen in the Netherlands, with Monty driving down from Germany. Surprisingly, we arrived within five minutes of each other. Then on to Wilhelmshaven, a large naval base on the North Sea, and to Monty's company base at nearby Sillenstede, where we spent a long weekend. Returning a few hours late to DeHaan, I found my penalty was a short posting on my own; it felt rather like being sent to Siberia. I drove my ambulance to where I was billeted and did all the necessary chores, including painting ambulances. It taught me a lesson about getting back to my unit on time.

I returned home in December of 1945 on the *Queen Elizabeth*. There were fifteen thousand of us: war brides with small children, returning troops and a fair number of Red Cross girls who had served in various capacities. Although we had one of the stormiest crossings ever in December, I remember being impressed most by the size of the ship, our walks around the great decks and our eventual arrival in New York harbour.

When I returned to Canada, I left behind a very charming young Captain—Monty, the Canloan officer with the East Yorkshire Regiment. In May of 1946, Monty returned to Canada and we were married in Toronto. After a reception in the garden of my parents' home, we left for the west where we have lived happily ever after.

Marion Stewart

"His spirit was wonderful and I never felt I could do enough for him"

Marion Stewart and her twin sister were born in Manila on the Philippine Islands where her father was a manager in a shipping office. When she was five, her family came to Victoria, B.C. to settle. She was working at Carmichael Silversmiths as a sales clerk when she joined the Red Cross. After the war she worked with the Red Cross Transfusion Service.

In 1941, I joined the Red Cross in my hometown of Victoria because I wanted to help out in the war effort. I quickly learned, however, that joining up was not enough to qualify for overseas duty. I also had to train as a nursing aide and put in some two hundred hours of volunteer work. Today when one hears the word "volunteer," it probably conjures up the idea of someone simply putting up her hand. In our case, to be an overseas volunteer with the Red Cross demanded several years of hard work.

My overseas journey with the Canadian Red Cross Corps started from Victoria on November 16, 1944. In Vancouver I was met by the commandant of the Red Cross and put on board the train for Toronto. Audrey Phillips of the Red Cross Corps met me in Toronto, and I stayed with her family for a few days before going on to Montreal where we met Isla Brown and the other Red Cross Corps girls. This made a party of thirty-six—almost a platoon—and it caused many heads to turn on our arrival in New York where we boarded our ship, the *Minnewanska*. We started our trans-Atlantic crossing in high spirits, happy to be on our way, but just a short way out, the ship developed engine problems and had to return to port. While the ship was being repaired we enjoyed a five-day visit in New York and were entertained by a good many people.

Finally we arrived in London just five days before Christmas when everyone was ready for Christmas leave. We were told where our postings were and then allowed five days of holiday. I travelled up to Edinburgh where my brother was training to become a doctor. After our joyous reunion and a brief visit, I made my way south to Leeds, where Audrey Phillips, Isla Brown and I were assigned for the next nine months to Seacroft Hospital under the supervision of a very strict matron. We certainly caused her a headache or two. However, we were determined not to be ordered around like children, so naturally we would not be very popular. The hospital had well over a thousand beds in twelve wards of almost a hundred beds each, spread over the large grounds. In February 1945, I was moved from the Y ward to the P ward which had been repainted, the bricks knocked out and the glass windows reglazed, making it the first ward of the whole hospital to return to peacetime conditions. However, we still had to draw the blackout curtains at night and had only one light in the hallway that led to the other wards.

In late March I started night duty on the Y ward, which meant five nights of twelve hours on duty and two nights off. It was sixty hours of work a week, but that was the way they did things then. Since we were not allowed to leave the ward during those twelve hours, we cooked our own meals in the ward kitchen. When I had to prepare the midnight meal, I would simply peel and fry some potatoes and then warm up some meat in the frying pan. Of course, I also made tea to accompany the meal. It was Spartan fare, but I always looked forward to it.

During the long night hours, the ward was busy with all the serious surgical cases, and I attended to many extremely ill patients. One night, ninety patients were admitted to the hospital; nineteen of them came to the Y ward. Some of the men were former prisoners of war who suffered from malnutrition and dysentery. They were thankful to be in real beds again. With so many new patients, the doctor arranged for many of the old patients to be transported to a convalescent home. As soon as men were able to walk after their surgeries, they were transferred to another hospital for a few weeks until they were fit to return to their units or be discharged from the Army.

I'll never forget one patient who came in with the first convoy and began making good progress once he was under our care. I used to give him drinks of milk every two hours during the night, and he quickly began gaining weight. His spirit was so wonderful that I never felt I could do enough for him. Unfortunately, his wounded arm, which had been healing nicely, suddenly became worse and had to be amputated. I accompanied him to the operating room, where he died unexpectedly during surgery. When I returned to tell the sister on my ward, she was so upset that she ran down to the operating room to find out what had gone wrong. She was told that he had been too weak to withstand the trauma of the amputation.

Losing this patient came as a shock to me—especially after he had held on for so long. Even though I had other patients that woke up throughout the night, there was none that had taken so much of my time or my emotional involvement. I'll always remember him as one of my grandest patients. He was six-foot-four, and I used to have to lift him up in bed, since I was the stronger of the two of us (he was just skin and bones). This brave young man had survived a march across Germany as a prisoner of war, but now he was gone—just like that—and it came as an enormous shock that weighed on me terribly.

I think it was because people carried such a weight of oppression all through the war that Victory-in-Europe Day (May 8, 1945) was such a explosion of feeling. It was as if it was all right to feel again. Quite a few effigies of Hitler were hung up around the town and then burned. Because I was on duty I was not able to join in any outside jubilations, but we did our own celebrating on the ward as everybody was ready for a good time. The lights and the wireless were left on until ten o'clock that night, and the talking never ceased. All the patients able to go home were given forty-eight-hour passes, which emptied the hospital of quite a number and made the work correspondingly lighter for us.

I had my own room, but it was very cold. Then one day I found a window open at the top, high up and hardly visible, and it was this that was allowing in the cold air. Needless to say, it became a bit warmer after I climbed up and closed the window. The room was small, but even smaller was the closet: I had to take out one thing before putting in another. The room was so Spartan and sterile, I tended to spend only my sleeping time there. I kept my trunk under the bed in readiness to move at a moment's notice. My mother's parcels from home always came as a welcome treat, with things like biscuits, cake, tea, tinned milk, clothing and toiletries. My father deposited ten pounds quarterly to my bank account. It was very much appreciated and helped to pay for necessities.

On the whole, my posting at Seacroft Hospital was interesting, except for feeling isolated at times. Since the hospital was quite a distance from town, we had to take the streetcar into town for any entertainment. But my friends and I enjoyed our trips to Ireland and Belgium on the leaves we were permitted. As for the very strict matron whom I mentioned earlier, she seemed to become less cross and more understanding as time went by. I think she became more accustomed to us Canadians and our more casual ways.

After nine months of waiting, Audrey, Isla and I received our transfers in late September of 1945 and three St. John's Ambulance girls arrived to replace us. The St. John's Ambulance girls were sent because no other Red Cross girls would come. We felt sorry for them but happy that we were leaving.

Our next posting was at Botley's Park Hospital, Chertsey, Surrey, only forty minutes by train from London. When we arrived, we soon discovered that, although Seacroft had seemed isolated and dismal, our new hospital was more primitive in some ways. We found ourselves living in huts divided into many cubicles, each for two people. There was none of the privacy we had at Seacroft Hospital, since we could hear everyone talking throughout the hut. The hospital was twice the size of Seacroft, with so many nurses that the matron could not begin to keep track of all of us as the previous matron of Seacroft had done. Still, there were many good features at Botley's. For example, almost all the girls rode bicycles rather than walk in the dark from our hut to the hospital dining-room, and this was pleasant exercise. Moreover, in our meals at Botley's, there was much more variety. Every morning there was jam or marmalade on the breakfast table, which we only had on Sundays before. We could also cook in our huts to our hearts' content. And we did for the evening meal—when we had something to cook! These may seem like small things, but they added enormously to our morale.

Many of the patients had broken or splintered bones, and quite a number were on plaster beds for spinal injuries. There was a young doctor who was doing marvellous work in removing discs from spines where the disc was exerting pressure and causing continuous pain. Even in cases of sciatica, he could give relief. I didn't know very much about it, but the patients put a lot of faith in him.

It was interesting to see how much innovative surgery developed under the necessities of wartime conditions.

I really enjoyed my first Christmas on duty. We had sixteen patients and the sister planned a festive day for them. All seven nurses stayed on the ward for dinner with the "up patients." The house doctor carved two small turkeys which were provided by one of the patients. How he came by the turkeys I never discovered, but I think we were the only ward lucky enough to eat turkey on Christmas Day. Mistletoe was hung throughout the ward, and the soldiers had great fun luring the nurses to stand under it. I think perhaps I may have been the only one who avoided being caught.

I completed the twelve months of work required by my contract on December 28, 1945. Since I was willing to stay on with the Red Cross, I returned to London where I was loaned to the Canadian Army to assist the war brides and children emigrating to Canada. The war brides were women who had married Canadian servicemen posted overseas during the war. They came from England, Holland, France, Belgium and other European countries. I was given a posting at the Brook Street hostel, a repatriation centre in London for war brides and their children. The hostel had been open for only two months when I arrived. It functioned well but was seriously understaffed. We could provide sleeping quarters for up to fifty women and children who slept in what used to be air-raid shelter bunks. At our hostel we would provide meals; our guests would usually stay for two days before starting their trip to Canada. A Canadian from Vancouver was our chef (he used to cook on the Canadian Pacific ships) and he provided great meals for staff and guests.

I remember when one baby had a cold, the medical officer told me to put a mustard plaster on it. Since the baby was only a few months old, I wasn't about to put a mustard plaster on him because it might have burned his skin. I put Vicks on him instead, and he was better in the morning.

In the spring of 1946, a staff member who had been in the hospital for ten days was ordered to take a week's leave. One of our guests agreed to fill in for her. She was not a typical war bride because she was a Canadian married to a Dutchman. She had been imprisoned by the Japanese in Java along with her two sons who were now fifteen and eleven years old. While her husband remained with his company in Java, she and her sons were travelling to Toronto to spend a year with her parents and recuperate from their years of imprisonment. We admired their great spirit after all that they had been through and their willingness to help out—even when they were supposed to be recuperating.

In May 1946 I accompanied a Dutch bride to Southampton where she was to board the *Queen Mary* bound for Halifax. The war bride was sick during our drive to Southampton, but that was expected because she was seven months pregnant, and a doctor and nurse were accompanying her to see her safely to Canada. She was a sweet nineteen-year-old woman who was travelling to Ontario where her husband was waiting for her. A week earlier she had been taken off the *Lady Nelson* when it was decided that she was not fit to travel, but now she was well rested after her stay at our hostel. When I think back to our drive to the *Queen Mary*, it still amazes me that we got our Dutch war bride to her ship before it left. First, a dog ran into our car and broke his leg, and naturally we had to report the accident to the local police station, and lost half an hour doing so. Later our carburettor became plugged, and the car stalled on a hill until we were given help from a passing truck. After that, we came across an American car that had run out of gas, so we drove one of the passengers into Southampton to buy some gas and then returned him to the car. Yet somehow we still managed to meet the *Queen Mary* on time. I saw the war bride to her cabin, which I was delighted to see she would have to herself, with her own wash basin. I did not see if she had a bathtub, but I doubt if that concerned her. She was happy simply to have made it to the ship on time. After making sure that she was settled in her cabin, I joined the medical officer in the officers' dining room, where we enjoyed a lovely sirloin steak dinner.

On another occasion, we had to send a war bride to a mental hospital. She was supposed to have gone to Canada on the *Queen*

Mary, but she missed the train at Waterloo and wandered around aimlessly until she was found by the police. They somehow verified that she was a war bride, even though she had no papers whatsoever when they brought her to us. We gave her a bath, washed her hair and supplied her with new clothes before we arranged for a medical officer to escort her to the mental hospital. She was with us for only a day but that was difficult enough, since we had to keep a watch on her the whole time because she was behaving so strangely. We never knew what she would do next. Some of the girls thought it was awful to send her away like that, but she was in no shape for a voyage to Canada and clearly needed hospital care.

We closed the Brook Street hostel at the end of September 1946, and I was re-posted to the Chesman Hostel, a smaller hostel on Fleet Street, where I enjoyed having a room to myself with a radio, after having shared a room for so long. I had received permission to extend my time overseas because my brother was being married in April the following year.

In October 1946, I accompanied another Red Cross girl, Marjorie, to Switzerland for a two-week vacation. There we saw the Golden Sphere, which had been erected by the League of Nations after the First World War. It was a haunting experience to see this earlier symbol of peace after World War II had taken untold millions of lives.

Although most of the ships carrying war brides crossed the Atlantic without problems, in November 1946, there was a serious accident when the *Letitia,* with a group of war brides on board, ran into a cattle ship just outside Liverpool. No one was seriously hurt, but the crew and passengers had to be taken back to shore. The war brides, their children and the Red Cross Corps girls (who were returning to Canada for Christmas) were sent back to Fleet Street for two weeks while the damage to the *Letitia* was repaired. Fortunately most of the English and Scottish war brides were able to return to their homes until they were recalled, so we had only the Dutch war brides and their children to look after. We ended up with a hundred mothers, each with one child. It was a bit of a blow to them, because of course they had been so excited about leaving for Canada. Nevertheless, we showed a film for the girls at the hostel everyday to help them pass the time more quickly. The Red Cross also provided clothes because so many of the war brides had their luggage mislaid in the aftermath of the collision. Some of them made new baby clothes from diapers, even putting smocking and embroidery on them for trim. A good many of the girls fell ill as the flu made the rounds, but most of them took the incident in stride.

Finally our work came to an end, and I returned to Canada on June 24, 1947, on the *Aquitania*. I travelled by train from Toronto to Vancouver with my brother and his wife. When I arrived in Victoria I had no prospect of employment. But then I learned that the Red Cross Transfusion Service had just started up six months before in Vancouver, so I applied to them for a position. In December 1947, I was asked to join the service after some of the girls who had been working in Vancouver wanted to go back east to work. My starting salary was $100.00 a month.

The Red Cross Transfusion Service had two nurses and five or six nursing aides that travelled all over B.C. to set up blood clinics in various communities, including Kitimat, Prince Rupert and as far north as Whitehorse one time. Sometimes we had to fly into these places to collect blood, but usually we travelled in a station wagon with one truck carrying all the cots, bedding and blankets. We had one other truck that was refrigerated to bring back the blood for processing. When we arrived at a site, we would unload the beds from the truck and set them up at the blood clinics. I would also sit by the bed with the patient and watch the bag fill up with blood to make sure there were no problems.

I worked with the Red Cross Transfusion Service until December 1978, when I retired. I was honoured to receive the Queen's Silver Jubilee Medal in 1977 for thirty years of service with the Canadian Red Cross. I count them as the most eventful years of my life, and they have given me many happy memories associated with those years.

Canadian Red Cross Corps members outside Canadian Red Cross H.Q., Burlington Gardens, London.
◀

Canadian Red Cross Corps members in their dress coats.
▶

Helen M. Egan

*"We found the drivers very
protective of us"*

Helen M. Egan was born and grew up in Bolton, Ontario. Before
joining the Red Cross she worked as a secretary and an
accountant, as well as helping in the family business.
After World War II she was married and ran
her own secretarial business.

In August of 1939 I chanced to see an article in a Toronto news-paper that the wife of an official from Finland was looking for women recruits to drive ambulances. I wrote to her offering my services and received a courteous reply stating that the newspa-pers had misinterpreted her meaning. She had, however, taken the liberty of forwarding my letter to the Canadian Red Cross So-ciety. When the Red Cross contacted me and asked me to join the Evening Division of the Transport Corps as a volunteer, my hopes were high that I would be sent overseas as an ambulance driver.

The Transport Division was quite an active group: drilling at the Armouries every Sunday afternoon, taking courses in motor mechanics, home nursing and first aid; and we were still working at our full-time jobs. I was in charge of dispatching drivers from amongst our own members for ambulance driving duties in the evenings and weekends. I also had to fill out a monthly duty roster of the number of hours worked. In the building that housed the ambulances, a crew of our girls remained at the ready for emer-gency calls every evening and on weekends. I can remember only two such emergency calls for our crew.

In August of 1943, I finally received notice that I was to be pre-pared to go overseas at a moment's notice. Soon after, five of us left Toronto for Montreal where we stayed overnight. In Montreal, five more girls joined our group and we headed for Saint John, New Brunswick, where one other girl joined us. After a few days in Saint John we embarked on the _Mosdale,_ a 3,000-ton freighter, for our Atlantic crossing. When we docked at Liverpool we were met by a Red Cross official who warned us to remain on board the _Mosdale_ for the night as they were experiencing nightly air raids. I passed this information on to the girls, and whether or not they stayed on board, I still don't know. The next morning we en-trained for London where we were met and driven to the Cana-dian Red Cross Corps House, "our home away from home."

After a week's hospitality leave, I was posted to the Canadian Nursing Sisters' Club—Maple Leaf No. 3—to the position of gen-eral duties. It was not ambulance driving as I had hoped, but I enjoyed the work and I also had a fair amount of time off and was

thrilled to see something of London for the nine months I was stationed there.

In April of 1944, after a few weeks training in handicrafts at Burlington Gardens, I was sent to Scotch Corner in Yorkshire to join
Unit No. 16 as a welfare officer. I was billeted with No. 10 until such
time as No. 16 was to be sent overseas. After six pleasant weeks of
double daylight saving time, three of us were switched to No. 2
Canadian General Hospital in Whitby on the coast, where we were
joined by Jean Lamb. Jean had already worked in Italy with the
Canadian offensive which had pushed up from Sicily, but she had
returned when the order came through that all married girls had
to return to London. On her way back, however, she received the
tragic news that her husband had been killed in action. Like many
courageous women who lost their husbands, she decided to continue working in the war effort; eventually she joined our unit.

My main role at the hospital in Whitby was to talk to the patients, who were wounded Canadian soldiers. I encouraged them
in learning handicrafts to keep them busy and make them feel
better. It was really a job that I created myself. Other women came
later to do the same thing, but I was the first. Looking back, I feel
guilty about one young chap who drew some fine pictures. One of
them was so good that I started using it for demonstrating, but
then he left before I could give it back to him. I still have it.

I also went around and helped the patients with letters home. I
remember that at Christmas I wrote to one young man's girlfriend, and she wrote back to say that she had found someone
else. It was a shock both to him and to me. It really made me wonder if I should continue with the letter writing when it brought
such disastrous results.

After Whitby, we moved with No. 2 Unit to Southampton, then
later to Ford Manor. One morning we were aroused at three
o'clock and given our last mail in England as we prepared to embark for the Continent. My mail included a letter from my sister
with a newspaper clipping of the D-Day landing in France. This
proved to be a good omen, since we arrived safely via hospital ship
at Mike's Beach in France on D-Day plus 63. The unit was trucked

to a position about five kilometers outside Bayeux, where we were again billeted with No. 10 Unit. I assisted for a short time on the night shift in the annex of the operating-room, doing odd jobs, mostly mending plastic gloves for the surgeons and pouring tea, etc. This was at the time the American planes had mistakenly bombed the Allies when a mix-up of flares occurred. We had many wounded men who had been injured by their own side.

After a short time, No. 10 moved up to Antwerp, Belgium, where we took over their patients and had a chance to develop a routine with our duties, since we stayed in this area until mid-November. It rained considerably, and we were glad we were equipped with high army boots to wade through the gumbo. We did have some nights of bombing near us, but it didn't scare me, because I knew they were not aiming at us. There was supposed to be an understanding that the hospitals would not be bombed. Each time a bomb was dropped nearby, it was reported immediately and eventually there was no more bombing.

At this time I was working with soldiers who had to be cleared before they could return to Canada. They were brought by twos and threes from outposts that didn't have the facilities to help them. I was there mainly to serve them coffee and talk to them while they were waiting to be cleared for their return to Canada. I found it amazing how well they controlled their emotions after all they had been through. It felt good to be there for them.

Our next move was to Ghent, Belgium, in open trucks over very dusty roads. Our hospital was set up in a three-storey modern building with terrazzo (stone chips set in concrete and given a smooth surface) floors, situated on the bank of one of the canals. It was interesting to watch the many barges being hauled along by a rope slung over the shoulder of, nearly always, a woman. Our billets were in what had been a collaborator's house about a ten-minute walk from the hospital. Since the hours were regular with weekends off, Jean and I again found the countryside a good place to explore, often hitchhiking in army vehicles. We found the drivers very protective of us; they would often go out of their way to deliver us to our destination.

*Aerial view of Antwerp, where Helen Egan was posted with
No. 10 Unit. The dock area is in the background.*

Canadian General Hospital No. 2 was a 1200-bed hospital. Dorothy King, who was in charge of our little group, worked in the office and recreation room. Isabel had the top floor, with Jean on the first floor; I had the second floor, which included the Officers' Ward. We each had from three hundred to four hundred patients to see every day. Everyone did a lot of walking on those terrazzo floors carrying baskets of supplies. To keep the boys employed and their minds off their wounds and problems, we interested them in working with crafts. Since we had a roll of coarse natural fibre resembling burlap, I asked the boys if they would like the crests of their units drawn on this material. Then they could work them with threads using the colours of their regiment. Once this idea caught on, I would often collect about fifteen of them in one day, take them to the mess, iron them and bring them back the next day. Incidentally, one of the officer patients was an artist and would draw these crests on the material by the dozen, which helped a lot. We also had kits of belts to be tied and needlepoint kits.

At the time of Victory-in-Europe Day (May 8, 1945), Jean and I were delegated to go to a processing unit set up just outside Brussels, where some of the former prisoners of war were flown in to be documented and refitted with clothes and necessities. We had a booth with Red Cross supplies alongside a similar one run by the British Red Cross. The prisoners of war would come through our tent in groups of twenty. Most of them were too stunned to take much note of what we were offering. It was an extremely emotional time for me as I saw how traumatized these men were. As I watched them pass through in their groups, I often wondered if they would ever fully recover from their experiences. But they were tremendous—they were such gentlemen, and they never complained. When No. 2 Hospital closed down in July, Jean was posted back to London and I went on to Brussels as a driver for two weeks while one of the drivers was on leave.

My next posting was No. 2 Casualty Clearing Station in Apeldoorn, Netherlands, to take over from Jean Ellis Wright. The colonel of this unit had been our family doctor years ago in Bolton,

Ontario, and several of the nurses had been with No. 2, so I felt at home immediately. The patients were anxiously waiting for their yellow tickets to arrive, because these tickets signified that they were on their way home. It was hard to get them interested in any of our crafts, since all they could think of was how to get their names on the roster for Canada. The war now being over, the doctors and nurses were more relaxed, and a group of us enjoyed a number of trips to Amsterdam for bowling and ice skating.

In early November, No. 2 Casualty Clearing Station sent its remaining patients to England and home, and the hospital closed down. Ten of us set out for a week's cultural leave in Denmark in two station wagons. When we arrived in Hamburg to stay overnight at the Leave Centre Hotel, six big German boys appeared out of nowhere and lined up by our car. As they did not look friendly, we scrambled out of there in a hurry, taking only part of our baggage with us. I had left my kit bag, and when we came to drive off in the morning, it and all the other small luggage was gone. Still, we were lucky they hadn't touched the station wagon. As you can imagine, there was a great deal of bitterness on the German side after their defeat, especially among the young men.

Our leave in Copenhagen was very interesting. We attended lectures in the morning and afternoon: all about Denmark and its five-year plans. It was fascinating to learn how Denmark was preparing a different kind of future, how they had learned from the war experience. The matron and I were entertained at a typically Danish dinner by a Danish family with only the twenty-year-old girl able to speak English, although the others tried from time to time, amidst great hilarity. It was a fascinating week, especially as we were assigned Danish escorts. We really appreciated the steaks, eels and seafood after all the army rations we'd had to put up with.

On my return, I went directly to No. 1 Hospital in Nijmegen, Netherlands. This unit had come up from Italy, with Pheme Walker in charge of the Red Cross personnel. On December 5th, the children of all the workers in the hospital were to be given a Christmas party and presents, which was their traditional custom. As we had a good supply of felt, I asked the patients if they would help: if I cut out toy animals, would they stitch and stuff them? One of the soldiers spoke up to say he was a tailor by trade; if I would give him the material, he would cut out the animals and see that the whole project was completed. He did an excellent job, and the stuffed animals were greatly appreciated by the children. It had been estimated that approximately five hundred children would attend the party, but nearly one thousand turned up, and the facilities and supplies were greatly taxed—including the strength of the nurses who were ladling out the rice pudding and chocolate sauce. It was a day to remember for everyone.

No. 1 Canadian General Hospital closed after the Christmas season. I returned to London to work in Burlington Gardens until the 1st of March, 1946. When I returned home on the *Isle-de-France,* I shared a cabin with twenty other gals, a cabin which in peacetime was meant for two.

After being away from home for so long and working as a volunteer, I felt somewhat at a loss how to pick up my earlier life. Fortunately my sister and brother-in-law welcomed me to their home on the farm. There I was able to complete a correspondence course in accounting, and this enabled me to find a job in Toronto where I returned to the normal peacetime routine.

I shall always be grateful to the Canadian Red Cross Society, and to Margaret Duff, in particular, who put my name on the roster for work on the Continent. It is most satisfying to know that I contributed in some small way to the war (and peace!) effort, and yet at the same time was able to enjoy every minute of my time with the Canadian Red Cross Corps.

Mary-Louise Harrison Ruttan

"The air became electric and
tense with excitement"

—

Mary-Louise Harrison Ruttan was born and raised in Hamilton,
Ontario. She graduated from a two-year dietician course at
MacDonald Hall before joining the Red Cross. In 1946
she married John Graham Ruttan with whom she
enjoyed fifty years of marriage until she passed
away in 1996. Her family remembers her
zest for life and love of laughter.

A revisitation to a special time over fifty years ago is not an easy jump. But reinforcing my fading memory with the help of a diary kept spasmodically and a file of letters surprisingly intact, I hope to portray something of the dramatic days lived in wartime England.

In August of 1943 I was faced with a difficult decision. I had the choice of becoming a home sister, with officer rank in an army hospital unit, or being part of the next draft to go overseas in the voluntary Canadian Red Cross Corps. Despite oh-so-wise advice from all sides, I followed my own inclination and happily accepted the latter. I think this was because I wanted to go overseas where I felt the "action" was, and if I were with a hospital unit, there was a possibility it might stay in Canada.

September of 1943 was an exciting month—arranging for uniforms to be tailored, packing a trunk of essentials, and preparing for a sudden call. This came later in the month, and Sheila Leather and I departed from Hamilton, Ontario. We were joined in Toronto by a few others, then more in Montreal and one more in Saint John, New Brunswick. We were a varied and happy group, getting to know each other and anticipating our adventure. We were in Saint John for several days awaiting our next move. The Red Cross ladies of Saint John were very hospitable. They even advised us to have wills made out and found a lawyer who did this for us free of charge. Sheila and I really appreciated the offer as we discovered we each had only about thirty-five dollars left in our leather pouches. We had been provided with train tickets, berths on the train and hotel rooms, but no meals! When and where we would be sailing was a deep, dark secret. There was a very small ship we could see sitting out in the harbour, and we wondered if this was perhaps the tug that would take us out to a ship somewhere.

We were finally aboard that "tug," a small Norwegian vessel named *Mosdale,* and learned that Captain Sunde, his pretty Canadian wife Fern, who was the wireless officer, and the crew had attended a ceremony in Cardiff, Wales, a couple of weeks before, where King Haakon of Norway had decorated them for having made over fifty trips across the Atlantic carrying more than 60,000 tons of food to Britain, all without benefit of convoy. This would be one more trip carrying us nine girls and two reporters from *Time* and *Life* magazines. We found out later that the crew almost mutinied before sailing, since most, if not all, of *Mosdale's* sister ships had been torpedoed. They sailed alone as they couldn't keep up with a convoy.

During the time we were on the high seas, Churchill made one of his famous speeches—"There is a convoy on the Atlantic at the present time being attacked by U-boats!" As a matter of fact, I felt like death anyway, becoming seasick as soon as the little ship was underway. We had to sleep in our clothes and have our life jackets and kit at hand in case we were hit, since we would have no more than a minute to get up on deck for the lifeboats.

We zigzagged across to Liverpool in thirteen days, at times near the Azores, I think, as it was so pleasantly warm. After landing, we went by train to London. We were met at a station in London that had obviously suffered considerable bomb damage, and taken to Maple Leaf Club No. 2 on Cromwell Road. We were greeted there, given a cup of tea and advised of the "Rules and Regulations," some of which were that we were not to marry for at least six months, and we were NOT to get pregnant!

We were assigned rooms at the top of the house, the fifth floor, since the boys who came to the club were on the floors below. (Some of the boys at times pushed the fifth-floor button for the elevator—always a big mistake, of course—and when the door opened the view was directly into the room I shared with several other girls.)

The next morning we were taken to our headquarters on Berkeley Square and greeted officially, then taken to offices to receive our individual ration coupons and unemployment insurance records. We were then *free* for ten glorious days!

An army friend, Ted, happened to be stationed close to London and had found out about my group's arrival through Canadian Military Headquarters. He came to town, took a room in a small Kensington Hotel near Maple Leaf No. 2, and we proceeded to partake of the colourful life and sights of London for a few delightful days. We also became accustomed to the wailing of sirens and the ack-ack of anti-aircraft guns booming out from Hyde Park.

During my leave I had also wanted to visit an old friend, Bill Robinson, who had been blinded by a booby trap explosion while on maneuvers with live ammunition. After several phone calls I finally located him at St. Dunstan's headquarters in London. He was going back up to the St. Dunstan's Rehabilitation Centre at Church Stretton in Shropshire the next day and asked me to meet him at Paddington Station and we could travel up together. In the meantime he would make arrangements for me to stay at the bishop's house next door to "Battlefield," the house where he lived and which he shared with other officers who had been blinded.

Meeting and greeting someone you have known, now blinded, is a heart-pumping trial. To talk normally without a wavering voice is impossible. Bill had been a mining engineer before the war and had never had to wear glasses, so why should he wear them now? It was a cruel sight. Bill, however, was wonderful. Somehow he was managing to take this tragic blow in stride. He talked and laughed easily and made me feel relaxed.

The next day Bill and I went bicycling on a tandem bike. After a couple of tumbles I got the feel of it, me steering and Bill providing most of the oomph! We went for miles through beautiful countryside, Bill telling me about the sights I was seeing along the way, and about his new life learning to be blind. He certainly seemed to be in good spirits. On the way back, it was starting to become dusk but Bill was determined to stop at his favourite pub. I was apprehensive about this, not knowing the area; soon it would be dark with no lights anywhere. However, I took my chances and somehow Bill guided me back. After dinner we went into the village again, this time to "see" a movie and I found that Bill could follow it surprisingly well without much explanation. The next day Bill took me to Shrewsbury, despite my objections, to catch my train back to London. He said he had to protect me from all the American soldiers about! I found two VAD girls to help him to his train back to Church Stretton. It had been an enlightening but traumatic two days.

Back in London with my leave over, it was time to get to work. A list was posted and I was down to be at Maple Leaf Club No. 1 to do general duties. This was my first introduction to Miss Duff (a Scottish lady in the navy blue uniform of the British Red Cross) attached to our Canadian Corps to oversee the personnel of the Maple Leaf Clubs. There were some girls who were not pleased with where they were posted, but I really didn't care as I was happy just to be in London.

While still staying at Maple Leaf Club No. 2, I met one of the girls there, Peggy Guthrie, who had been stationed in Londonderry, Ireland, for several weeks. She knew many Canadian Navy officers because they were frequently in Londonderry. One of them wrote to her to say that a group of navy officers was coming into London for a long weekend. He asked if she could round up some of the Canadian Corps girls for a party, and Peggy asked me to join them. It developed into a very pleasant party, indeed, and during the course of the afternoon, two more navy types joined us. They had been to a posh wedding near Guildford, and had then come up to London and checked into the Savoy Hotel. They knew about our party so came across the street to join us; they were Jack Ruttan and Ken Meredith. The following afternoon I was called to the door. It was Jack Ruttan, suggesting we go to the Sunday afternoon tea dance at the Grosvenor Hotel on Park Lane. That brief weekend was to have a very large influence on the rest of my life, though I had no way of knowing that at the time.

The job at Maple Leaf No. 1 kept me busy, since it was a popular place for Canadian boys of the Army, Air Force and Navy when they came to London on leave. In fact, it became "home" to some of the boys. It was apparently a treat to hear our Canadian voices, especially for those boys who had been in England for years. We laughed and joked with many and tried to cheer up those who were lonesome. Some of the younger boys really didn't know what to do with themselves, other than locate a pub. We tried to steer them in other directions, telling them about free concerts, museums, wonderful historic places to visit, and the superb shows of all kinds—music halls, plays—all kinds of wonderful things to see and do in London, the most marvellous city in the world. Sometimes they would look at us as if we had rocks in our heads, since for many of them the only worthwhile place to be was back at the old corner drugstore.

The club was filled to the roof during the fall of 1943 and spring of 1944. Sometimes we had to make up extra beds on the floors of the lounge and writing room. We worked long hours serving meals, scrubbing tables, making beds, manning the telephone and reception desk, and generally making ourselves useful, while at the same time talking and laughing with the soldiers, and listening to often horrendous stories, particularly from Navy and Air Force boys.

There were a few light-fingered boys so we had to have radios, lamps and other things bolted down, and tried to watch that sheets and blankets weren't stolen—anything they could trade on the black market. When my young brother Ted, who was in the Air Force, came to the club, I warned him to be careful, so he put his watch carefully under his pillow, but in the morning it was gone! Of course, most of the boys were great fellows, and we certainly had lots of fun. We got to know some quite well, especially Air Force boys who were crew in bombing raids over Germany, since they had more frequent leaves. All too often we were saddened, however, when we heard of boys who were missing.

The hours we were on duty were long—before 8 a.m. until 7 p.m., with a couple of hours off in the afternoon. Sometimes we had more hours off in the afternoons; then we worked 6 a.m. to 11 p.m. We had one day off a week, and were usually free on the preceding day by 4 p.m. My brother Hugh, who was an officer in the Royal Hamilton Light Infantry, often came in with his pals. The air raids were frequent at this time, usually at night, but this didn't deter us from getting out and about whenever we could. We soon learned the importance of leaving wherever we were in time to catch a tube, as they closed down by midnight, and taxis were almost impossible to find, especially when an air raid was on.

The tube stations were an unforgettable sight. Families occupied bunks stacked against the walls, and the overflow made up beds on the platforms between the bunks and the trains. We had to step gingerly over sleeping bodies to reach the doors of the trains. I think they felt safer in the tube stations than in air-raid shelters, or perhaps they liked the companionship, confusion and noise.

When the bombing raids were in or near our area, we were urged to go to the basement, so that we would be away from flying glass. One night I watched for a while from a little balcony. It was quite a sight with the searchlights scanning the skies and many planes overhead. I saw one plane come down flaming into the Thames only a few blocks away. Hopefully it was one of theirs, I thought. Then a flare floated down in front of me; a bomb usually followed a flare, but that night it didn't. I was lucky. Another night, a barrage balloon was hit and came down in front of the club. And on another night, there was a spectacular sight as huge flames lit up the sky. We found out later it was a paint factory.

There were not many dull moments, and often, unexpectedly, old friends would arrive. Occasionally we would even accept a blind date. I particularly remember one such date at a British Army officers' mess on the outskirts of London. This was a bomb disposal squad. Although a lively party ensued, I recall vividly being conscious of the faces of the men. I can only describe them as ageless. I saw that same sort of face on a few Air Force boys that came to our club.

Christmas came and the club was overflowing as usual. We managed to find a lovely Christmas tree, and we got the boys to help us put it up and decorate it in the dining-room with strings of popcorn, cranberries, bows and ribbons—whatever we could scrounge, mostly out of parcels from home. As we decorated, we all sang the good old Christmas carols. On Christmas Day we served a traditional Christmas dinner with turkey and plum pudding. The tables were decorated gaily with a Christmas stocking for each of our guests, containing socks, cigarettes, candies and oranges. After that, the tables were re-set, and we girls sat down and the boys served *us*. It was great fun.

In February, I was entitled to a week's leave. It had been a bitterly cold winter with very little heat in our club so the thought of going down to Cornwall was appealing. I consulted Dorothy Pearson who was working for Lady Donegal at our headquarters. Lady Donegal had many friends and contacts thoughout Britain who offered hospitality to Canadians. It was arranged that a friend and I would go to visit Mr. and Mrs. Hallings-Pott (I thought it such a delightful Agatha Christie name) on their thousand-year-old farm near the southeast coast of Cornwall.

The bombing raids were heavy and frequent around this time in London, but in Cornwall it seemed utterly peaceful with the sun shining, birds singing and daffodils blooming. We rode bicycles along the coast, walked miles over the fields, and had wonderful meals with real eggs and milk, which we seldom had in London. In the evenings we sat around a roaring fire and discussed the day's happenings while listening to the BBC News and "Lord Ha-Ha" broadcasting from Germany.

Then it was back to the fray, now rested and bursting with health. This was a good thing because at the club we heard we were losing our cook, whose place was to be taken by the Canadian Red Cross girls, more of whom were coming over all the time. We also heard that our good man-of-all-work was leaving us. He had been essential for fixing the many broken windows. In a letter I wrote home, I said at that time, "On Tuesday I had to take charge of the linen, a job I had never done before. As no one had time to teach me, I had to figure out the job for myself. As a result I worked an extra couple of hours in the afternoon. Yesterday my job was to make every bed in the house—just 110 or so! Some of the boys gave me a hand so I got through them all!"

I received word in March that I was to start office work at our headquarters, as it had been discovered that I could type and do shorthand. On April 11th, I reported to General Price and found I was to work most of the time for Mrs. Matthews, keeping records of Canadians in various hospitals in Britain and arranging distribution of parcels to them. I was now a "business girl" and went to work every morning in my uniform. I had to move to Corps House in Queen's Gate Terrace. It was a wrench leaving my pals at Maple Leaf No. 1. There had been lots of drudgery, to be sure, but such fun as well.

I biked to work every morning in less than half an hour, and worked from 9 a.m. to 6 p.m., with lunch in the top-floor canteen —also "elevenses" and afternoon tea—and biked back to Corps House for dinner. Saturday morning we worked 9 a.m. to 12 p.m. or sometimes until 1 p.m. If friends were in town, we often went to the theatre and dined somewhere after; other times we went out for dinner and dancing. All the theatres had adjusted their time-tables to start at 6:15 p.m. to enable people to catch the trains before they stopped for the night.

The army boys in the south of England at this time were not allowed leaves, so fewer were coming into the Maple Leaf Clubs. There was a strong, almost visible feeling of anticipation. The invasion of Europe had been expected for many weeks, but now news of the great event was anticipated almost daily. While working at headquarters we had to be on fire watch duty. This involved staying overnight and taking turns at fire watch. It also meant sleeping on cots in the warehouse basement. One of my friends came to keep me company for a while one night, but he didn't seem his usual self. Rather distracted and jumpy. Next morning I was out early at 6 a.m. on Piccadilly Circus selling poppies for the British Red Cross. Suddenly news came bursting forth—this is D-Day! Now I understood the edginess of my friend the night before: he had known but couldn't tell.

I returned to the office in time for breakfast and such excitement! Not much work was done that day. We had our ears glued to the wireless in Lady Donegal's office, which was next to ours. In a few days my edgy friend of a few nights before disappeared, as expected. He was on some secret work. Soon more news of the great D-Day invasion came in, including the long lists of casualties. Despite these, we were told that the invasion was going well and that there were not as many casualties as expected. Everyone had been on tenterhooks for weeks: June 6th, D-Day, had finally come and the war in France was beginning.

One night about 11 p.m., ten days after D-Day, the air-raid alert sounded, and almost immediately in Corps House we heard a plane very low over our roof. Then the engine stopped. A moment later, and not far away, a great crash made us jump. The "All Clear" wasn't heard until next morning at nine-thirty. Soon after that, the "Alert" sounded again. There was much speculation, as this was clearly different from the earlier air raids. We soon had the answer. This was the beginning of a period of several months when the Germans sent pilotless bombs from the Pas de Calais area in France to the south of England, including London. These were the infamous V-1s, nicknamed "buzz bombs." The damage they did was mostly to the upper sections of buildings they hit. As a result, we were not allowed to sleep on the two top floors of Corps House. Those of us who had rooms up there had to do some scrambling around every night to find a free bed or sleep on the floor. (It is wonderful how well one can sleep on the hard floor, when necessary.) We also had frequent fire watch duties of two-hour stretches, so hours of sleep were sporadic.

A woman named Maizie worked with me at Maple Leaf No. 1 and we became great pals. Her bedroom was next to mine, and somewhere we found an electric heater which we shared. One week she had the heater and the next week I had it. It surely helped us through that freezing cold winter of '43/44. In the spring Maizie left London to drive ambulance for the British Red Cross. When I saw her a few weeks after she had started, she told me that she loved the work. She was out all hours, day and night, picking up men brought back from France in planes and taking them to hospitals at various places around the country. She said, "The work is great but the living conditions are horrible. We're practically starving, the food is terrible, no social activity, and we're kept behind barbed wire, except when we go on call and an occasional twenty-four-hour leave. The Englishman in charge of us hates Americans, so we never see any of the Americans who are in the airfield next door, and he isn't much fonder of Canadians."

Mary-Louise Harrison (Ruttan) and Muizie Din with their heater at Maple Leaf Club No. 1.
◄

Mary-Louise Harrison (Ruttan) and Peggy Guthrie at Maple Leaf Club No. 1, January 1944.
▶

Nevertheless, she looked well—very tanned and healthy looking. Sometime in the following weeks, she married one of the Air Force men she had met at Maple Leaf No. 1, and I had the honour of being her bridesmaid. Her bridal gown and my bridesmaid's dress were sent over to the Corps from Eaton's.

The news we received during those many weeks after D-Day was quite horrendous. The Canadians were playing a big role, holding their own and pushing forward slowly, though with a great many casualties. It was early in August, when the fighting was in the Falaise Gap and Caen area, that I received word that my brother Hugh was missing in action. Vague bits of news filtered through over the next few weeks which made us hopeful that he might have been taken prisoner by the Germans. He had, apparently, led a night patrol to reconnoitre and locate a German unit. They had been attacked, and only two men returned. They reported that Hugh had been wounded in the legs.

At this time I had a ten-day leave coming up and was planning a trip to Scotland with Peggy Guthrie, when I received a letter from Pamela Taylor in Yorkshire. This was a girl Hugh had met quite recently and had raved about. She invited me to visit, so I arranged for a day en route to Scotland. Pam met me at the station, madly excited; she had just received a telegram that Hugh was in a hospital in Penarth in South Wales. It was arranged that she and I should visit a friend of her father's who lived in Penarth, so we could visit Hugh in hospital there. His complete surprise was evident on his bedraggled face when we walked into the ward. There were dozens of beds occupied by the soldiers who had been sent back to England from a German hospital in Paris. When the Americans began bombing Paris, the Germans started to leave the city. They left the hospital in a hurry, taking only the walking wounded with them. The Americans then came into Paris, took over the hospital and shipped the remaining wounded back to England.

Hugh was wounded in his thighs and one knee, and we were told it would be several weeks until he would have the use of his legs—otherwise he was okay. His story was quite dramatic: his pa-

*Mary-Louise Harrison (Ruttan) with her brother Edward P. Harrison
at the Churchill Club, London*

*Pamela Taylor, Hugh Harrison & Mary-Louise Harrison (Ruttan)
with Hugh to receive the Military Cross from King George VI.*

Mary-Louise's brother's wedding in Yorkshire, England, 1944.

trol had been ambushed, and he had been shot, but he had lain hidden in a wheat field all night. He was found by a German the next morning and taken into a German depot where he was put in front of a firing squad. Because his uniform was completely covered in mud, the Germans at the depot thought he belonged to the Canadian Third Division. In the nick of time, a German Intelligence Officer arrived on the scene. He identified Hugh as belonging to the Second Division. "Take him to hospital," he said. His almost being shot by a firing squad was a result of some Third Division Units allegedly shooting their German prisoners. Hugh was eventually transferred to a hospital in Paris. He said the American bombing of Paris was the worst bombing he'd ever been through.

A few months later, Pam and I were invited to attend a ceremony at Buckingham Palace where Hugh was decorated by King George VI with a Military Cross. It was awarded to him because of some extraordinary things he had done in action a week or two before the time he was taken prisoner. Then again, a few months later, I went up to Yorkshire to be a bridesmaid at Pam and Hugh's wedding.

During the summer of 1944 there were fewer people coming into London. The buzz bombs continued to harass London and the south of England. The tube stations were full to capacity every night with London families. There were fewer boys coming into the Maple Leaf Clubs, and those boys who did manage a London leave said they almost felt safer in Normandy. We were extremely busy at headquarters keeping records of Canadian casualties, Canadian hospitals and records of supplies being sent to the hospitals.

With double daylight saving time during the summer, it was daylight until about 11 p.m. By the end of September we went back one hour and, with the days becoming shorter, it soon was getting dark by 7:30 p.m. Everyone took to carrying torches because of the blackout once again. There continued to be surprises when unexpected friends turned up. Jack Ruttan came to town on a few days' leave for the first time in months, bringing fourteen bananas, a great bag of almonds and a bottle of Spanish sherry for which he said somebody had offered him five pounds—obviously he had been busy in the Mediterranean area—a wonderful treat! We went dancing at Ciros and to the theatre.

At the end of September of 1944, I was asked to drive ambulance for the British Red Cross. Despite the descriptions of the group that Maizie had been with, I rather wanted to go. But we had to have family permission, because of the danger involved, and my father strongly objected. After much thought, I decided to stay on in dear old London and continued for a time being secretary to Mrs. Matthews, until she went back to Canada with her husband. For a few weeks after, I worked in the colonel's office while the girls there were away on leave. Then I was asked if I would like to have a switch to the Ontario Services Club. Having been at our headquarters for a year, and as there were now fewer jobs there, I was happy to have a change of scene. I didn't start working at the Ontario Services Club, however, until February of 1945.

All that autumn of 1944 was a busy time for me; I was working in the office at headquarters, and visiting Canadian boys I knew in hospitals. At Christmas time we managed to find a little two-foot tree which we placed on a table in a windowed alcove. We decorated it with strings of white Life-Savers, bows and odds and ends. We all had friends coming and going, and many an evening became a party of sorts. The buzz bombs gradually became fewer, but were replaced by the V-2 bombs. The V-2s did more damage than the buzz bombs, but somehow they didn't seem so bad, since the air-raid sirens didn't go off to warn us, and there was no apprehensive waiting as with the buzz bombs. When a V-2 hit its target we would hear a great crash and we would know some place else had been hit. It was sad but we simply couldn't or wouldn't worry about it—life just had to carry on.

One of the hospitals I visited around this time was at Basingstoke where there were badly wounded boys, many with faces horribly injured. Some suffered not only from their gruesome injuries, but were also terribly bitter; they knew they had been the victims of mistakes by our own side.

Before starting the new job at the Ontario Services Club, I had a week's leave at a lovely country home in Dorset. It was a large home with about twenty bedrooms and quite a formal lifestyle, with an ancient butler in attendance. He had been retired, but was back at work again in a limited way, because so little help was available for households. The family dressed for dinner every evening but, stupid me, I hadn't thought to bring an evening dress. I felt a bit gauche. However, I saw a lot of the surrounding country—Thomas Hardy country—and it was delightful.

The Ontario Services Club on Lower Regent Street was an attractive and popular place. It was constantly crowded with all ranks and all Allies. We worked different shifts every day, and we had one day off a week, except Saturdays and Sundays, since those were the busiest days. Somebody I knew would come into the club almost everyday, back on leave with news of the front, so everyday was different.

The first day I started, Jack Ruttan turned up, bringing gifts of silk stockings and Elizabeth Arden lipstick, this time from New York. We went to several marvellous shows, such as *Hamlet* starring John Gielgud, and dining and dancing after. Most of the girls working at the club were fairly recent arrivals, and at first they found the work exhausting, as did I after a year of secretarial work. But we soon got into the swing of it and it really wasn't nearly as hard work as at the Maple Leaf Club. Hard work or not, it was fun and we all thoroughly enjoyed it.

It wasn't all fun, however. Reading over letters home, I find one, dated March 5, 1945, that I certainly remember:

> I am feeling very upset. You will remember I mentioned many times in letters over the past year—my friend Tony Eaton, husband of a friend of mine at Mac Hall. He was here two weeks ago, having just finished a course called the "flying o-pip," meaning flying observation post—on tiny Auster planes. He was to be the squadron leader of his group and all the officers under him just worshipped him. He won the Military Cross in Italy where he was wounded twice (he was an artillery officer). He was so proud of his new wings and thrilled at having passed through the course successfully (out of 70, only 35 passed). Well, he was killed last Thursday night in a collision with a Mosquito. Tony was a wonderful friend—I can hardly take it in, it is such a blow!

During the spring of 1945, almost every day we saw in the skies enormous armadas of our planes setting out to pulverize the enemy. We were having no air raids at this time that I can recall, and gradually there were fewer and fewer V-2s. Confidence was in the air—surely it wouldn't be long now until the "Great day of Victory."

It all started quite suddenly about 2 p.m. on May 8, 1945. The air became electric and tense with excitement. Flags of the four nations began appearing at every window in every building around Piccadilly and Regent Street, in fact, everywhere. Rumours were flying, but as yet no definite word. I saw an Air Force boy weaving up Jermyn Street with a Luftwaffe helmet and a flag sticking out of it. He was blowing a whistle. There was a horse and cart loaded with flags, with the horse draped in the Union Jack. The streets were jammed. Everything suddenly seemed to break wide open, and everyone was waving flags and wearing red, white and blue pompoms; the men who entertained line-ups of people were singing lustily and standing on their heads.

It was indeed Victory-in-Europe Day. What a mob in the club. I

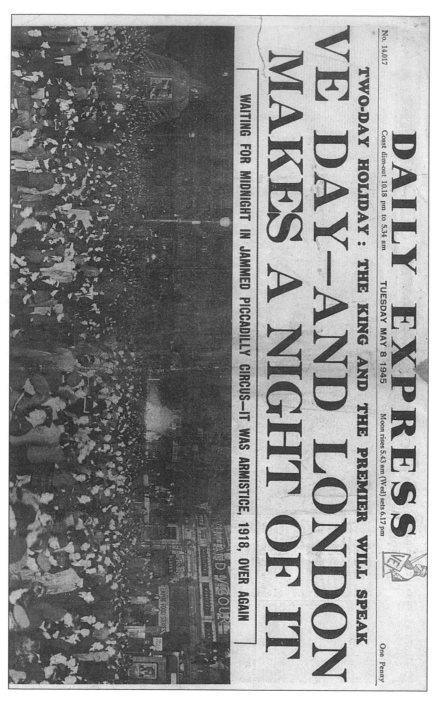

The front page of the Daily Express, London, V-E Day.

had never seen such crowds; we were run off our feet. At 3 p.m., Churchill came on the radio and everybody became silent listening to his words. Then everyone stood up for the playing of "The King." Church bells were pealing riotously. Planes were zooming over rooftops. People were milling in masses up and down every street. It was *wonderful* being in London at that glorious time.

The following weeks were exceptionally busy as the boys from all the services came flocking into London. Many were there awaiting transport home and having a final "fling." The war in Europe was over, but the war against Japan certainly was not, and many were volunteering to go on to Burma and India. In a few weeks the Corps girls who wished to go home could apply, although it was emphasized there would be plenty to do for many months. I decided to stay on.

In July the "hot" thing was a coming election, with Mr. Churchill standing for re-election. The Labour Party, however, was producing strong competition. The Corps girls, as civilians living in Britain, had a vote (the soldiers' vote) which was interesting, as we had also been allowed to vote in the federal and provincial elections at home. I cast my vote for Winston Churchill, of course, but to no avail. Mr. Attlee of the Labour Party was the winner. All the world was overwhelmed and thought the British an ungrateful lot. In a way, though, it was understandable; the people were tired of war and everything connected with it.

On Saturday morning August 11, 1945, crowds of people poured into town; there was celebrating and then things seemed to calm down. About midnight on the 14th, somebody came yelling up the stairs of Corps House—"The War's Over!" August 15th was officially declared Victory-in-Japan Day. Everybody hopped out of beds and bathtubs and onto the street. A great bonfire was lit in front of the house and everyone started roaring about, singing and dancing, mostly dressed in pyjamas and housecoats. We seemed to be the only ones who knew, but very soon all the dead-looking houses came alive and people gathered from every direction. There were firecrackers, dinner bells, whistles—whoopee!! Somebody started to sing "The Maple Leaf Forever" and "O Canada," so there was no mistaking who had started the fun. But London people, when they decide to, can whoop it up with the best of them. So this was the beginning of madness again all over London. We became so busy in our club that queues were actually forming, and Major Armstrong from Ontario House came over to try to establish order. Again, we were run off our feet.

I couldn't have been too utterly exhausted, though, since after dinner I set off with two other girls for the city. I described that night in a letter:

> We went by tube to Mark Lane Station which is the nearest to the Tower of London—and what a sight it was!—all flood-lit, looking like a setting in an opera—indescribably beautiful—all silver and black. We walked over Tower Bridge, the light glittering everywhere away up the river—a very different sight from the times I had looked up and down the Thames seeing nothing but vague misty forms on the banks and only streaks of searchlights in the sky. The Royal Mint, across the road from the Tower was flood-lit in red light. We walked on to London Bridge and then on to St. Paul's Cathedral. This sight I shall never forget—black ruins all about for acres, and the great cathedral all bathed in light standing above it all, with the gold cross on top of the dome gleaming—a breathtaking, unbelievable sight.

Throughout the fall of 1945, our club was kept extremely busy, with once again the boys from all the services pouring into London, awaiting ships to take them home. And then gradually the crowds began thinning out. Early in December, along with several other Corps girls and hundreds of young men, I was on the *Queen Elizabeth*, homeward bound.

It was with many mixed feelings that I embarked on this journey: glad to be going home and looking forward to Christmas there, of course, but all too aware that a very special time in my life was ending. There had been many grim days and worrying times, but they were overlaid with fun, adventure and irreplaceable memories. Certainly it changed my life. Perhaps one day I would write about it all!

Helen Perodeau

*"It was awesome to see
all those ships"*

—

Helen Perodeau was born and grew up in Westmont, Que. She married
in 1941, and her husband was posted overseas in 1942. She went
overseas with the Red Cross in 1943. After the war Helen's time
was spent bringing up her four children. The family moved to
Sidney, B.C. in 1970. From 1980–83 she was an Executive
Assistant to the Minister of Finance of B.C. and from
1983–86 she was a member of the B.C. Board of
Parole. In 1997 she joined the Honorary
Board of Governors of the
Victoria Foundation.

Honesty requires that I start out by saying that "patriotism" and "service" were not the motivating forces behind my desire to go overseas during the war. With my upbringing they should have been, but it was "my man" I was after—again. Giles and I had married in December 1941, but then he was sent overseas in May 1942. Like many other brides during wartime I was desolate, and tales of the lovely English lassies dallying with the "flower of our Canadian manhood" were filtering back to us. After landing a job with Canadian Industries Ltd., I began to look for a way to go overseas, and the Red Cross seemed to offer the best chance of getting to England.

The Red Cross did not send anyone overseas who was under twenty-one years of age. I had over a year to wait, so during this time I went to evening drills after work, and on weekends I packed parcels for prisoners of war. The glorious news that I would be going overseas came shortly after my twenty-first birthday.

Such excitement and such a flurry of activity getting ready! My sister Mardie and my father, who was the commissioner of the Canadian Red Cross Overseas Corps, were already in England, but security was uppermost in all our minds, and I, for one, certainly did not want any German U-boat captains to know when I would be on the high seas. I did not know our actual date of sailing, but I was *so* cryptic in my letters that neither Giles nor Mardie could figure out what I was talking about.

We sailed from Halifax in September 1943. Our elation was only slightly dampened by the fact that in order to board our ship we walked *down* the gangway from the dock. I soon found out that our "ship" was actually a banana boat, but in spite of my doubts, it proved to be equal to the task of getting us across the ocean. Still, with all the banana boats put into service on the Atlantic run, one wonders what happened to the bananas—and the plantation owners!

The formation of our convoy was the first of many overwhelming sights for me; it was awesome to see all those ships as far as the horizon and probably beyond. The logistics and organization of it all still boggles my mind. Since that crossing, which included several nights and days of severe storms and exploding depth charges, I have had a deep respect for the men of the Allied and Merchant Navies. There was one storm that was so tremendous that I did not mind at all, because I figured that no sub could keep any ship in its sights in such bad weather. It was also interesting and comforting to learn that the ships trailed log booms behind them so that the following vessels would not "rear end" the ship ahead while travelling in total darkness. I remember when depth charges went off, our ship gave a disturbing shudder that made me think we had hit a rock—rather naive of me considering that we were in mid-Atlantic by this time!

Upon arriving in England, I enjoyed a far too short but very sweet reunion with my husband in Seaford where he was stationed. Then it was on with the job. I began as a cook in the basement (where else in London?) of Corps House. When the building that was to house the Junior Officers' Club became available, a group of us were sent to scrub it from top to bottom and to whip it into shape for the "grand opening." And that we did. We scrubbed and scrubbed, and I still can't see an ornate wrought-iron bannister without experiencing a small shudder. But it was fun working at the club after it opened. In hindsight, I think the greatest compliment I received from a soldier was that I was as great to behold as crisp lettuce—although I didn't appreciate it at the time.

We all took turns at different jobs in the club, except for cooking. My least favourite was making the beds. The poor occupants had to be up and about so that the beds could be made by a certain time in the morning. Sometimes this task was accomplished with great difficulty, as not all the occupants were willing or able to accommodate this arbitrary time frame.

I was probably unduly sensitive to the fact that my father was overseas commissioner for the Canadian Red Cross. Needless to say, when I became pregnant, I thought I had not only let him down, but also his "girls," the Red Cross and even the Allied Cause! I was wrong. Dad was delighted at the thought of being a grandfather. The "girls" were grateful that I had paved the way for them. And the Red Cross and the Allied Cause did not seem to suffer without my efforts for them.

Because of my pregnancy, I had to leave the Red Cross, but I continued with volunteer work. I spent my days packing parcels for prisoners of war, and I moved in with Dad and my sister Mardie who shared a flat on the top (ninth) floor of Cranmer Court. The flat had an unobstructed view of the Battersea Power Station across the river. The Germans were always trying to knock out this power plant, and when they missed, our building was next in the line of flight. I saw my first buzz bomb before I knew what it was. I was sitting in the kitchen writing to Giles when I heard an odd sound. I looked out and saw this strange thing flying by right outside the window, just over the rooftops. It seemed so close that I felt I could reach out and touch it.

The V-1s, more commonly known as buzz bombs or flying bombs, were the first of the German "secret weapons." They were sent off from locations in northern France that were remote from the Normandy beachhead. The V-1 was a bomb with wings and a motor on a timer set to cut out over the desired target. The V-2s were rockets that were launched from the German's secret base at Peenemunde and hit their targets without warning. Many people were more upset about these bombs than the V-1s, but I was never one who wanted to know what hit me!

We heard that sometimes the Canadian and British fighter pilots would attempt to fly alongside the V-1s to tip up their wings so that the buzz bombs would go off course. If you are interested in seeing one, the Canadian War Museum in Ottawa has a genuine buzz bomb—one that didn't explode. The public soon learned about the buzz bomb and its little idiosyncrasies; people came to know that when they heard the engine cut out it would plunge to earth and explode. You held your breath as it put-putted closer, and then there was a marvellous feeling of relief when it kept on going, even as you experienced a faint feeling of concern for anyone who *was* under it when the motor cut out.

Despite how frightening the bombs could be, I can remember

*Princess Marina, Duchess of Kent, officially opening the Junior Officers' Club
in 1944. She is accepting a "Mountie" (RCMP) doll. In the background
is the fearsome Miss Duff.*

Christmas party at the Junior Officers' Club.

*Registration Desk at the Junior Officers' Club, with Helen Perodeau
signing in a Canadian soldier.*

*The Queen leaving the war-time headquarters of the Canadian Women's Club in
London. Beside Her Majesty is Mrs. Lee (Toronto), Overseas Commandant of the
Canadian Red Cross Corps, which furnished a guard of honour. Behind her is Major-
General C.B. Price, overseas commissioner of the Canadian Red Cross Society.*

*Christmas Party, at Corps House, for men from Canadian General Hospital No. 7,
Taplow, England.*

being out one night in a London "pea souper." It was astonishing
how quickly one lost all sense of direction in the fog and yet had
little sense of fear. It strikes me that it was much safer then to walk
the streets of London in the blackout than it is now to walk along
our well-lit streets. So much for progress.

During the nightly bombing raids, my sister and I would go to
the third-floor landing. She had a theory that, if a bomb hit nearby, the debris thrown up by the blast would not reach that high,
and if it went through our roof, it would not penetrate to the
third floor. No one else in the building seemed to share this theory; we were always alone on the landing. We did, however, receive
some strange looks from third-floor residents who had to step
over us as they left for their air-raid duties. One of them was a top

general of the Airborne Division. Some nights he'd be on fire-watch duty, and come out of his flat looking very spiffy and brave, only to find these two disheveled females on the floor of the landing.

Dad, as a member of the Home Guard, spent many nights with a rocket anti-aircraft battery in Hyde Park. He, too, had a humiliating and embarrassing experience. It occurred one night when through his headset he thought he heard the order to fire, and fired off his rockets. The rest of the batteries thought they must have missed the order, so they fired off theirs, and all the rockets in Hyde Park went off with nary a German plane overhead. I do believe Dad was demoted from corporal to private.

The travel ban that was imposed prior to D-Day came into effect before I could be shipped home, so our daughter Ann was born in the Canadian Military Hospital at Horsham. Giles managed to come over from Holland to see us before Ann and I sailed home in April 1945—on a larger ship than going out, I was happy to note. Only after the journey did I learn that during this stage of the war the German U-boats were making an all-out, last-ditch effort to sink as many ships as possible. We were not in a convoy, which is probably why we took the "scenic route" home via the Azores.

When I arrived home I contacted some of the regimental wives. It had been a long lonely war for them, and talking to them made me appreciate even more my great good fortune in being able to serve overseas and share some of my husband's wartime experiences with him.

Eileen Graham

*"I will never, never
forget those pictures"*

—

Eileen Graham was born in Belfast, Northern Ireland. When Eileen
was two years old, her family came to Canada and settled in
St. Catharines, Ontario, where she grew up. She was
working for the Public Utilities Commission when
she joined the Red Cross Corps. On her return
from overseas she worked for the Blood
Transfusion Service in Edmonton. In
1950 she married and in 1955
she moved to Sidney, B.C.

It was 1941 when I decided to change my job in St. Catharines, Ontario from Bell Telephone to the Public Utilities Commission, so that I could work in the daytime and take part in the Red Cross courses at night. We took courses in map reading, ambulance driving, first aid, gas warfare, etc. I also drove a salvage truck for the Red Cross two or three nights a week. We covered different areas of the city, picking up items which people had placed in their driveways for recycling: newspapers, cardboard, fat drippings and metal. The fat and the metal went into making bombs. All the salvage was for the war effort.

The ambulance training was something different, since we trained in emergency first aid. There was no notion of going overseas at the time; the emergency first aid was something we wanted to learn, and we did it.

In 1943 they called us in to ask if anyone was interested in going overseas. A group of us said yes, and we began working towards that goal. We had to have permission from our family, but my father didn't like the idea. He told me, "I won't let you go over there to drive an ambulance. In the First World War they used to drive them near the trenches—no way." "All right," I said, "I will go as a general duties volunteer." Father agreed, but he advised me to go to London where it would be safer. And that is what I did when I was called up. I went as a general duties worker in July 1944.

There were sixty-three of us in our group that went overseas, the largest group at that time. We sailed in a convoy that included three aircraft carriers and a hundred ships. Our ship was the *Glenstrae,* a small meat freighter. The convoy took seventeen days to cross the Atlantic, with beautiful weather all the way. We walked around and around the ship to get exercise and the ocean was as smooth as a mill pond. One morning, however, I woke up very ill with seasickness; the motion of the ship had changed during the night. I struggled up and attempted to make it to my lifeboat station, but reached only the first deck when my legs buckled under me. Since I couldn't make it any further, I crawled back down to my bunk. After a while the head steward came down to see me

Convoy assembled in the Bedford Basin, Halifax, N.S.
(Public Archives Canada PA-112993)

and asked why I didn't attend the lifeboat drill. I told him, "I tried, but I couldn't make it." He replied, "If it was the real thing you would have made it—you've got to get up to the lifeboat deck." Later he sent me oranges; he talked tough, but was soft as putty underneath.

Our ship made the journey safely enough, but not long afterwards we heard that she had been blown up in the Mediterranean while in another convoy. We were very saddened, for we had gotten to know all the crew members. They had been extremely kind to us and we had made a lot of friends. Then they were just gone.

When we arrived in Liverpool, our first sight of England was the docks area where there was hardly a building left undamaged. It was devastating. In fact, all the way down to London on the train, we saw buildings reduced to rubble from the bombings. When we arrived in London, I was assigned quarters in Maple Leaf No. 2. The blackout was on, of course, and I had never seen anything so black in my life. There were no lights at all, no street lights, no lights showing from the houses, so we just had to feel our way in the blackness.

Then there were the buzz bombs (V-1s). We arrived right in the middle of them. They started in the spring of 1944, and they were coming over hot and heavy that July. The buzz bombs were terrifying. They sounded like motorcycles—put, put, put—and you could see their fiery tails. Sometimes they would be high in the sky and sometimes just skimming over the top of the houses. When the noise stopped, the buzz bombs sometimes dropped straight down, but they frequently glided for a while. Since you never knew where they would go, you took shelter right away. We used to have at least a dozen a night. Sometimes we would stay in our beds, depending on what part of London they were hitting. Occasionally they became so bad that the girls who ran the Maple Leaf Club No. 2 would tell us to bring our mattresses downstairs to the lounge and sleep there. We were always nervous about taking a bath, since the alarm could go off while we were in the tub.

The first job I had was at the King George and Queen Elizabeth Officers' Club. I made beds. Another girl and I were assigned to the club, where we made beds by the hundreds. It was our job to change the linen, a task that took the whole day. After two or three weeks of bed-making, we received our permanent jobs; I was assigned to the Ontario Services Club in Piccadilly. Because of the buzz bombs, the opening was delayed, as the men who had been working on the club were recruited to repair the damage elsewhere from the bombs. We were there for the opening in September 1944.

The Ontario Services Club was not a place for overnight stays; it was a day club, and we closed about nine or ten o'clock each night. We had a lounge, cafeteria, library and information desk. One of our most exhausting days was Christmas 1944, when we served pretty close to a thousand turkey dinners. From first thing in the morning until we closed that night, we were going steady. By the time we closed, it was full blackout and a heavy fog blanketed the night. We were also in the midst of a bus and tube strike. In order to find our way home to South Kensington, we had to link arms five abreast, with one girl putting her hand against the building and the one at the other end dragging her foot against the curb. The girls at the house were waiting with our turkey dinner, but we

Red Cross Corps storage room with parcels sent from Canada for prisoners of war.

were so tired we could hardly eat it. We didn't even open our presents; we just left them under the bed. We recovered quickly, however, and the next day it was back to work.

I was appointed officer in charge of Corps personnel in August 1945 until the club closed at the end of February 1946. From there I was house officer for our residence at Onslow Gardens in South Kensington. These were terraced houses, five storeys high. Before the war, these houses had beautifully landscaped gardens behind them, but now there were huge tanks of extra water for fire fighting. We had two of the houses, the connecting wall on the main floor having been knocked down to make an office. We had a large lounge, office and dining-room on the main floor, and four floors of rooms for sleeping. We had our own cooks who did the meals. There were sixty-three girls staying at the house.

When the Army opened up the prisoner of war camps, the boys poured into London and our Club at Piccadilly. Many of them were terribly excited to be free and meeting Canadians again. Others were so traumatized by their experience that they were very withdrawn, and we had to be careful how we treated them. Often we couldn't break through their silence to get them to talk to us, and so we asked some of the boys to help them.

I recall an event that illustrates the extraordinary gratitude that the prisoners of war felt for their parcels. It happened to a woman in Canada who was packing parcels for the prisoners of war. While at work, she lost her diamond engagement ring, and she assumed she would never see it again. At the end of the war, however, a gentleman looked up the Red Cross office from where the parcel had been sent. He came to return a diamond ring he had found in his parcel several years before. He had not hesitated in returning it, he said, for he was so very grateful for the parcels he received while a prisoner.

The other incident I wish to relate about the German camps occurred right after the end of the war in 1945, when there was an exhibition in London of life-size black and white pictures of people in the concentration camps in Germany. It was in a long gallery where you could walk along the corridor and nearly touch the pictures on the wall. You felt as though you were actually walking among the people in the camps. I will never, never forget those pictures; they have haunted me ever since. The purpose of the exhibition was to show the public in Britain the horrendous acts against the people in the concentration camps.

I came home in July of 1946. Over thirty of us came back on a troopship which was so packed we could hardly sit on the deck. We landed in Halifax, and the train was there to meet us. By the time we returned to Canada, all the excitement of people returning home from war was long past. For me, it was an especially difficult time since I had lost my fiancé when he was shot down over Hamburg in the last weeks of the war.

In the beginning, I went back to my old job at the Public Utilities. In 1947, however, when the Blood Transfusion Service of Alberta was ready to open, I went out to Edmonton to join the team. Dr. Stanbury, who had originally been in charge of the Blood Transfusion Service in England, had suggested to the Canadian government that a similar service be organized for Canada. When he had interviewed me in London, I thought it sounded interesting. There must have been thirty or forty girls in Edmonton when the service started up. I was hired as a driver for the Red Cross Blood Transfusion Service and was with them from 1947 to 1951. British Columbia was the first province to have its building ready. Alberta was second and we used the old army hut at the airport.

We drove converted desert ambulances, with all the necessary equipment, to clinics throughout Alberta in all kinds of weather. We sent out advance information on the date, time and place of the clinic. The snow would sometimes be three or four feet high. We drove through blizzards in the winter and through gumbo in the summer. Sometimes when there was an emergency out in the country—often in the middle of the night—we would take the blood out to the small cottage hospital. We also used army surplus trucks, one of which was made into a refrigeration truck. Station wagons were used to transport the girls to the clinics.

About twelve of us girls would go out into the surrounding towns to collect blood. Sometimes we would stay overnight if we had to travel a great distance. The blood would be brought back to the depot in Edmonton where it was processed. In some small towns, we would collect fifty bottles, and in larger towns, we could get 150. When we arrived in a town, we would go up and down the street looking for the butcher. With his permission, we would use his refrigeration and put the bottled blood on the floor among all the meat hanging above. It was the only place large enough to keep it cold.

The Edmonton depot covered the territory north of Red Deer while the Calgary depot looked after the region south of Red Deer. We flew to Whitehorse at one time and to Yellowknife at another to do a clinic. The Air Force flew us up with all the equipment.

We had many burn cases in Alberta, because the fuel the farmers used out in the bush was highly volatile. These burns from the fuel were often terrible, and blood plasma was needed in the treatment. One night there was a bad snow storm and blood was needed at Hay River, which was quite far north. I phoned the Royal Canadian Mounted Police to ask them what was the best route and what the roads were like. The police officer responded, "You're not going out tonight," and I replied, "Yes, we are." But he insisted, "No women are going to go out on the roads in a night like this." Finally we agreed that he would take the blood to the end of his district, where a police car from the next district would pick it up, and pass it on to another until it reached Hay River. The relay worked.

In 1950, while still working for the Red Cross, I married Eric. We settled in Toronto in 1951, and in 1955 we made the move to Sidney, B.C. My son Bruce was born the next year. After retirement, I rejoined the Red Cross as a volunteer in the Blood Transfusion Clinics. For me, it was "once a Red Cross volunteer, always a Red Cross volunteer."

Betty Bussell Simone

*"I shall never forget seeing
thousands of bombers"*

Betty Bussell Simone was born and grew up in Edmonton, Alta.
She attended the University of Guelph in Ontario. She then
moved to Toronto where she worked for National Trust
before joining the Red Cross. In 1945 Betty and three
other Corps members founded the National
Overseas Club and formed its first executive.
In 1954 she graduated as a private pilot
and met her future husband
Peter Simone.

I was married on June 23, 1941, and ten months later my husband Arthur Bussell, a bomber pilot, was shot down and killed while he was on a mission over Germany. It was then that I decided that I wanted to contribute to the war effort. I joined the Red Cross Corps, and twelve of us sailed from Halifax in late August 1943, on the *Pacific Enterprise,* a cargo liner—to give it a dignified description. Also on board were three American professors who were going to London to join the War Information Office. The journey took twelve days. We were part of a very large convoy, with some ships sailing from New York and joining our convoy at sea. We were so important with our cargo of bacon, explosives and *us* that we sailed in the front line, next to the commodore. When we docked in Liverpool I was amazed by my first impressions of England: the sight of millions of chimney pots and then all the open fields en route to London. Somehow I had always thought England would be solid with houses.

We were met at Euston Station and driven with all our gear to Maple Leaf Club No. 2, a club for servicemen of different ranks, where we were billeted for a couple of months until Corps House on Queen's Gate Terrace was ready. Once we were settled, most of us went on landing leave—I travelled to Sheffield to visit my husband's relatives.

I must say that on my arrival in England, I was so thrilled to be there that I was beside myself. Still, when I returned to London after my leave and began to experience the nightly air raids, my initial excitement quickly evaporated. I reported to the Civilian Relief Clothing Department at Red Cross headquarters in Berkeley Square to begin my new job as secretary to the deputy director, who was also the wife of our assistant commissioner. She was in charge of collecting clothing coupons for people who were bombed out. I counted the coupons and kept the books and reports, as all the coupons had to be accounted for to the authorities. In a large adjoining room where the huge supplies of clothing and quilts were kept, I also assisted in putting packages together for the people who had lost their homes. Layettes were given out to every baby born with a Canadian father. It was wonderful how the Canadian Red Cross was able to keep up with the demand for supplies. The bombings created great stress for the people of Great Britain, and they deeply appreciated the efforts of the Red Cross, especially the efforts of Canadian women who contributed so many hours of sewing and knitting to make the clothes that we were distributing. The Red Cross girls were also grateful recipients of lovely warm sweaters, scarves, stockings, gloves and woolen bloomers, known as "romance killers."

As you can imagine, there was a great deal of correspondence regarding the layettes—some hilarious you can be sure, for some of the mothers-to-be did not really know very much about the supposed Canadian father of their child. When I look back now I find it hard to believe that I spent some two years in the layette department, with additional canteen duty at the clubs and fire-watch duty at Corps House and the office.

At Corps House we did chores that included serving dinner to the other girls in the Red Cross. Much of this was basically routine. What kept us sane was the lively social life we led when friends would come down from the bomber squadon on leave and we would all go out for dinner and dancing at the Strollers Club. How we managed to keep going at the rate we lived amazes me. We could go out for the evening, arrive back at Corps House, spend the rest of the night in an air-raid shelter with buzz bombs going off all night, and still get up to go to work for eight hours after very little sleep. But we were young and I don't think many of us had any idea of what we were getting into in our zeal to help out.

Prior to D-Day some friends of mine from Edmonton invited me to bring several of my Red Cross chums to a picnic and dance hosted by the South Alberta Regiment, a tank corps stationed just south of London. It was particularly interesting for us because we were allowed to climb down into the tanks. I think they were Shermans. They had gained the nickname of "Ronsons," since they tended to go up in flames when they were hit. We found it inconceivable that several men could travel in these confined, darkened tanks under fire with very few viewing windows. The regiment was preparing for the D-Day invasion which we all knew was coming soon. The visual obstacle walls and ditches in the nearby fields confirmed the extensive training preparation for the invasion.

I shall never forget seeing thousands of bombers going over London the night of June 5th. At the time we had no idea that this was the beginning of D-Day. Nearly a year later, crowds of us gathered outside Buckingham Palace where the Royal Family came out onto the balcony, and we all celebrated VE-Day. The next day I was part of the vast crowd when Churchill spoke to Londoners and made special mention of those of us who had come across the seas to help with the war effort. But among my memories of those thrilling youthful days "over there," the most outstanding, heart-stopping day was when I attended a Royal Investiture at Buckingham Palace. It was at the invitation of a friend, Charles Semple of Toronto, to see him invested with his Distinguished Flying Cross in May 1945. Another friend and I went together (spit and polished to a fare-thee-well) and sat right in the middle of the front row of spectators. King George VI sat on a ceremonial platform about ten feet from us. After the investiture an official Royal Canadian Air Force photographer took pictures of all of us in front of the Palace, so we would have a permanent reminder of this unforgettable day.

I count myself lucky to have been right in the middle of the action at such a historic time. I must admit that had I not been called home due to my mother's illness, I might still be there. I hated to leave, but I did in July of 1945 when I returned first to Edmonton and then to Toronto, where I had enlisted.

Margot Elmsley

*"It was a little oasis for
the war brides"*

Margot Elmsley was born in Victoria, B.C. While growing up she lived
in the Ontario cities of Ottawa, Kingston and London. Margot did
volunteer war work in Victoria, Ottawa and Calgary before going
overseas with the Red Cross. After the war she focused on
raising her family wherever her husband was
stationed, which included Winnipeg,
Ottawa and Washington, D.C.

I remember very well when World War II broke out, for I heard the news at a supper dance at the Empress Hotel in Victoria. When I returned at about two in the morning, my father was sitting in the den, and I told him that the war had started. My dad was in the Army all his life, so he was prepared and ready for the onset of war. In fact he was glad to know that Canada was going in to support Britain against Hitler.

My future husband Tony was in the Permanent Force Army and completing a course in England when war broke out, but to his chagrin he was sent to Victoria—as far from the war as possible. We were married in November 1940, and left the same day for Debert, Nova Scotia, where my husband had orders to report to whichever division was assembling there prior to going overseas. To Tony's great disgust, however, he was sent to Army headquarters in Ottawa, where we arrived just before Christmas in 1940.

It wasn't until early in 1943 that Tony finally left for England. He was a mechanical engineer with the Royal Canadian Ordnance Corps. This was a support section of the Army that repaired and did the maintenance on the guns, tanks and other vehicles.

After my husband left for overseas, I moved to Calgary. I went partly because my parents were there at the time, but the main reason was that a Canadian Red Cross detachment was being formed in Calgary, and I felt my chances of getting overseas would be better with a new group. Why did I want to go overseas with the Canadian Red Cross Corps? I'm sure that ninety-nine percent of the Red Cross girls will agree that it was mainly to be near our husbands. At the same time, I felt that even though I could work hard to help in the war effort at home, I would be very far away and living very comfortably in comparison to the British civilians—and I wanted to be a part of the action.

Even before Tony went overseas, I had started a business course in Ottawa after hearing that the Red Cross needed office workers in London. I knew even then that I was going to try to get overseas after Tony went over. When I went to Calgary, I finished the business course and then did volunteer work for two years before I was finally assigned to go overseas.

In Calgary I worked days and evenings as a Red Cross volunteer. I believe the Calgary detachment was the first in which all the members were trained as general duties workers in order to fit in where needed. I had to learn first aid, handicrafts and large-quantity cooking at the Veterans' Hospital. I was trained to fit in any place where I was needed: as a cook, someone to work with patients doing handicrafts and first aid, or someone to do office work. It seemed I was everywhere. I did filing, typing and shorthand in the Red Cross office. I went to the blood clinic where we prepared the blood plasma. I worked in the hospital kitchen with the cooks.

After the large-quantity cooking I did at the Veterans' Hospital, I could cook for two people or one hundred and fifty, but nothing in between. We also did hospital visiting, which entailed going around to see patients, doing little things for them and keeping them company. A lot of them were from Australia and other places in the Commonwealth. Most of the men were in the Air Force, because we had many Commonwealth Air Force training centres around Calgary. When an accident occurred, the men would be sent to the Veterans' Hospital. There we would help with the handicrafts and write letters for the men.

It was all very interesting, but I think the most rewarding part was working at the Red Cross Reception Centre which was in the old railway station. We would welcome the troops and the war brides with their babies as they came through on the trains. This was where the war brides could rest, wash themselves and change and bath their babies. In the reception centre we had a bathroom, a change room and a kitchen where we served food. We would make tea and sandwiches and help the war brides in any way that we could. It was a little oasis for the war brides.

Hospital trains brought wounded servicemen from overseas through Calgary, and we used the reception centre as a base for these trains. We would go on the trains to chat to the patients, provide refreshments, take messages and make phone calls for them.

I would quite often meet people I had known before, and it was very, very touching. I remember one time that I saw a lad whom I had known in Victoria. He had been a beautiful dancer, but when I saw him again on the train, I realized he had lost a leg—one of those things that make you feel so sad.

Canada had prisoner of war camps filled with German soldiers, and most of these men had jobs in the camps. I met one prisoner of war who had been cutting trees and had a tree fall on him, so he was on his way to hospital and had to stop in Calgary. After the war, the Germans were sent home, but many of them returned here to live. Even as prisoners of war they had fallen in love with Canada.

Finally, in March 1945, the great day came when two of us departed for Toronto. From there we travelled to Montreal and then to Halifax where our group sailed on the hospital ship *Letitia,* which was luxurious compared to the usual transportation. We had a wonderful voyage. The lights were on all the way and the weather was fine. There were sixteen of us Red Cross girls in the group. On board were also a few airmen who were being returned to England; I think some were psychiatric cases.

Although the bombing was over when I arrived, the aftermath was a sight I will never forget. I saw bombed-out buildings, exhausted faces and women's blue legs, because most of them went without stockings on the coldest day. For these women, the pair of nylons that each of us saved to take in our luggage was the present most appreciated.

I was assigned to Maple Leaf Club No. 2, one of four clubs in London established by the Canadian Red Cross. Maple Leaf No. 2 looked after troops coming back from the Continent. There were quite a few Canadian servicemen in the clerical departments for the armed forces in London. They had offices in Harrods department store which was close to our club, so they came to the club for lunch every day. The troops returning from the Continent on leave would be put up at the club, since we had rooms where they could stay. They could leave their possessions with us and go on leave to Scotland or other places without worrying about their gear.

After I was installed at Maple Leaf Club No. 2, I went down to Surrey to meet my husband. He had recently returned from the Continent to go on a course, and as a surprise for me, had rented a cottage near Bramley, about midway between Camberly and London, as a place for us to spend weekends together. As a general duties worker, I had two days off during the week and Tony had the weekends off. Consequently Tony and I could almost never get the same time off. However, when I switched from general duties to full-time cooking, I had three weekends out of four free to spend with Tony. I was certainly grateful for my large-quantity cooking course in Canada. Later Tony was stationed at Borden, Hampshire, and I saw a great deal of southern England from a jeep.

I enjoyed my time at Maple Leaf No. 2. We were a happy group, and the men who came to the club were cheerful and felt that the club was home. We were responsible for most of the chores in the club—making beds, serving in the dining room, maintaining the front office and many other things. The men were always willing to help us around the club, so our shoes and belts sparkled from spit and polish and our luggage was graciously transported to taxis when we went on leave.

Sometimes my creativity as a cook produced odd results—such as vanilla in the gravy instead of browning (or was it gravy on the vanilla ice cream?). In the kitchen there were four permanent cooks, with two on duty for each shift. While we sometimes had paid helpers to peel vegetables and clean up, much of the time we had to do those things ourselves. And we were cooking for about one hundred and sixty people!

On Sundays we had a buffet lunch, but as there was only one cook on that day, we took turns putting on the meal. When it was my turn, I used to have to do most of the preparation myself. I was petrified and would start at six in the morning to get the lunch ready in time. We did have a funny Irishwoman who prepared the vegetables and another who washed the dishes, but half the time we wouldn't have hot water and we didn't have proper soap, just bars of soap and hard, hard water so there would be no suds at all.

In addition, the paid staff were quite often ill, and then we would have to do it all.

The men would come down to the kitchen to sit and chat, and when they saw we needed help, they would carry things for us. They were also great dish washers. I think these men were expressing their gratitude to Maple Leaf No. 2 for the way in which it boosted their morale, giving them a home away from home and supplying them with extras that they would otherwise not receive in wartime Britain.

I remember one time that I managed to visit Tony on a weekend. After our time together, I was waiting on the platform at Guildford to catch a train back to London. I noticed a train standing by, and at each window there were dark turbanned faces. At that moment, a British officer approached me and asked if I was travelling to London. When I answered yes, he invited me to travel in the special train. The train was repatriating Gurkha troops from a prison camp in Germany to Britain, and from Britain they would travel home to India. It proved to be an interesting trip, but what struck me was the utter silence of those rows and rows of men. The Ghurkas are such a proud people, and I often wondered what they had had to endure in the German prison camps—when the Nazis were so contemptuous of dark-skinned races.

My husband and I returned to Canada within two weeks of each other in March of 1946. I came back on the *Isle-de-France;* Tony came back two weeks before me on a Liberty ship. We found ourselves back at headquarters in Ottawa for a year, and then we were posted to Winnipeg and "army life." As an army daughter, I knew in part what to expect, but there is no doubt that my time with the Red Cross had given me a liking for the camaraderie of military life and for all the good friends one makes when people work together as a team.

Eleanor Wallace Culver

"Then the dreaded route marches started"

Eleanor Wallace Culver joined the Canadian Red Cross Corps in April 1942 and trained in Halifax as a VAD at both the Children's Hospital and the General Hospital. She also drove heavy military trucks as part of her training before going overseas. After the war Eleanor and her husband raised nine children (five daughters and four sons) in North Vancouver. Eleanor and her husband reside on Thetis Island where she enjoys gardening and weaving.

B y the time I went overseas with the Red Cross, six of my brothers were wearing the uniforms of the armed forces. One brother was among the first Canadians to be awarded the United States Air Medal for rescuing fellow airmen from a downed airplane in Alaska. Four brothers were on overseas duties by the time I arrived in England in 1944. Later, one of my younger sisters also joined the Red Cross in England.

Travelling to Montreal to join the Red Cross and board a ship for the crossing to England was the first time I had been out of Nova Scotia, and the first time I had left the home where I grew up as one of fifteen children. On the ship, I shared a cabin with five other girls. The crossing to England turned out to be a pleasant trip of fourteen days. Our ship travelled in a large convoy with a calm sea and wonderful weather. It was July 1944.

While in England, I stayed at Maple Leaf No. 4 before being stationed at a hospital, and it was here that we were exposed to the buzz bombs, which I found frightening. Because I was billeted on the top floor, I asked if I could sleep in the lounge on the first floor. Permission was reluctantly given for me to take my sleeping bag down there after it was closed to the officers. Feeling rather foolish, I went to sleep as the sole occupant of the lounge and woke to find myself surrounded with sleeping bags, all occupied. On another night we received permission to sleep under the pool table in the games room. I had a good night's sleep and woke to realize that the roof over the pool table was made of glass. Once, when a buzz bomb was passing over, we were amused to watch one of the girls lean over and put her head in a waste paper basket.

Soon after my arrival and a short leave, I was sent with five other welfare officers to No. 18 Canadian General Hospital in Colchester to receive training from an occupational therapist. Along with ward duties, this training was scheduled to last for three weeks, but after six days, four of us were chosen to join No. 21 Canadian General Hospital to prepare for duties on the Continent. This hospital had arrived in England from Canada only three weeks beforehand. We turned up in our Red Cross uniforms, much to the amusement of the matron and colonel. We

Marching to tent camp at Southampton

Smiling bravely at the Adjutant after a long route march.

Queue for washing mess tins at Southampton tent camp.

Settling in for the night at Southampton tent camp.

had to make a mad dash with the matron to the army depot in order to outfit the four of us. Our uniforms were the same as the nurses' except that we had the Red Cross badge on our berets. We were each issued a khaki shirt, tie, battle jackets and pants with high boots. The pants were baggy and kept in place with leather gaiters to match the shoes. We were told we could bring our Red Cross uniforms but there was no promise that we could wear them.

Then the dreaded route marches started. Eventually we had to go on marches with all our equipment on our backs (a small pack, gas mask, water bottle, large pack, blanket, trench coat and ground sheet—this did not weigh less than sixty pounds). After a while we got used to the weight, but riding as we did for ten miles standing up in a truck was not easy. We had to be helped into the truck and out again.

We eventually began our trek to the Continent. This meant stopping at two camps en route. These were tented camps where we paused, awaiting orders to move on to the next camp. Each camp was at least an overnight stay. One camp, which was American, was particularly memorable for the wonderful large tins of fruit and the generous meals. We eventually received orders to proceed with full gear in trucks to Southampton on the coast where we boarded ship for the crossing to Dieppe. When we arrived, we were trucked to the small town of Neufchâtel, thirty miles inland. There we went to a former German hospital and found it occupied with German prisoners of war and refugees. The prisoners were put to work building huts for us and the refugees went elsewhere. We were housed two to a tent, which we occupied for about four months. The weather was horrible: first we had to cope with constant rain and mud and then snow that turned to slush. We ran out of water, saved tea to wash our teeth and were generally miserable. Our living conditions affected our morale until it became very low.

During this period of living in tents, I had numerous nightmares about the London buzz bombs. One night I woke up to flashes of light and sounds of explosions. Of course, I immediately thought of the buzz bombs, but no, it was the mess tent going up in flames and the cans of butter exploding as a consequence of misguided culinary virtuosity. In the morning all that was left were rows of the dreaded bully beef. No justice!

Strangely enough, some of the staff at the hospitals took a dislike to the Red Cross. I am not sure why, but perhaps it was because of our volunteer status. I recall that after getting settled and organizing our Red Cross games room, we began to have problems with the matron. She let it be known that she didn't want Red Cross people in her hospital. This was a woman who would start mess meetings with "Miss Reid and me" and proceed to murder the King's English. She continually interfered with our activities. Our colonel also proved to be less than helpful, and I recall an incident that demonstrated how inept he could be. We had a visit from the Vaniers. Madame Vanier was head of the Red Cross in Paris and the aunt of Pat Davis Nicholl, one of our Red Cross girls. We were all called on parade, and the colonel thanked the Vaniers for coming by saying, "We enjoyed your visit and when you come back again, we hope it won't be too soon." We had anticipated that he would do something stupid, but this was beyond our expectations. Not long after, a shipment of rum being transported to the front for the soldiers allegedly found itself in the hands of our colonel. Later, I had a ride to Dieppe in one of our trucks, and the driver told me that he was taking cigarettes that were intended for the Red Cross to the black market in Dieppe—a black market that was run with the help of the colonel's mistress.

Yet the activities of the colonel and the matron also created some unintended humour. One day I watched one of our orderlies approach the hospital with a large stick tucked under his arm as he escorted four German prisoners he had captured. When I asked him how he had accomplished such a feat, he pointed to his stick and said he had been told he wasn't doing his part in the war effort. As a result, he went into the woods and rounded up the Germans. He told me that it was easier than catching rabbits, and then off he went clutching his stick, a big grin on his face. The Germans looked as if they were looking forward to beds and a meal.

At this point, our hospital moved up and into an established hospital at St. Omer, France. Meanwhile the matron continued to thwart all the work of the Red Cross girls. It got so bad that a Corps member came from England to try to ease the situation. She made an appointment with the matron, but first she called on the four of us Red Cross girls, Deborah Davis Emmans, Pat Davis Nicholls, Sheila Griffiths and myself. She listened to all our complaints but said that she found it hard to believe that the matron, whom she had found earlier to be very pleasant and cooperative, could behave in such a way. Off she went for her appointment, while we waited together for her return. She arrived back looking ashen, and asked, "Where is your whiskey?" (We all received a monthly ration.) We watched as she drank and her colour returned. Now she believed all we had told her. She said she couldn't reason with the matron—it was hopeless. Later, Colonel McKenna came twice to help with the situation, and on the second visit, he asked us to hold on for a little longer, and if the situation didn't change, he was going to withdraw the Red Cross from the hospital. Fortunately, the matron was finally removed and we remained. The matron was transferred to the military hospital at Bramshott where she quickly became known as the Beast of Bramshott. She was obviously as popular with the nurses there as she had been with the nurses at No. 21 Canadian General Hospital. She was last seen standing at attention when Haile Selassie was inspecting one of his hospitals in Ethiopia. There is a God.

The hospital at St. Omer also operated a small annex hospital, with a staff of fourteen nurses and doctors and one Red Cross volunteer. We took turns doing duty there. That's where I was on May 8, 1945 when Churchill announced that the war had finally ended. We had waited forty-eight hours for this announcement, and had saved our liquor ration for the big celebration. But by the time the announcement was finally made, we had lost interest in having a party and just went to bed early. Interestingly enough, this annex was near the coast by Dunkerque where a small pocket of Germans had been cut off and were still resisting capture. Driving from the annex to St. Omer at night, the sky was lit up with the fighting that was still going on.

Eventually I left St. Omer and said goodbye to the three Red Cross girls I had worked with since arriving in England. I moved to another military hospital at Ghent, Belgium. There I discovered our infamous colonel was a patient with eye problems. I declined to visit him with my goodies in a basket. From there, he was discharged from the Army.

Obtaining permission to go on leave was very frustrating, since it involved placing your name on a list of nurses waiting for the opportunity to leave the Continent or visit places like Paris or Brussels. If you were lucky, your name would be drawn, but you had no choice as to whom your travelling companion would be. If your name didn't come up, you had to wait until the next list appeared. A few of us finally travelled to Paris on leave, but found ourselves in a disreputable hostel with some of the windows missing. We called Madame Vanier, and when she arrived at the hostel, she agreed that we should expect better accommodation— bless her! We were then billeted at the Officers' Club. No problems in getting dates once we were there!

At our hospitals, the Red Cross closets were kept supplied with a great assortment of kits to create cushion covers, wall hangings, etc., plus toiletries and writing materials. We coordinated a drop-in centre for the patients, and we visited the wards each day with baskets over our arms as we dispensed articles according to the needs of the individual patients. We also wrote letters that the patients dictated to us. I remember one patient who would always instruct me to end his letters with "when I get home, first thing, it is going to be GUTS." Finally I asked him what GUTS stood for. His answer: "get up them stairs." Another patient who was a nice young man from the coast of Newfoundland would give excuses as to why he couldn't write himself. Later I found out that he was illiterate. This was when Newfoundland was still quite isolated, so it would have been difficult to get a proper education.

After doing duty at Ghent, I was moved up to Nijmegan in the Netherlands for a short time, and then I joined Deborah Davis Emmans in Wilhelmshaven, Germany, to become part of the Ca-

Building shelves at Sande, Germany, 1946.

nadian Army Occupational Force. We were members of a staff of ninety female officers with ten times that many Canadian military officers. There were three officers' clubs as well as great music and good food. If you dated one officer, you would be joined by a group of them before long. We had a wonderful colonel and matron. One day they arrived on an inspection tour just after we had put the kettle on in the store room to make coffee, a task that was not part of our duties. We quickly shut the storeroom door and stood at attention. The colonel said he wanted to inspect the storeroom, so in he went and was quickly lost in the steam. He came out, saluted and moved on. The next thing we knew, he was back —informing us that he had come for his cup of coffee.

While on duty at this hospital, I became acquainted with an officer I had met earlier in Dartmouth, Nova Scotia in 1943. He became my constant escort until he returned to Canada some months before me. We met again three years later in Montreal and were married in Victoria in 1950. Our first child was born in

1951 and by 1961 we were the proud parents of nine wonderful children. We are now the grandparents of twenty-one children.

I returned to Canada at the end of July 1946 on the *Queen Mary*. Also aboard was Al Capp. We all followed his cartoons in the *Maple Leaf* magazine where he had just run a contest for a drawing of the ugliest woman in the world. When we asked how it was decided, he said he had got out of that situation by saying it was too ugly to print.

After arriving in Halifax, I did escort duty on a train travelling from one of the docks to Montreal. I couldn't help smiling when one of the escort officers said that her niece badly wanted to come to the dock to see the war brides walking off the ship in their long white dresses and veils! My memory of that trip is of lines of terry-cloth napkins draped around the cars and crying babies, not to mention the smell. We stopped at one station beside a train from Montreal carrying disenchanted war brides on their way back to England (the war brides could return, fare paid, within a certain time frame). To our dismay the two groups had a chance to compare notes, which did not help the morale of our group.

Since 1946 it has been a great source of pleasure to be part of the Red Cross Overseas Club and to keep in close touch with so many interesting members. Now I must go back to helping my husband lay 25,000 bricks on the driveway surrounding our house —not exactly how I expected to be spending my eighty-first summer!

Leah Halsall

"You have to be a good sailor"

Leah Halsall was born in Tientsin in northern China. During her
childhood she lived in Tientsin, Pei-tai-ho and Shanhaikwan
before moving to Hong Kong where she attended boarding
school. After her tour of duty with the Red Cross Corps,
she worked as a medical record librarian in Victoria.
Now retired, she takes a keen interest
in the outdoors, archaeology,
anthropology and politics.

W hen war was declared on September 3, 1939, there was no apprehension of danger in Hong Kong, but by 1940, people were being evacuated, mainly to Australia. My Uncle Ted, who lived in Chilliwack, British Columbia, was concerned about me and contacted the Immigration Department to have me admitted to Canada. My youngest brother had already been living with him since February 1939, after the deaths of our parents in 1938.

On May 20, 1941, while I was in downtown Hong Kong shopping, I saw a cruise ship in the harbour. When I returned from shopping I was told to phone the Japanese NYK Line. I was advised that I had to be on the ship that I had seen in the harbour by ten o'clock that night as my uncle had booked passage for me to Canada. There was, of course, a mad rush to get everything packed and to obtain my Japanese visa. I sailed at six the next morning for Japan and changed ships in Yokohama to come to Canada. I travelled to Vancouver, and lived in Chilliwack for a year where I studied at the local business college. I then wrote my exams for a job in Ottawa, and on my birthday in 1942, I arrived in Ottawa to begin working for the Department of Veterans Affairs (DVA). I eventually became a private medical secretary in the DVA Canadian Pension Commission.

After Laurentian Terrace was built as a residence for female government employees, I moved in and made many friends. One day in 1943, Miss Juliette Robert, our resident nurse, announced that she was conducting a St. John's Ambulance course in first aid and home nursing which I promptly signed up for. This proved to be a very useful decision. I did not know about the Ottawa Voluntary Aid Detachment of the Canadian Red Cross at this time or that there was overseas service involved until Joan West (Hunt), a good friend of mine from DVA, told me she was going overseas in November 1944 to serve with the Canadian Red Cross Corps. I decided that I, too, would like to serve overseas in the Canadian Red Cross Corps as part of the war effort.

Part of my reasoning was that my father had had connections with the American Red Cross. In 1919, while in Siberia as a Canadian Army adjutant, he was asked to organize the post-war relief in Siberia because he had studied and could speak Russian. He accepted the position and was demobilized from the Canadian Forces. In 1920, he was sent to China to organize the post-flood relief after the flooding of the Huang Ho (Yellow River). He remained in the American Red Cross on a part-time basis for several years and attended the International Red Cross Conferences in the Philippines and Mexico.

In February 1945, I went to the Voluntary Aid Detachment Headquarters of the Canadian Red Cross for an interview and was accepted for duty on February 17th. I later received my navy blue uniform and everything that went with it. We had regular meetings in the evenings, where we did a lot of drilling and furthered our knowledge in first aid and home nursing. We were jubilant when VE-Day arrived on May 8, 1945, and happy to be asked to march in the parade celebrating the end of the war in Europe. We looked smart in our navy blue uniforms as we marched past Prime Minister Mackenzie King at the Parliament Buildings.

After the war, the troopships were kept busy for the next few months bringing back the Canadian servicemen and women. Finally, the Canadian government made arrangements for the ships to bring over the war brides and their children to Canada. This activated the Canadian Red Cross Corps to increase the number of escort officers. From the first girls who crossed the Atlantic during the U-boat era to the last girl to join up, the escort officers would number ninety-four.

With the influx of war brides and children, life changed for me in the Ottawa VAD. I started going to the railway station in the evening to meet them. We were assigned a number of war brides that we had to find and unite with their husbands. We also visited the hospital where British military servicemen were patients. These men were former prisoners of war from Japan.

Since I had to put in two hundred volunteer hours in nursing, I worked at the Ottawa General Hospital on the evenings when I was on call. I would work all day at the office, report to the hospital by seven at night and finish working at 2:15 in the morning. There was a drastic shortage of nurses and doctors because many had joined the forces during the war.

I was teamed with another girl, Barbara, and we were given a choice of where we would like to work. On the first night we tried the men's ward, where we were teased a lot. On another night we worked in the maternity ward. Finally we settled for the children's ward, which we really enjoyed. We had to look after all the formula feeding—quite a job since there were only two of us. The nurse on duty had to do her charts, so the two of us had to change all the babies, clean them up and do anything else that was necessary. There were many children in the ward—from tiny babies with pneumonia to fourteen-year-olds—and they all came under our tender care. The sick babies kept us on our toes, and we were busy most of the night. Thank goodness no crises occurred during the time we worked there!

In the spring of 1946, our commandant announced that she wanted one of us to go to England as an escort officer. She explained to us, "You have to be a good sailor to take the place of one of the girls who suffers from seasickness." I put up my hand immediately. "I'm a good sailor," I said. Because I had had the experience of being on ships in the Pacific Ocean, I was selected to go overseas as an escort officer in the Canadian Red Cross Corps —despite not having completed my two hundred hours of hospital duty. I was told that my headquarters would be in London and my main job was to assist the war brides and their children on their voyages to Canada. I went to see Captain Simpson at DVA and had no trouble getting six months' leave of absence from my job.

As I had to have uniforms, all my measurements were sent to Eaton's in Toronto. In no time at all, back came my navy blue suit and great coat as well as other clothing and accessories for outside and non-duty wear. I also received uniforms for my on-duty wear on the ships—blue dresses, white aprons with the large red cross in front and white veils with a small red cross in front.

I left Ottawa for Halifax at the beginning of June. On June 6, 1946 all the escort officers awaiting transport boarded the *Lady Nelson*. When we docked in Southampton on June 16th, the military transport met us and drove us to the railway station. We caught the train to London where we were met by our transport girls. They drove us to 80 Brook Street in the Mayfair district, the home of the escort officers. It had a marble staircase and had once been quite palatial. We were to be given $30.00 a month and $5.00 for our laundry.

Upon my arrival at Brook Street, I was very happy to see my brother Walter. When he told me that he had decided to settle in Victoria, British Columbia, and asked me to join him later, I recalled the words that my father used to say to us as children: "When I retire, we will live in Victoria. You will love Victoria." So I told my brother I would join him when my tour of duty had ended with the Canadian Red Cross Corps, and I had put in the required month's work at the Canadian Pension Commission following my official resignation.

During my stay in London, I was given a tour of the Mostyn Wives' Hostel in order to learn what the escort officers did when they were on duty in London. They were expected to make up hundreds of beds for the war brides and children to occupy during their night's stay in London prior to their departure by ship to Canada. The escort officers also served supper and breakfast, as well as setting and clearing the tables.

Finally I was informed that I would make my first trip escorting war brides and children from Southampton to Halifax on the *S.S. Queen Mary.* I had already seen this magnificent ship, all 1,020 feet of her, a few weeks earlier while staying at the Nova Scotia Hotel in Halifax, so I knew what to expect. The escort officers always boarded the ship the day before the war brides and children, so on June 28th, we were picked up from Brook Street by the transport girls and taken to the railway station. After a pleasant train ride, we boarded the *Queen Mary.*

The *Queen Mary* was carrying around 2,400 war brides and children on this trip. There were fourteen escort officers. Ten of us were assigned to the cabins, which meant we would each have about 240 war brides and children under our care; two girls were in charge of the day nursery and two girls coordinated the distribution of items to the war brides who had filled out lists of their children's needs. These items had been packed by the Red Cross Corps girls at Burlington Gardens headquarters. They included layettes, knitted baby clothes and other clothing made and donated by Canadian women through the Canadian Red Cross Society. Our duties on the *Queen Mary* started at 9 a.m. and ended at 9 p.m., but we could be on call for twenty-four hours.

On June 29th, we were ready with our lists of names of all the war brides and children who were coming aboard. We were supposed to check every war bride and child. We asked them questions and looked for signs of ill health. On this trip one of our escort officers recognized signs of a blue baby being brought on board; the finger tips and around the mouth were blue. Mother and baby were sent to the hospital infirmary for further checking by the ship's medical officer, with the result that the baby was kept in the infirmary for the rest of the voyage.

Those of us with cabin duties were assigned to blocks of cabins so that there would be no duplication. Every day we checked each cabin to make sure that the war brides received help when they needed it. The excellent food on the *Queen Mary* actually created some problems because it was so rich. We gave out aspirins, laxatives and sunburn lotions, and we organized baby feedings. We answered many questions about Canada and calmed the fears of some of the brides. Rough seas caused a lot of seasickness. If anything serious occurred, we sent the war bride or child to see the medical officer in sick bay.

After completing my first voyage as escort officer on the *Queen Mary,* I boarded the *Lady Rodney* in Halifax on July 7th or 8th. The *Lady Rodney* and the *Lady Nelson* were two very small ships out of Montreal. Although we called them "banana boats" because of their pre-war West Indies runs, their crew were wonderful and their food terrific. Captain LeBlanc of the *Lady Rodney* kept a fatherly eye on all us girls.

On this particular crossing, the weather grew worse each day until we finally realized that we were heading for the eye of the storm. At the height of the storm, we all stayed in our cabins for breakfast. At around noon, I decided to go to the dining-room for lunch and found that I was the only occupant. After lunch, I went out on deck and was almost washed overboard by an enormous wave that looked like a curtain on a concert stage. I was lucky to escape from most of the wave and make it back to my cabin. We arrived in Southampton on July 17th, and some of us were immediately taken to the *Queen Mary*. We boarded her to resume our usual routine and sailed the next day.

I remember an incident that occurred a couple of days later. Shortly after 8 a.m., we were just finishing our breakfast in the restaurant when a huge wave hit the *Queen Mary* amidships. It caused thousands of dollars of damage and, I believe, a broken leg or two. We grabbed everything we could on our table and were able to continue with our breakfast. But within ten minutes the stewards came rushing to our table to tell us they were having problems in the main dining-room and needed our help. When we entered the dining-room, we were met with complete havoc—crying children, fainting war brides, seasickness that had hit several women, broken dishes, upturned chairs and food everywhere. With the help of the stewards, we half-carried the women to their cabins, and it was eleven that morning before we had reunited the last child with its mother. The rank smells emanating from the devastated dining-room just about did me in, but once I finally hit the fresh air, all was well and my breakfast decided to stay put! We arrived in Halifax on July 23rd.

The *Lady Nelson* returned us to Southampton where we landed on August 8th and entrained for London. Since I was on leave in London, I had a great time with the two captains I had met on board who took me to a movie one afternoon. Afterwards, I went to the ladies' room to freshen up before dinner and found myself with four young women wearing lots of make-up, who obviously knew each other, and were chatting away. One of them moved right up to me and busied herself pulling up her stockings, but the sudden silence of the women behind me alerted me to the fact that something was happening. Sure enough, my purse was open so I moved it to the counter. Much laughter behind me! I never said a word and left the room. I'll bet I was the only member of the Canadian Red Cross Corps whose wallet was nearly pinched by a "lady of the night." At dinner, I ordered rabbit, which I thought would be stewed and taste like chicken, but this restaurant fried it rather solidly, and when I tried to cut it, the rabbit went flying off my plate and landed near some other customers. The three of us became hysterical with laughter.

On August 25, 1946, fourteen escort officers boarded the *Queen Mary,* and the next day almost 2,000 war brides and children came on board. I did not know it, but it was to be my last voyage on her. We proceeded to our staterooms on the main deck and settled in. My room-mate and I had twin beds in our large room and a private bathroom. It was very comfortable, much like a good hotel. I always slept with my portholes closed, and during bad weather they were never opened.

Following our usual routine, we departed from Southampton early on August 27th. The sea gradually became rougher as we approached the open Atlantic. On August 28th, between midnight and one in the morning, my roommate and I were awakened to the sound of falling objects in our stateroom and bathroom. Our beds had moved as well as our chairs. We got up immediately, and I realized that another huge wave must have hit the *Queen Mary* amidships. It appeared that the ship had stopped, but we still felt a lot of motion underfoot. We straightened the beds and other furniture and put back all the fallen objects. As our portholes were closed, we suffered no water damage. No one knocked on our door for help, so we took it for granted that things were under control elsewhere. It was back to bed, and before long we were sound asleep.

When we went to the restaurant that morning we were in for a shock. I believe it was Kay Douglass (Ruddick) who told us that the wave had entered the opened portholes on the top deck, hitting the bridge and entering other areas. Captain Illingsworth's cabin was drenched. A lot of people were seasick. The reason why the ship had stopped for a couple of hours was because the electrical equipment had been affected. Our escort officers worked

Leah Halsall as an escort officer aboard the Lady Rodney, November 1946.

like Trojans, taking care of the babies, with lots of help from passengers. That day the crew had a massive clean-up job to do in the cabins (lots of seawater-soaked mattresses) and elsewhere in the ship.

Amazingly, things settled down and so did the sea. The brides who could make it to the deck came out to sit in the deck chairs and get a sun tan. I was up on deck as well, warning the war brides that twenty minutes in the sun was long enough. But quite a few ignored my advice, and later that day I had to supply sunburn lotion to those in my cabins. One girl was in tears as she did not want her husband to see her looking like a red lobster.

On deck was Prime Minister Mackenzie King, returning from the Paris Conference. He looked very comfortable in his large deck chair with his cap on and a blanket covering him. I deeply regret that I was rather shy and did not go over to speak to him and tell him that I had seen him many times in Ottawa when I was returning to the Daly Building after lunch and he was on his way to have lunch at Laurier House. Also on board was Lester Pearson, who was the Canadian Ambassador to Washington, and there were other VIPs as well.

On the morning of August 30th, we listened to Mackenzie King make a short speech of welcome and offer congratulations to the war brides. We arrived in Halifax on August 31st and the war brides and children were disembarked and transferred to the care of the Red Cross VAD train crew.

The _Lady Nelson_ once again returned us to Southampton. While in London, towards the latter part of September, I was assigned the task of taking care of a four-year-old child named Mattie, who was going to join her father in Vancouver. Our escort officer team left for Liverpool and boarded the _Scythia_. When Mattie and I met, she put her hand in mine, and there was an instantaneous rapport between us. I took her to the dormitory and after settling her in, we had dinner. Bathtime arrived before long, and I filled the tub with warm salt water which I tested before placing Mattie into it. The next thing I knew, I had two arms around my neck, two legs around my waist and a whimpering child to comfort. I

The Queen Mary.

The Lady Rodney in War Garb.

ended up taking her out of the tub and washing her from the hand basin.

The more I thought about Mattie's reaction to the bath water, the more I was convinced that she must have come from a cold-water flat. So I changed my tactics on subsequent nights and put her into cool water to start with, gradually pouring more hot water in until she became used to it. By the end of the week, she was enjoying her experience, and I had no more problems with her.

The day after we sailed, I checked her clothing needs and then went to our supply room to pick out several pretty outfits in her size. These I exchanged for her well-worn but clean clothes, which I promptly threw out of the porthole in my cabin. Mattie was quite willing to have her hair cut in a short style with a fringe, so I made an appointment for her at the hairdressing salon on the ship. She was very pleased with the result. That night, I chose one of the prettier dresses for her to wear and tied a ribbon through her hair. She made a triumphant entrance with all eyes upon her. I don't think there was a single person who did not return her smile of greeting. As the days went by, she became the ship's favourite passenger. It was a real wrench to part with her in Halifax, but she had to be turned over to members of the Red Cross VAD train crew to continue her journey to Vancouver. Wherever she is, I hope she enjoyed her childhood with her father and grandparents and went on to a happy adulthood.

Within days, we boarded the former hospital ship *Letitia* which was soon in England again, where I was told that I would be returning on the *Lady Rodney*. As things were winding down with regard to the number of war brides and children awaiting transportation to Canada, it was decided that my trip on the *Lady Rodney* would be my last crossing as an escort officer. On November 5, 1946, we embarked on the *Lady Rodney*. The ship's galley was out of bounds to the war brides, which meant that we would have to make the formula and deliver the bottles. It was fortunate for us that the majority of the babies were breast-fed. The medical officer gave us the instructions to make the formula and we organized ourselves for an around-the-clock routine. Two girls went on duty at about one o'clock in the morning to make the formula, and four of us had our schedules for delivering the formula bottles. I went on duty at seven in the morning to deliver my share of the formula bottles.

At one point we had very rough weather, causing most of the war brides to become seasick. I recall an incident when I was taking both tomato juice and formula to a mother. I must have carried the bottle of formula against the expansion bracelet of my watch, because I suddenly felt a burning sensation on my wrist. As I tried to move the bottle, the tomato juice spilled, making quite a mess of my pinafore. I had to get more tomato juice, and when I arrived at the war bride's cabin, she thought I was covered with blood and imagined that the war had begun again.

There was another incident when I was in the galley and a stewardess came in and said that the Dutch war brides wanted some tea. She had a full tray of tea all set to go, but turned to me and said, "I can't take this—it's too rough." I assured her that I could take it, but once I began walking with the tray in both hands, I found it almost impossible to keep my balance in the gangway. Then I had to go up a flight of wide stairs; fortunately, from there on I more or less sailed with the motion of the ship right into the Dutch war brides' cabin, without spilling a drop! Even though they were sick, the war brides all started to laugh when I "sailed" into the cabin.

The sea finally calmed down and the war brides were able to enjoy the sunshine on deck. We entered Halifax harbour on November 14, 1946. Captain Donaldson of the Canadian Army Service Corps and his staff came on board, as they always did when our ships arrived in Halifax. They checked on everything that had occurred on the journey with regard to the war brides and children and were informed of their eventual destinations in Canada. After their business was finished, they took care of our transportation to and from the ships in Halifax. Captain Donaldson always arranged dates for us which took place in the evenings at the officers' mess.

As this trip was my last venture with the war brides and children, I made my fond farewells to the wonderful friends I had made over the past several months, some of whom I have kept in touch with by correspondence. With the formation of the Overseas Club in late 1945, I was able to meet many of the Canadian Red Cross Corps girls at the reunions I attended.

As a footnote with regard to the escort officers, the last official war bride ship to arrive in Halifax was the *Aquitania* in January 1947. The total number of war brides who came to join their husbands in Canada was approximately 48,000 with about 21,000 children.

I arrived in Victoria on New Year's Eve, 1946. My brother Walter had arranged for me to board at Loretto Hall run by Catholic nuns, but he was out of town when I arrived. As it was New Year's Eve, the other residents were out on the town and I was all alone. I cried my eyes out thinking of the wonderful evening I would have had if I had stayed in Ottawa. Things soon brightened, however, and I lived at Loretto Hall for several years, making close friends that I still have today. It was a happy, wonderful place to live. Today this heritage residence is a beautifully preserved bed-and-breakfast and restaurant on Belleville Street.

Because I had training in medical stenography, I soon went to work at St. Joseph's Hospital, which was close to Loretto Hall. A few years later, I studied to be a medical record librarian and held this position until my early retirement from Victoria General Hospital (formerly St. Joseph's Hospital) in 1982. Eventually all my siblings came to live in Victoria, fulfilling my father's desire for all of us to live here. My father made it back to Victoria in a different way as I had his ashes buried in Ross Bay Cemetary.

I am happy to say that I am still enjoying my retirement, particularly with the four hiking groups I belong to. I shall never forget the eventful overseas experiences I had with the Canadian Red Cross Corps, and I am still grateful that I was able to go overseas when the need arose for "a good sailor."

Peggy Leigh McRae Fairey

"The celebrating and rejoicings
were unbelievable"

Peggy Leigh McRae Fairey was born in Vancouver, B.C. where she
attended Crofton House, a private school for girls. After the war,
she and her husband settled in Vancouver, and Peggy returned
to her accounting job that she had left to join the Canadian
Red Cross Corps. She has two daughters and a son.

I joined the Canadian Red Cross Corps at its beginning in the 1940s because I wanted to help in the war effort. Many of my colleagues at the large insurance and real estate office in Vancouver where I worked as the assistant accountant had already left, or were planning to leave, to join the war effort. I didn't want to work in an office, cook or become a VAD. I just wanted to drive, and there was a section for drivers that appealed to me. We were trained at the Beatty Street Armouries by Army sergeants. It was quite an efficient programme: we learned about hand signals, mounting and dismounting from a vehicle and all the regular repair duties.

Before we could be sent overseas, we had to do a certain number of hours of volunteer work. I also had to take a St. John's Ambulance first aid course and two or three mechanics courses. The Ford Motor Company taught one of the courses and the General Motors car dealership in downtown Vancouver also took us under its wing. They provided books and overalls for us to wear. The Ford Motor course, which was taught in Burnaby, was very good because they had a car motor that was constructed to show the internal working parts. There was a lot to learn but I loved it.

When at last the notification for going overseas came by a phone call for me at my office, I discovered that I was expected to be in Toronto in two weeks. I had to tell my boss, who was none too happy about a further reduction in his staff, arrange for medicals, apply for a passport, pack and cope with the thousand and one details that had to be attended to. But finally my friend Coralie Somerville and I climbed aboard the train, and off we went—still panting from the frantic rush. We soon found out, however, that the Red Cross was no different from the Army—"hurry up and wait."

While we felt that we had already been well-trained for the job, the officials in Toronto made us take a map-reading course, a motor-mechanic's course and a gas-attack course. We also had to do stretcher-bearing drills. All of these we had done in Vancouver, so we were a little irritated. The trainers didn't even think we could change a dual tire on a truck. But Coralie and I said, "Try us!" We had learned how to do it in Vancouver, and we showed them we could do it.

After we had been in Toronto for a while we were asked to do some ambulance driving for Christie Street Hospital. About six weeks later we were on our way. Our departure had been delayed because all ships were needed for the D-Day invasion. At the time, of course, we had no idea why there were no ships to take us overseas.

When we finally arrived in Montreal, there was our ship. It looked tiny—a little freighter that was very, very old. This was to be our home for nineteen days. With sixty-four Red Cross gals on the *Glenstrae,* I pitied the poor crew and other passengers. It was a memorable experience, for we joined a convoy that was one of the largest to cross the Atlantic during World War II, but we never felt a sense of danger. Because we travelled south through the Azores, the weather was warm, and we were happy to lie out on the deck and sunbathe. On board we met a group of English boys who had been evacuated to different homes in the USA and were now returning to England. Another passenger was a man who had worked for the Bank of Montreal in Vancouver and was going to work for the Bank of Montreal on Lower Regent Street in London. There was also a man we called "the spy" because he looked so mysterious. Oh you can make up wonderful stories while you're travelling!

While on board, we were told that we must always carry our life jackets, but that was not a problem because they were actually rather soft and comfortable to sit on. Having a bath was quite a procedure: we had to call for the "bath steward" who would bring fresh water with which to rinse ourselves after our sea water baths.

After landing in Liverpool, we caught the train to London, where we stayed at the Red Cross Junior Officers' Club. From there we were sent on embarkation leave. I went with a friend who was visiting her boyfriend. When we came back we were advised that we were to be seconded to the British Red Cross as ambulance drivers. At Red Cross headquarters, we were told that we were now on our own. "Don't come to us with your problems, but

Convoy of Red Cross ambulances.

good luck, etc." Then off we went to Chester for our first posting. Chester is a very old walled city near Liverpool and close to the Welsh border. We were actually based in a small detachment just outside of Chester. Here we met the first English girls we would be working with, some of whom remained with us until we returned to the Canadian Red Cross. One of them took me under her wing and taught me how to drive an Austin ambulance, which was quite different from the ambulances I was used to driving. We remain friends to this day. As ambulance drivers, we picked up wounded servicemen from the ships at the Liverpool docks. Our first patients were Italian prisoners of war who had the mumps. I remember thinking, "This is what I'm here for?" I believe they had been brought to Liverpool on a captured Italian ship. After the patients were put in our ambulances, we were told which hospitals to take them to. There was a communicating door between the driver and the patients, which was usually left open so the driver could talk to them.

From Chester some of us went to join the Swindon Convoy.

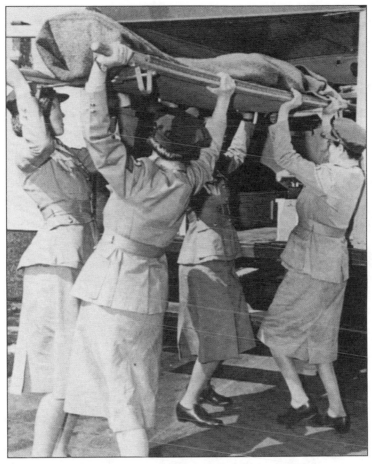

Red Cross Corps members loading a stretcher into an ambulance.
(Courtesy Toronto Telegram Collection, York University).

This was a mobile convoy, which meant that we kept all our possessions in a barrack box in our ambulance. It was like being in a camper—your ambulance was your home. Wounded servicemen were flown from the Continent and taken to an area where medical personnel checked them over and sorted them according to their nationality and type of wound. Then arrangements would be made as to their destination. The men were brought in all muddy and dirty from the battlefields. They would be cleaned up and then someone would help them, if they wished to, write a letter to

Peggy Leigh McRae Fairey with her ambulance. RAF, Broadwell, 1944.

Peggy Leigh McRae Fairey's hut (l) and mess hall (r) Lydiard, 1944.

View from Peggy's window in British Hospital No. 5, Brugge, 1945.

Repatriation Celebration, Brugge, 1945.

their family. We would then transport the men to the various hospitals. There might be one ambulance full of head injury patients, another for burn patients and yet another full of walking wounded. At different times, we could have all Canadians or all Americans or all English. We often drove all night, so I can assure you we didn't get up very early in the morning.

The British were short of personnel to drive ambulances and counted on the Red Cross and Order of St. John's to provide drivers. Being seconded to the British Red Cross, we were generally alone in our vehicles. Only if a patient was being given plasma did we have an orderly. The American and Canadian Forces had their own drivers and co-drivers.

After the Swindon Convoy and a stint at Charlton Park, six of us went to London where we were given two trucks and two ambulances to drive to Paris. From London we drove to the Torquay docks where we stayed overnight. The next morning we drove on to a landing transport barge which took us to Ostende. From there we were told we had to drive to Paris. Since we had no idea how to get there, we asked some people for directions. The only signs on the road said "Maple Leaf Up" and "Maple Leaf Down." The main traffic on the road to Paris was made up of convoys.

After we had been driving for a long time and feeling quite tired, one of the girls said, "I've got a friend who is the matron of a hospital that's nearby and maybe we can stay there overnight." Of course by this time we would have stayed anywhere, just to get a little sleep. We found our way to the hospital and luckily the matron had an empty ward, so we took it over for the night. The next morning we returned to our vehicles. We were taking them to a small country hospital near Paris, which had previously been under German control but hadn't been used for a long time. Now the British had taken it over and were getting it ready to take in British people who had been caught in France during the war and had not been able to return home. We left the vehicles at the hospital and caught the train to Brussels to join our convoy.

We ended up in Denhaan near Ostende, Belgium, and from here we drove patients to France and Holland. Each trip was a new adventure. I remember quite clearly the day the Allies crossed the Rhine. We were picking up servicemen from an airfield close to the Rhine and the battleline was not far away. But even though we were close enough to know what was happening, we were in no real danger. We were also transporting many Dutch soldiers to hospitals closer to their homes. I recall a time when I was driving a Dutch soldier to a hospital, and I asked him where he lived. When he told me, I realized it was nearby, so I said, "Let's take a drive around that way before I take you to the hospital." When we arrived at his family's home, they all climbed into the ambulance with him. I remember thinking how great it was for him to see his family and for his parents to see their son before he went to the hospital.

My future husband Bill and I had been good friends back in Canada. While Bill was on leave in England, we decided to get married when the war ended. Because the Canadian government didn't have a foreign marriages act, we had to obtain permission from the Canadian Ambassador to Belgium, the Canadian Red Cross, the British Red Cross, the Canadian Army and last but not least, my parents. We had a civil ceremony in a fourteenth-century Gothic hall. It would have been better had we understood the Flemish language. Later in the day we were "churched" in the chapel at the 5th British General Hospital. The drivers of our convoy gave us a beautiful reception at headquarters.

It was while I was stationed in Brugge that we helped the prisoners from Belsen. As each prisoner got off the train, his name was announced on a loud speaker which could be heard throughout the town. We were there with our ambulances to take the prisoners to the hospital. Most of them were young and wore fatigues, but they were so emaciated that you can't imagine what a horrible sight they were. These men looked numb and seemed to drift in a daze. Some were met by their families, while bands played and marched through the town, with effigies of Nazi leaders strung across the street. The celebrating and rejoicings were unbelievable. Although the prisoners were extremely weak, they tried to go along with the mood of the people. One young man stood silently, his arms full of flowers, almost in a trance, while his British mother told us how she had married a Belgian soldier during World War I.

At the end of 1945, I left the unit in Antwerp and returned to England. Although I was on my way home to settle into married life, I had mixed feelings about leaving, since Bill was still in Holland and I would have to leave him behind for the time being. After years of war, it was hard to know what to expect of the future. When you are part of the war effort, you become used to people making all your decisions for you. You just do what you have to do.

I travelled back to Canada on the *Queen Elizabeth*. It was a much shorter voyage this time—just five or six days. We had many Scottish troops on the ship with us and when we entered Halifax harbour we listened to a wonderful performance as the pipers lined the deck and played for us.

Shortly before Christmas I arrived back in Vancouver to meet a new part of my family, for I now had in-laws. After the New Year, Bill also returned home. We hadn't made any plans for our future, so that task was ahead of us. In the meantime we found a small apartment and attempted to settle in. We discovered, however, that we were strangers in our home town. Our old friends had moved away or had not returned from the war. But to our surprise we were soon surrounded by many of our overseas pals who came to live in British Columbia.

What beautiful friendships we formed while we were overseas. I feel that the love, friendship and understanding I gained during the war years is still very precious to me, and I shall be forever grateful to the Red Cross for choosing me to go overseas. I especially treasure the lasting friendships I made with the British Red Cross drivers. When we visit each other, we seem to pick up where we left off at the end of the war.

Grace Maynard

*"You people in the Red Cross
saved our lives"*

—

Grace Maynard and her three sisters were raised in the little town of
Scott, Saskatchewan, a wonderful place in which to grow up. She
was a scholarship student at the University of Saskatchewan in
1939, completing undergraduate and graduate degrees
after the war. A career woman, she also served as a
volunteer in social services and the arts.

I went overseas in January 1945 as part of a team of four who were to visit camps where liberated British Canadian prisoners of war were interviewed. We were to obtain from them their opinions about Canadian Red Cross food parcels as well as other relevant information about the Red Cross services. Margaret Wilson, who later worked in the Canadian Red Cross head office in Toronto, was our leader; the other two women were the late Norma Gershaw, who was sent to southern England to meet Canadian Army personnel, and Joan Magee Campbell who was stationed in Bournemouth and met returning Canadian Air Force personnel. Margaret and I went out to camps where returning British prisoners of war were interviewed. But more of this later.

I left for overseas from Ottawa where I had moved after studying for a year at the University of Sasatchewan. In Ottawa, I worked for the Inspection Board of the United Kingdom and Canada, ending up being concerned with women's working conditions in factories. I lived in an apartment with three other girls, and when one went into the Navy I decided I would go too, even though I was working as a volunteer at night for the Red Cross. After some delays relating to categories of functions which I would perform in the Navy, I joined. Three days later the Red Cross asked me if I would like to go overseas. I had previously put my name forward for a position where public speaking was required, and this experience had appealed to them. Fortunately, I had a friend who knew somebody at the right level of the Navy and I was allowed to resign.

About six weeks later I was in Halifax about to leave for England. The picture of me that accompanies this story was taken in Halifax. It may not be noticeable, but the hat is stuffed with toilet paper to keep it from falling over my ears. It was taken after I had been sightseeing in the city, in the rain, before boarding the banana boat which was hardly big enough to hold twelve Red Cross girls and about ten Merchant Navy captains who were returning to England after their ships had been torpedoed. Other authors of these stories have mentioned walking *down* the gangplank to board their ship. Ours was like that too. We also found that it took sixteen turns on the only deck to make a mile!

We sailed first to New York, met up with a partial convoy, then turned north towards Newfoundland. As part of a large convoy we passed close to the Canary Islands; later I believe we were on the first passenger ship to sail up the English Channel since the war started. Inasmuch as I was seasick most of these three weeks, I missed most of the on-board activities, but I did see that the lounge was criss-crossed with ropes for passengers to hold on to when the ocean was rough. Two ships were torpedoed to starboard.

We were greeted in London and moved into Onslow Gardens, where I went into a freezingly cold dormitory, the end of which had been blown out, and then not too well patched. I would go to bed wearing socks, great coat, long underwear with flannel pyjamas, balaclava, etc. Fortunately two other Red Cross girls asked me to room with them and things greatly improved. Our only warmth was from a "wee" fireplace.

It was common for three of us to have baths in the old-fashioned tub using the same water because there was not enough hot water. We had one egg for breakfast per month. The bombing of London was still continuing, but we were taught that if you could hear the bomb, you obviously had not been hit. We were really quite relaxed about it all, even though we did have drills and retired to the basement at times.

While waiting to interview returning prisoners of war, I was assigned to work in headquarters at Burlington Gardens where a group of us read letters from women who claimed they had given birth to Canadian babies. They were entitled to layettes and, depending upon the certainty of birth, to some financial support. The layettes sent to these women were wonderful; most of the sweaters, leggings, etc., were made by Canadian women. Many of the Red Cross volunteers would work between assignments in the layette department. One met a great many other Canadians through these assignments.

Needless to say, some of the letters were amusing; others were tragic. One amusing letter read something like this: "A Canadian

soldier came to stay at our home, and thanks to him I am pregnant, as is my daughter, but that is not why I write. I want to complain that he stole our bicycle." Probably this type of story is as old
as war itself.

Our headquarters was in the centre of London. On occasion
we would time the activities of the French prostitutes who fre-
quented the area. Our boyfriends, coming to pick us up to go out
to dinner or to the theatre at about 5 p.m., were often accosted by
a French prostitute, but others would quickly intervene, explaining: "No, no, he belongs to the Red Cross."

When the large numbers of prisoners of war started returning
to England, Margaret Wilson and I, who were on the British "detail," would leave early each morning from London to go to the
reception camps. Upon arrival, we would be assigned to a location
about eighth or ninth in the sequence of interviews; the military
naturally took precedence over us.

The questionnaire we had them fill out asked questions such as
"How frequently did you receive food parcels?"—with a space of
about three and a half inches for the answer. For many, this was
sufficient, but for others who had been five years in prison camps
and who might also have been marched across Germany, the
space was clearly not enough. These men wanted to explain that
the parcels had been received regularly during most of the war,
but towards the end, on the marches, this was not so. Many of the
men wanted to tell us about their experiences and I subsequently
received letters from some.

We had been told that we should attempt to standardize conditions under which the questionnaires were answered. This became impossible. One time we might be in half of a bombed-out
airport hanger with some men leaning against the wall. Another
time there might be chairs and tables. Even so, I doubt these different conditions changed the answers significantly.

The questionnaire was four pages long, and there were detailed questions that asked what kind of food the men liked,
whether they liked chocolate better than coffee, etc. It turned out
that what they liked best was Canadian bacon. The men often

used the parcels for bartering or for entertainment, putting on performances by making costumes from the packages. Some of them sent me pictures of the concerts they put on.

We interviewed the prisoners of war from March until July. There were hundreds and hundreds of prisoners of war returning. I remember that they emptied the prisoner of war camps on the Continent quickly and brought the men back by the planeloads. We went down to see some of them land in England. Some were men from Dieppe who hadn't been on British soil for five years. Many of them had had a dreadful time on the death marches, as they called them. The Germans would clear a camp and march them across Germany in order to keep them away from the frontlines.

Victory-in-Europe Day was spent in a camp among former prisoners of war. For many the war had been over for years but there were tears and hugs and much joy. An Irishman came over to me, and we cried together when he said: "If only you knew how you people in the Red Cross saved our lives by sending us food parcels." I was told this over and over again. I felt totally inadequate receiving their thanks, for here I was a young woman overseas conducting interviews when there had been all those women back home knitting socks, gloves, mitts, scarves, sweaters, as well as all the other people who had worked so hard to make sure the parcels were there for the prisoners of war. I was receiving the thanks for them and had contributed so little.

After we completed our assignment, Margaret Wilson compiled the results of the survey in Toronto. I was posted back to headquarters in London and again did a variety of jobs. One involved going to Holland and bringing back Dutch women who were married to Canadians and were over seven months pregnant. I made two such trips. The captain of the ship insisted any baby born on board must be named after him. As well, I helped in the hostels where war brides stayed for several days before continuing their journey to Canada. This "helping out," working in the layette department and performing functions as required, continued until the summer of 1946 when I returned home.

And what were some of the things I learned from this experience? One realization was the ease with which most of the Canadian women had moved among the various "classes" in England. One night I might be sitting on the curb in front of a local pub and the next night, dressed appropriately, dancing at the Astor. So many British people had been taught their "place"; generally we had not. I had read about this in books but had not experienced it until I went overseas.

In addition, I learned something about the breadth of sexual behaviour that was acceptable. As an example, I went with a boyfriend to a country home for a weekend. I was asked if I wanted to sleep with the boyfriend or by myself. This would not have happened at home at that time (or so I think). A similar incident took place one evening when two couples (I was one of the women) were saying goodbye, and the other woman wanted to know if a physician friend who had been her partner for the evening wanted to come home with her. He declined.

I returned to Ottawa and to a life which eventually led to marriage, a divorce, degrees from three universities (Carleton University, the University of Colorado and Stanford University), and a realization that the gods have been generous and I have been lucky (except on the golf course). Now, after a second marriage, I live in Victoria and think this place is wonderful.

I am deeply grateful that I can, at long last, tell the story of the gratitude that the British prisoners of war expressed to the Canadian people who contributed to the Canadian Red Cross parcels during World War II, and the belief of many that their lives were saved because of those parcels.

Edith W. Muttart Sparke

*"I was ready for anything, or
so I thought"*

Edith Sparke was born and raised in Edmonton where she attended
Normal School to become a teacher. She taught for nine years and
then worked as secretary to the president of Union Oil Co. in
Vancouver before joining the Red Cross. In 1952 she married
Richard Sparke, the acting manager of a tea plantation in
India. They returned to Canada in 1955, where she
enjoyed a varied career in teaching, secretarial
work and court reporting until
her retirement.

I shall always be grateful for the new horizons that opened up for me when I joined the Red Cross. Although it took me a long time to make the grade to go overseas, it doesn't matter now as the whole adventure was worthwhile and exciting. I marched in the Beatty Street Armouries, learned to double-clutch 15 cwt. (hundredweight) trucks on the old Vancouver flats, graduated to the streets of Vancouver to drive for the Blood Donor Clinic, learned to read maps for our orientation trips on Sundays, and even drove during the street car strike transporting hospital personnel to and from work for several weeks in dense fog. It was all very challenging.

With all this preparation, we were eager to start for England, but no overseas calls came for what seemed ages, and although we were kept busy at home, we were all eager to leave as soon as possible. Many people at the time questioned whether women should go overseas, but my family supported my decision. My eldest sister Rena, who lived in Vancouver, helped keep up my morale in those long months of waiting. My father had been dead for some time. My mother agreed that I should make my own life. After all, I had already been working away from home for many years. By this time I was self-supporting with a munificent monthly salary of $200.00.

When I was finally called overseas in early 1945, I was ecstatic and made great preparations. I had never been to England and I was ready for anything, or so I thought. I gave up my excellent job with the Union Oil Company, and I also gave up my room (we didn't rent apartments in those days) when I arranged to visit my mother in Edmonton before going overseas.

I had no sooner arrived in Edmonton by train than a wire came from the Vancouver Red Cross to return immediately. There was no reason given. On my return I found to my dismay that the group scheduled to go had been cancelled. I was in shock. I explained the situation to Union Oil, but I had already been replaced. Jobs were scarce at this time and there was no unemployment insurance. Union Oil was sympathetic, however, and placed me in their credit department. It was all very embarrassing, to say the least, and I finally decided to write to Toronto to explain my situation. Three weeks later, word came that I could go—not as a "driver" but as "general duty." By this time I would have gone in any capacity.

I can't remember all the names of the people I went over with at that time, but I know we had a good group and that we travelled on the *Letitia*—travelling southwards towards the Azores to avoid any danger. My only problem was that my main luggage was late in being delivered to Halifax, so I had to leave Canada without it. We arrived at Southampton in approximately three weeks. All I'd had to wear during the crossing, and would have for two months afterwards, were the clothes I had packed in my duffel bag and haversack.

At first I was stationed at Corps House at Queen's Gate in London; then I was assigned to help set up a new hostel in a five-storey London house called Onslow Court. A group of us scrubbed floors and walls, set up beds and made everything ready for the Red Cross girls coming back from the Continent or from other parts of England, either on leave or on their way home to Canada. We served breakfasts, coffee breaks and afternoon teas. Some readers may recall those old British homes with the kitchen and laundry in the basement and the living-room on the second floor. It was in this environment that I had the opportunity to meet and come to know many Red Cross girls.

I recall one fateful day at the hostel when I started to run my bath and decided I had time to have a cup of coffee downstairs. We had been warned never to use more than six inches of water at any time, but the taps were so slow that I didn't worry about taking my time downstairs. I was totally immersed in a lively chat with the others when someone called out that something was leaking badly. I dashed upstairs and, of course, the bath had run over. I was extremely upset but everyone rallied round with sheets and towels from the laundry to help mop up all the water. It had poured down the stairwell from the fifth floor to the bottom floor. What a mess! I was worried for some time that I would receive a reprimand, but I never did.

After working at the hostel for several months, I asked to be transferred. I was finally assigned to the handicraft department at Burlington Gardens, where I taught two two-week handicraft classes—first to a group of British women and later to a group of Dutch women. I taught the British Red Cross women so that they could pass on the skills to others who would be teaching handi-crafts in England. The Dutch Red Cross women became inter-ested in the programme and sent some of their members over to England for instruction. The skills I taught included soft toys, string and woven belts, embroidery, tapestry work, rug-hooking, weaving, leathercraft, slipper-making, glove-making and tooling. It was all very interesting, but not really my forte.

During this time I was one of several Red Cross workers invited for a weekend at Leeming Air Station. We were billeted out and treated like royalty. One of the highlights of our weekend was going for a ride in a Lancaster bomber. The day before our flight we were taken on a tour of the inside of the bomber. The climax came just as I got into the Perspex bubble at the front and was lying flat on my stomach looking out through the bombsight. There was a huge roar overhead and someone said, "There's a Liberator in from Canada." I started to crawl back as fast as I could so that we could see the crew unload. Just as I was going through the doorway, I tripped and fell. My whole left leg was bruised and the inside of my right leg had a large purple bruise. I had to stay in sick bay for the rest of the day, but I was determined not to miss our flying debut scheduled for the following day. None of us had any idea what it would be like to be up in the air. Nevertheless, the following morning we were duly gowned in Mae West suits, and the next thing we knew we were up in the sky. The whole experience was overwhelming. I had never encountered such noise. I was so petrified that I sat frozen in my place until we landed. Despite all this, I was glad to have had the experience, for it gave me a better understanding of what it must have been like for the bomber crew. How they kept their focus under such trying conditions, I do not know.

My next assignment was at Colonel Frost's Office where I did all his secretarial work. Then I became involved in handling R. B. Bennett's correspondence as well. Before he became a Viscount, R. B. Bennett had been Prime Minister of Canada from 1930 to 1935. He was known for his prodigious memory of people and facts on a wide range of subjects. Being a lifelong bachelor, he had ample time for dictating letters and memoranda in his later years. After retiring from Canadian politics in 1938, he moved to England the following year and was made Viscount in 1941. When I started working with him, he was chairman of the Canadian Red Cross Overseas and director of the Coal Board in England, but he no longer had a permanent secretary.

In the beginning I worked only on Fridays, but before long I found myself spending long weekends at Box Hill, Surrey, taking dictation for as long as four hours at a stretch, and having to transcribe the work in my bedroom on an old rickety Underwood typewriter on my dresser. It was a very uncomfortable situation, as I had always been accustomed to using a proper typewriter, desk and chair. Typing under such awkward circumstances may well have helped me later to reach a speed of 240 words per minute as a court reporter. I don't remember all the details of the correspondence, of course, but it was fascinating to learn about the many aspects of the Red Cross all over the world. I saw then how large the organization was and how it coordinated help to many different areas of the world.

I must tell you about the first time I arrived at Lord Bennett's estate on my own, having taken a taxi from the station. The butler opened the door, and I was led through a dark cave-like area with tropical plants, stalactites and stalagmites, and fireflies darting about in the gloom. I was then led into a beautiful, bright foyer with a wide winding Italian staircase. I remember following the butler up this staircase and along a hallway overlooking the foyer, and then into the most gorgeous bedroom I had ever seen. One wall was completely lined with glass drawers of all sizes, all carefully marked with the contents. I was in uniform and my only luggage was my haversack. As soon as the butler left, I dashed to the bathroom which had mirrored walls and oh!—hot water pipes to put the bath towels on. Pure luxury for most of us during wartime.

Later on I discovered a movie theatre, a library lined with books in blue leather bound by the Blind Institute, greenhouses and highland cattle grazing peacefully in the rolling fields beyond the home. Viscount Bennett wrote to people all over the world as well as keeping up his business correspondence. His regular secretary for many years was now preparing the meals because help was very scarce. For me it was a learning experience which has stood me in good stead ever since.

In September 1946, I returned to Canada on the _Mauritania_ with 1,800 war brides heading for Halifax. Since we had no responsibility for the brides, the voyage was quite uneventful until we arrived in Halifax harbour and were trapped in a fog so thick that we couldn't dock for three days. You can imagine how difficult it was for the war brides and their babies; they even ran out of diapers. After we finally docked, I visited relatives on Prince Edward Island before travelling on to Toronto where I stayed with Euphemia Walker. She and I had met while I was in sick bay with my bruised legs and she was there with jaundice. We had become great friends and now her family offered me a position as an executive secretary in their business, York Knitting Mills. Thus my "unfortunate" accident on the bomber was ultimately fortuitous.

As a late arrival overseas, I realize my life was not fraught with the dangers so many of my colleagues encountered. I would have been there if the word had come. At any rate, I feel I was fortunate finally to go to England, and to make friendships that have lasted over these many years. Those friendships and the formation of our Overseas Club that continues to bring us together at meetings and reunions have made all the difference in my life.

Claire Watson Fisher

*"It was quite magical, and
possibly dangerous"*

Claire Watson Fisher was born and raised in Montreal. She was studying
Art History in 1942 when she joined the Red Cross to train as a
nurse's aide. After the war she enjoyed a career as an Art
Consultant, as well as taking on curatorial and
administrative positions in art galleries
in Montreal, Ottawa and Toronto.
She and her husband retired
to Victoria in 1988.

In 1940 when England was alone in the front line, I was deeply affected by a news photo of St. Paul's Cathedral surrounded by flames and reports of heavy damage to the city of London. Having been to a school directed by British teachers where British History was an important subject, I felt especially close to England and wanted very much to be there at that time, to be involved in the war and help in whatever way I could. My father who had emigrated to Canada from England as a young man, understood these sentiments and encouraged me. After considerable thought I joined the Nursing Auxiliary of the Canadian Red Cross in 1942, requesting overseas service.

I trained for a year at two of the major Montreal hospitals and at St. Anne's Military Hospital, eventually becoming a qualified nurse's aide. Following a long waiting period, I left Montreal on November 24, 1944 with a group of Red Cross girls bound for New York and the ship that was to take us to England. We departed with a sense of high adventure, and the account that follows of my experiences overseas is extracted from letters written home from England and France. I believe they reflect the times and the vivid impressions that have lasted to this day.

In New York the American Red Cross arranged for us to be driven directly to our ship. It was tantalizing to glimpse the streets, the tall buildings and the shop windows, knowing that we would not be allowed to spend time in this exciting city which many of us were seeing for the first time. Our ship was the _Rangitiki,_ an old passenger/cargo ship recruited from the Vancouver to New Zealand run. She had seen better days. We were told that the passengers included women and children returning to England, as well as some important personnel. A pilot took us through the submarine nets at the entrance to the harbour and out to sea where we were to join a convoy. It was an impressive sight to watch the convoy form and surround us. There were ships in all directions as far as we could see. In the middle of the convoy, as we were, we felt very safe.

We had been at sea for about a day and were gradually getting used to our crowded quarters when the ship's engines suddenly stopped; there was not a sound. The ships ahead of us disappeared over the horizon, those astern passed us. We were soon alone on a vast empty sea. Following an anxious period, we were informed that one of the engines had broken down and that we were returning to New York for repairs. While we were waiting for some temporary measures to be taken, I took an evening walk on the upper deck. It was a bright moonlit night with a star-studded sky, and our darkened silent ship afloat on a shining sea. It was quite magical, and possibly dangerous.

We were escorted back to New York by a destroyer at very slow speed. On arrival we did not know if we would have permission to disembark. However, after waiting in suspense for some time, we were told that those with relatives or friends in New York could get off. Fortunately I had a family friend living there who I knew would take care of us if necessary.

Without much difficulty, twelve of us found rooms at a hospitality house run by the Salvation Army, and the American Red Cross took charge of us. We were issued passes to the theatre, concerts, movies and radio shows; the most generous hospitality was extended to us by Americans as well as by some Canadians living in New York. The concern for our welfare could not have been greater if we had been shipwrecked. We spent our days exploring the city and enjoying the entertainment offered to us in the evenings.

After eight days spent in New York we were escorted back to the ship on December 7th and set sail again. This time the convoy appeared to be even larger; it was comforting to awaken each morning to see the ships in the same position. During the voyage, we were each responsible for an unaccompanied child and for taking turns to entertain the children in the nursery. In the evenings, we joined the ship's passengers to entertain ourselves by organizing concerts, singsongs, card games and general fun. We arrived in England on December 21st, docking in Liverpool. The crew, as well as some passengers, lined up to wave goodbye and to sing "O Canada," as we were the first to walk down the gangplank. At last I was on British soil and filled with the most intense excitement.

We travelled to London by train and were driven through the city by bus to Onslow Gardens. We spoke in hushed voices as we passed the remains of bombed-out houses, some with staircases still intact and bits of furniture strewn about. We saw many patched windows and buildings with scorched and blackened fronts. It was a foggy, grey, dirty and damaged city, but I immediately fell in love with London. We made the best of the few days before our postings by exploring the city, mostly on foot. We were saddened at the sight of so much damage, not only to homes but to so many buildings of historical significance. There was St. Paul's just as I had seen it in the news photo, but now it was surrounded by gaping pits, the buildings around it completely destroyed. During this week, we got lost in the blackout several times, learned to ignore the buzz bombs, and had a lot of fun with friends who had arrived before us. On Christmas leave, they were able to escort us to their favourite haunts.

On December 29th, Peggy Drysdale, Peggy Eakers and I were posted to Mount Vernon, a British Emergency Medical Service (EMS) hospital in Northwood, Middlesex, just forty minutes from London by underground. The hospital had been expanded to accommodate a thousand beds by the addition of huts built around the main building. The patients were both military and civilian. My first assignment was on an orthopaedic and general surgery ward where the patients were of many nationalities, having belonged to various units—paratroops, the underground, or attached to British or American Armies of liberation. I recall nursing Poles and Russians picked up in Europe; a Dutchman who had been in the underground; a London fire fighter; two old men, victims of a buzz bomb; a taxi driver injured in a London raid; and several British soldiers. One soldier had been an opera singer and serenaded us daily with song; he was very good and brightened our day. The patients and British nurses were friendly and kind to us and did everything they could to make us feel at home. They expressed great interest in Canada, asking many questions about the landscape, the climate and the way of life.

Those who were VADs know that the work was arduous and involved very long hours, alternating drudgery with considerable responsibility for the patients. Since the hospitals were short of domestic help, we were often called upon to dust, sweep and clean the wards, but there was always a laugh at the end of the day to share with my roommate Peg Drysdale as we nursed our aching feet. I enjoyed working with the British nurses, many of whom had lost their homes and families in the raids over England; these young women had a wonderful sense of humour and a simple courage.

Our days at Mount Vernon passed pleasantly although the matron was cold and severe. We got through the blackout by groping our way between the huts at night. We even managed to enjoy the food rationing as we carried around our pots of rationed jam and sugar, often speculating on whether we would have custard and brussel sprouts for the fourth time in a week.

As the end of the war approached, the blackout restrictions were lifted at Mount Vernon. On May 1st, we gleefully took down the black curtains and removed the shatter-proof tape from the windows. There was a rumour that soon a day marking the official end of the war would be announced. Finally we heard on the radio that Victory-in-Europe Day would be on May 8th. By great good luck, Peggy Eakers and I had the day off so we went up to London. It was an incredible sight. People were everywhere, a vast, jostling, good-natured crowd. Flags and bunting hung from the windows in a colourful display. There were bands and impromptu parades, with singing and dancing in the streets—a great feeling of joy and release in the huge crowd milling around us. We confided that we felt a pang of loneliness. We were strangers in this celebration by Londoners who had endured the war for six years, through blackouts, bombings, rationing, fatigue and danger.

We decided to walk through the familiar places—Piccadilly, Trafalgar Square and Westminster, and finally to 10 Downing Street where a large crowd was waiting to hear from Churchill. Then in the afternoon, we heard his eloquent speech announcing the official end of the war. As he finished speaking there was a peal of bells from Westminster Abbey. At dusk we saw the lights of London for the first time in all the familiar streets. We were in front of Buckingham Palace when there was an audible gasp from the crowd as the Palace emerged from the gloom in a sudden blaze of light—it looked like a fairy castle. We went to Trafalgar Square and joined in the dancing with some Canadian servicemen we knew and were able to enjoy our own celebrations of victory. When we returned to Mount Vernon our patients wanted to hear every detail of the celebrations and enjoyed vicariously the tales of our adventure.

In July, as we had requested, Peggy Eakers and I were transferred to Black Notley, an EMS hospital in Braintree, Essex. Our new hospital was further from London, but the atmosphere was more pleasant; the matron was welcoming and often invited us to tea. My first ward was medical; many of the patients had been prisoners of war and were suffering from serious stomach ailments. I spent most of my time in the kitchen as they had to be fed a special diet every few hours. Soon I was dubbed the Diet Queen. The patients often asked about Canada and made a point of telling us how they admired the Canadian soldiers. The ward was always full of jokes and laughter; the men had been there for some time, but their spirits never flagged in spite of their daily diet of baby food. I was assigned to other wards in the next few months, but the first was the most rewarding.

Our contract was to be terminated on December 30th, so we agreed to help with the Christmas festivities. On Christmas Eve, a few of us decorated the ward, making it festive. Then we joined the men in singing some rousing carols. It was fun, as was the next day, one of the best Christmases I have ever had.

At the end of December, I left Black Notley Hospital and returned to London. Having agreed to stay on in England for a few months, I worked in the office at 3 Burlington Gardens, helping with various projects. One day Colonel Frost asked me if I could speak French. I told him that I could, since my mother was French Canadian. He said that a Canadian Red Cross relief project was being considered for Normandy, it being the most familiar area to Canadians because of the battle fought there in 1944, and that a French-speaking person would be required if this concept developed. The idea had first been proposed following General and Madame Vanier's visit to the battle area and their concern for the devastation and the people's suffering. At that time General Vanier was the Canadian ambassador to France.

Early in May, I was asked to accompany Marion Bigelow, also with the Red Cross, to Paris to report on the feasibility of such a relief project. Marion had served as a welfare officer in Italy and Belgium and had been on the Continent for two years during the war. We were asked to formulate a tentative working plan for distribution of supplies, and to make arrangements for office and living accommodation, all of which depended on approval from Canada. In Paris, we contacted Madame Vanier, who was our Red Cross representative. My first impression of Paris was riding in the embassy car with the Canadian flag on the bonnet, Madame Vanier pointing out the various streets and buildings with knowledge and appreciation. It was a very special experience. During the next few days, we met with the president and director of the French Red Cross who were enthusiastic about the proposed project and assigned a liaison officer to accompany us. This person was familiar with Normandy and the needs there.

On May 5th, we began our travels through Normandy where the great battle of Normandy had been fought starting on D-Day, June 6, 1944. It ended in Caen and Falaise three months later, with the closing of the Falaise Gap by the Canadians, British and Americans. During that time, more than forty thousand civilians were killed and countless others wounded, and an area stretching from Cherbourg to Le Havre was devastated by the air, sea and land battles. The route carried us through the "Falaise Gap" battle area, and in spite of the lush green fields and blossoming apple trees, we were moved by the sight of the desolate stark ruins of what had once been peaceful Norman towns and villages. Not one community was intact; there seemed to be ruins everywhere. Many areas were now flattened fields of rubble with only a church spire or a grey stone wall left standing as a grim memorial to its former life.

A street in Caen reduced to ruins by the bombardment.

The majority of these villages now had flimsy prefabricated huts to house people who had lost all their possessions, and as many families as possible were crowded into them. These huts had been sent from five different countries. They varied in size and shape, and those with flat roofs and composition walls had wilted under the rainy Norman climate. We were told that household utensils were in short supply; it was not uncommon for a family of five or ten to have only a few plates and glasses and one cooking pot. Frequently, gorse or boughs were used as mattresses, sheets were rare, and there were no blankets.

We had determined that we should concentrate on the two Departments of Normandy most desperately in need—La Manche and Calvados—and we asked to meet the officials of the French Red Cross in those areas. We were first introduced to the Comtesse de Kergolay who was president of the French Red Cross for the Department of La Manche. The Comtesse's thirteenth-century château had been used as a "mental hospital" following the bombing and destruction of Saint-Lo. The gatehouse on the property was occupied by nuns who had lost their school for orphans, and the stables were used for storing French Red Cross supplies. We were later to see more "mental hospitals" as they were called; they were sheltering and caring for people who had become deranged during the battle for Normandy.

The Comtesse took us to meet the Prefect of La Manche, who told us that of the six hundred communities in his Department, only fourteen remained unscathed. Although there was no real shortage of food, as Normandy is a lush garden, everything else was in short supply, including milk, as livestock had been killed during the battle. We found that the French Red Cross was efficiently organized for distribution of relief supplies through the Departments in Normandy and the cantons, each with a president and chief social welfare nurse, who were aware of the immediate needs. It was evident that this organization would simplify any distribution we were contemplating.

We proceeded to Caen where we were taken to the Château de Villers Bocage to meet the Marquis de Clermont Tonnerre, the president of the French Red Cross for the Department of Calvados. The drive to Villers Bocage, through the area of heaviest battles, was made doubly startling, as we passed through a violent thunderstorm. Battered stumps of trees with their branches stretching out like mutilated limbs lined the roadside. Rusty tanks lay abandoned in the fields or crumpled in the ditch, and here and there a solitary wall was etched against a black sky when flashes of lightning illuminated the scene; the remains of the war surrounded us.

Monsieur de Clermont Tonnerre was to become our faithful friend and advisor; he had the same selfless devotion to his work that we found in many others working in the French Red Cross. His château, which had been spared in the battle, had been converted into a hospital as well as a hospice for the nuns who were nurses there. We heard from others that the Marquis and his three sons ran an ambulance service to their hospital for civilian wounded during the battle. All four were later awarded the Croix de Guerre.

We received very good advice from the Marquis on how we could set up a plan for the proposed depot and handle the shipments from Canada. In Bayeux, the only town in Calvados which had been spared in the battle, we found a house suitable for accommodation. The French Red Cross offered to lend us a 15-ton Ford truck for transport of supplies, and the British Army's town major assured us there would be no difficulty in drawing food rations through their unit. On advice from the French Red Cross and the various social workers we met, the essential supplies required were listed. These were to include household utensils, such as sturdy crockery, glasses, cutlery, cooking pots and pans, as well as layettes, children's clothing, women's clothing, work clothes for men, shoes, blankets and sheets, hospital dressings and supplies, milk and vitamins.

Marion and I wrote a report of our findings and submitted it to Colonel Frost with our recommendations, requesting that special consideration be given to providing clothing for children. We returned to London and awaited approval from Canada. We had not been there very long when we received instructions to leave for France as soon as possible to set up the Canadian Red Cross Civilian Relief Depot in Normandy, to be located in Bayeux.

Marion, who was to be the director, and I, the interpreter and secretary, were joined by Marg Evans who was to be our driver. Marg had been an ambulance driver seconded to the British Red Cross. Both Marion and Marg were from British Columbia. In the months ahead our designated roles were greatly expanded to include much more complex duties.

It was early June when we reached our home and office in Bayeux which was located at 4 rue des Terres, Place du Château, overlooking a small park. The owner had moved back into her house after five years of having it requisitioned to various military units, first to the Germans and then the British. We were told that it had been Montgomery's headquarters for three weeks after the D-Day landings. This lady, Mademoiselle Guilbert, moved all her furniture back into the house and was delighted to be in her own home again after such a long absence; she appeared not to mind sharing it with us. She joined us at most meals, and as she could not speak a work of English, I did my best to translate the conversation.

The house was large, the furniture exquisite Louis XV, and there was a beautiful garden at the back with well-cared-for flower beds. Marg and I shared a large room overlooking the garden; we were awakened in the morning by birdsong and the chimes of the nearby cathedral. We had an excellent cook named Angelle, who worked wonders with the British Army rations. Since there was no heating system, our housekeeper would bring us a jug of hot water for washing each morning.

Our office was at the front of the house overlooking the main street; we had hung the Canadian flag above the front door, and many visitors called to wish us well. We always welcomed the British major, who was the resident officer in charge of the British camp, and who was to give us invaluable help throughout our stay. As a special favour he had a hot bath laid on for us at the camp once a week where we bathed in a Nissen hut, which had a lovely bath and lots of hot water. Most important of all, our British Army friends offered us two five-ton trucks for use when our major shipments arrived. They also gave us the use of the army railway siding at Bayeux.

During the first few weeks, our house seemed to become the British officers' mess, as they were most envious of our lovely quarters. They would come for morning cups of coffee or tea, and for a drink in the evening when we invited them. Mademoiselle Guilbert, a petite woman with sharp eyes, always sat with us in the living-room, busy with her knitting, and would remain there without saying a word until the last person had left. Having observed the steady stream of male visitors, she had set herself up as our chaperone. We tried to curtail these visits as much as possible, since it always meant working long hours into the night to catch up on our work. But it was difficult to draw the line, as we depended on these people for help. However, when the shipments arrived, they did not call on us.

Towards the end of June, a small shipment of supplies was due to arrive in Dieppe to get us started with our distribution. It was agreed that I would go to Dieppe to supervise the unloading of cases and accompany them to Paris by train, there being no direct rail route from Dieppe to Bayeux. Feeling very responsible for these shipments, we had decided that we would stay with them from beginning to end. We were perhaps over-zealous in our determination to prevent any pilfering, but we considered this to be our main responsibility.

While waiting on the dock in Dieppe, I noticed a stone obelisk in a square overlooking the sea not far from the harbour. I walked up to it, and on it were inscribed the names of those who had sailed for New France from this harbour in the seventeenth century. Great excitement—I saw the name of an ancestor on my mother's side of the family—Le Moyne. On seeing this I had a sense of belonging in Normandy; it was a wonderful feeling.

The cases arrived safely and I accompanied them to Paris. There I was met by Marg in the 15-cwt truck we had christened "Annabelle." Marg and I had lunch at the British Officers' Club, and, as luck would have it, met some Canadian officers who asked what we were doing in France. We told them about the job ahead of us, that we had only a two-seater truck to get around in, and that there were three of us. We explained that it was awkward to carry out our advance planning in this way. After listening sympathetically, a colonel offered us his staff car, which he said he no longer needed. It was delivered to Bayeux the following week.

From Paris, Marg and I drove to Bayeux with our first supplies. This route led us through incredible devastation. Everywhere, there were remnants of houses and rubble which had not yet been cleared away. However, the countryside was beautiful at that time of year, and the lush green landscape and fields of red poppies lifted our spirits. I decided that I would try to ignore the ruins surrounding us, as we would be driving through them for several months, and to concentrate instead on the lovely countryside.

The mayor of Bayeux had given us the use of a large warehouse in the centre of town. Checking it, we found it to be secure and stored our first small shipment there. We often included the

Transporting and distributing relief supplies, Normandy, 1946.

mayor in the "official" dinners we sometimes gave in our house, as well as his wife, the presidents of the French Red Cross in the departments we were to serve, and always the town mayor. Through generous loans and interest in our work, we now had at our disposal a staff car, a 15-cwt truck, two large trucks and a warehouse. At last, in late June, we had all the support we needed and were ready to carry out our official work.

In the days ahead, we were to distribute the few supplies that had already arrived, but mainly we were planning the major distribution. We went out every day to visit areas requesting assistance. With the help of the social workers and the French Red Cross, we were able to determine which towns, villages, schools, hospitals or orphanages were most in need. In many cases, we visited families living on farms that had been spared, or living in prefab huts. On these occasions, we were always offered a tot of calvados, a potent Norman liqueur made from apple cider, which we were obliged to accept. This became difficult after the second one, when there were several visits planned, so we devised a discreet way to dispose of the calvados in the back gardens, after the second visit of the morning.

We had now become friends with Stanislas, Monsieur de Clermont Tonnerre's youngest son. Stani, as we called him, was often our guide on these trips, since there were no signposts to guide us, just a criss-cross of roads among the rubble, with here and there a Bailey bridge. We very much enjoyed having him with us as he had a great sense of humour which helped us through these days.

On July 20th, the first big shipment arrived in Rouen for delivery to Bayeux in sealed freight cars. Two Canadian soldiers had been sent out from England to help us organize the warehouse, to guard the crates there and to drive the trucks. The soldiers were sent to Rouen to check the shipment onto the train and accompany it to Bayeux. Here I joined them at the railway siding, and we checked each crate onto our trucks. There were seven hundred crates and we kept our eye on them until they were safely locked in the warehouse; we were determined to assure security at every step. In early August, five hundred more crates arrived. The total value of these two shipments was over two million dollars in today's currency.

The warehouse was now crowded to the ceiling, but was organized in a way to enable us to identify the contents by the markings on the crates. These were stacked in groups according to the nature of the goods contained. The relief supplies were of superior quality; they had been packed with loving care and were exactly as requested. All this work was done by volunteers in Canada; and much of the clothing had been handmade, as well as all the layettes.

Following our visits of the previous month, we had formulated our distribution plan. We had selected a number of strategically placed centres in Calvados and La Manche, which had secure space available, and we shipped a large number of crates to each centre for later distribution. The French Red Cross assumed responsibility for guarding these. In some cases, one or two crates would be delivered directly to a hospital, school, orphanage or shelter. This type of shipment would be handled by our two trucks. The crates in the selected centres would be unpacked and sorted into bundles by French Red Cross volunteers. These would then be delivered by our 15-cwt truck with Marg at the wheel.

All these deliveries had to be worked out on a tight schedule according to need, and then coordinated so that all three of us could be present when the goods were handed out. This had been requested by Madame Vanier, who believed it important that we be personally involved and talk to the people as much as possible. On occasion, I would be called upon to make a speech in French replying to the town mayor's eloquent thanks to Canada for its generosity. The first time I was taken by surprise but did my best to express appropriate sentiments. Later, I memorized a speech composed with the help of Madame Vanier and felt more confident.

During this period, we would go to Paris once a month to report to Madame Vanier. It was a privilege to have known this wonderful woman whose compassion, love and kindness were evident in everything she did. The Vaniers welcomed us into their home in the Canadian embassy and referred to us as their "family." They were a distinguished couple, much loved in France, and great humanitarians. There was a spiritual quality about them which touched us, and a warmth that came from the heart. We always looked forward to these visits.

We were aware that the relief supplies were filling an urgent need. Gifts of flowers were often left on our doorstep, and we received numerous letters of thanks. These would be sent to Canada along with our reports; we hoped those responsible would hear of this appreciation. The expression of thanks always mentioned the special care taken in making and preparing the clothing: for example, a dress would have a pretty brooch attached or a pair of

Marion Bigelow distributing relief supplies, near Caen, 1946.

trousers would be accompanied by a pair of braces.

Monsieur de Clermont Tonnerre, his wife and their three sons always welcomed us into their home in the Château de Villers Bocage. We were often invited for lunch or dinner to meet their friends and share family events. Their château was immense; I think one of the largest in Normandy, and some of the beautiful furniture had been moved back in. They still spoke of war, the battle, the liberation, and Monsieur would tell us sadly that he would never recover from the humiliation of the German occupation. Monsieur once showed me my mother's family name in a rare book listing the names of old Norman families. We felt at home there, and we loved this family for their kindness to us and for their simple courage.

The titled French families of Normandy had been active in the

French Red Cross during the battle. Often their châteaux had been used as hospitals or shelters. They were still involved in the Red Cross and many wore their uniforms. These wonderful people included us in many of their family events and we were always welcomed into their homes. In this way we were fortunate to see some of the lovely old châteaux of Normandy, most of which had been spared during the battle as they were set back from the towns and villages. A few of them became distribution centres when we handed out supplies in the area.

On one occasion we were invited to tea at the Château de St. Come de Fresne. This was the home of the Comte and Comtesse de Berenger and their daughter Antoinette, who became my friend. St. Come is a small village between Arromanches and Courseulles, so on D-Day the Berenger family was in the middle of the landings, the British on one side and the Canadians on the other. The Mulberry Harbour ended at the foot of their property and could be clearly seen from their home. The Mulberry was a pre-fabricated harbour that was towed across the Channel from England and erected at the landing site, providing a road to shore over which the tanks, trucks and equipment were driven. The family had hidden in the woods during the battle. Antoinette, who was a young woman at the time, often spoke to us of those days.

At the time of our stay in Normandy, Monsieur De Berenger was planning a museum as a memorial to the landings at Arromanches and was busy collecting information and photographs. In the meantime, he had assumed the role of official guide to all those who came from abroad to visit the area. The day we were there for tea, he took us on a tour of the beach in the company of some British officers who had been there on D-Day. He showed us where the Mulberry Harbour had joined the beach, which road the tanks had taken and where the troops had swarmed ashore. He also had a telescope, so that as we listened to his vivid descriptions, we could easily envision the whole scene, especially since most of the Mulberry Harbour was still there, as well as rusty equipment strewn on the beach.

One night in Bayeux our house was shaken by a terrific explo-

Title page of collection of thank-you letters from French children to the Canadian Red Cross, 1946 (courtesy of Red Cross Archives).

A thank-you letter from a French child, Colette Guillemot age nine and one-half. (Courtesy of Red Cross Archives).

sion. We thought that a cow or a horse had stepped on a land mine in a nearby field, as sometimes happened. In the morning there were crowds of people on the main street just a step from our house, and police everywhere. A clothing merchant, who had just finished redecorating his shop and had obtained new supplies of material ready for the grand opening, had had his whole shop blown out with a time-bomb, including the windows in the two shops next door and the one across the street. This merchant had been a collaborator during the occupation, having entertained Germans in his home and made deals with them, accumulating a lot of cash, which he was now using to establish his business. He seemed to have no trouble finding merchandise while others in Normandy, who had lost everything, could not find or afford it. We thought the bombing of his shop was an act of vengeance; fortunately no one was hurt.

Our work was at its maximum in August, September and October. Sometimes we would be on the road seven days a week over a period of three weeks. Every day brought a new event, a new person with a story to tell, a new tale of bravery and courage. People wanted to talk to us and seemed to find some kind of release in recalling events of the battle and their part in it. For us, every day was a rich experience.

I recall that on one day we gave out relief supplies to ninety-two families in Villers Bocage which had been almost completely destroyed. As planned, the people came to a distribution centre and we were able to talk with them whenever possible. In this way we also gave out supplies to twelve hundred people in a small town near Rouen. On another day there was a major distribution near Courseulles where the Canadians had landed on D-Day. And so our days went, each one eventful and different from the other. There was always much emotion expressed by the people in the towns and villages where we carried out these distributions, and frequently bouquets of flowers were presented to us.

Our major distributions were often clothing to children. The letters of thanks they sent always touched us. We noted a few of them received from little girls before forwarding them to Canada:

"Long Live Canada, I love Canada and my pretty pink dress. I send many kisses and say thank you," signed by a nine-year-old. "I thank the kind lady who gave me the lovely red river suit," from a little girl aged seven who drew a flower on her letter. "We have lovely dreams in our beds since we have such lovely pyjamas," wrote another child aged ten.

One day, Marion and I went to a small community outside Le Havre to visit an orphanage where there were over a hundred children, to give them supplies of clothing, bedding, milk and vitamins. The children had set up long tables under the trees and invited us to a picnic. As we approached, they all stood up, grinned, and sang a verse of "O Canada," then presented us with a bouquet of flowers. It was a happy day; we were touched by the children who were so endearing. The director told us that he and the children had lived in a barn for two months during the battle. Once, when an Allied plane had crashed in a nearby wood, some of the children had taken the bodies before the Germans could get there, wrapped them in the parachutes and buried them in a secret place, marking the graves and tending them with flowers.

The quantity of supplies which had been sent from Canada enabled us to benefit entire institutions as well as individuals. We were able to assist the Institute Lemonier, where two hundred boys were being taught a trade and receiving their schooling. This institute had been in the target area for aerial bombardment and shelling from the sea during the battle for Caen. The building was demolished, but the boys and their teachers were rebuilding it when we were there. Fortunately we were able to outfit all the boys as well as provide bedding for them.

We also gave to many of the refugees who were living in crowded quarters in Bayeux. They had lost everything, but were fortunate to find room in the one town in Calvados that had been spared. As it was not possible to give to all of them, we gave clothing mainly to the children sheltering in our town.

During our time in Bayeux there were occasional diversions to alleviate the difficult days on the road. On a late summer day, we were invited to a wedding in the small town of Canisy. The bride

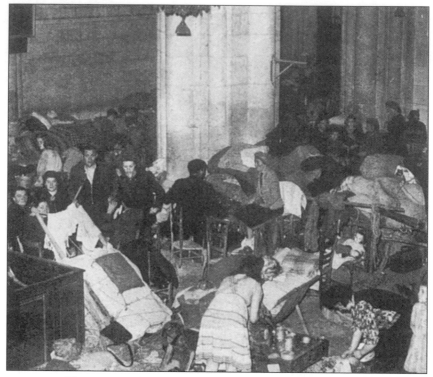

_The interior of the church of S. Etienne. Some 1,500 people found
refuge here after losing their homes in the bombardment._

was the daughter of the Comtesse de Kergolay of Saint-Lo. Saint-Lo had been destroyed during the battle, so the wedding was to be held in Canisy. The bride wore a simple white gown and rode through the streets of the village in a horse-drawn carriage. Her groom rode on horseback preceded by four men wearing colourful costumes, also on horseback. They rode along the main street, followed by the villagers, all two hundred of them on foot. The bride had eight attendants—four little girls in white and four little boys in red velvet. The Bishop of Coutances came to marry them in the tiny church, followed by a civil service in the town hall. After the ceremony, we, as well as all the villagers, were invited to the reception at the Chateau of Saint-Lo, where we were served champagne and chocolate éclairs.

In contrast to this, we were invited on another occasion to the wedding of the Mayor of Bayeux's daughter. The wedding took place in Bayeux Cathedral, which was crowded with society people from Paris and the noblesse of Calvados. The bride wore a beautiful gown fashioned by a Paris couturier, and she had eight attendants wearing elegant gowns. After the ceremony, the mayor gave a reception in the town hall, complete with a lavish display of black market food and liquor. We thought the simpler wedding had been more fun.

We also entertained in our house in Bayeux when the occasion arose. Mademoiselle Guilbert, who had lived in Normandy all her life, knew a great many people in the country, and would sometimes bring home wonderful farm produce to share with us. On one such occasion, we gave a dinner party, knowing Angelle would prepare a gourmet meal with this new supply of fresh food. We invited the Prefect of Calvados, the Marquis and their wives. Mademoiselle Guilbert provided some fine wines. The Guilbert family was known in the town to have a famous cellar of vintage wines, and during the German occupation, Mademoiselle Guilbert had buried it in nearby farmland. The wine was returned to her home, along with the furniture, before our arrival in Bayeux. It was a gracious gesture on her part to offer it to us, and needless to say, our dinner party was a great success.

In August we heard that our Prime Minister, Mackenzie King, was in France visiting the battle area of Normandy where the Canadians had fought, as well as the Canadian cemeteries. He was in Bayeux on August 11th, and we were invited to attend the official lunch on that day which was held in the town hall. We were placed at the head table, and I was seated directly opposite Mr. King, as I was expected to translate the conversation. My memory of him is that he was quite affable, his sharp blue eyes darting about the room, and he occasionally asked a question about someone he had noticed. He also asked about our work in Normandy.

After lunch, we were told that Mr. King wanted to visit our working place, which was an event we had not expected. We had lent our Canadian flag to the town hall for the occasion and it was draped over the front balcony. I thought we would surely need it for this honoured visit. As the guests left the table, we agreed that Marion and Marg would rush back to the house to tidy up a bit, and I would bring the flag. With the help of the waiter, I managed to retrieve it from the balcony. I wrapped it under my arm and ran through the streets to our house just in time to raise it in front of the door as several official vehicles drew up.

Our entrance hall was soon filled with people milling about the Prime Minister: his aides; Brooke Claxton, the Minister of Health; the Military Attaché; and several gendarmes. We wondered why they had come since there was not much to see. Fortunately, there was a large map of Normandy in our office with all the distribution centres pinpointed in red. They showed interest in this, so Marion gave a brief resumé of our work. Then Mr. King had his picture taken with us and they left. It had all taken place in about ten minutes. We thought it was a very politic gesture on their part and hoped we had not disappointed them.

One morning we were surprised on awakening to find a bivouac of tents in the park in front of our house. A representation of the 69th Brigade had arrived from Germany to take part in a ceremony in Bayeux Cathedral. This British unit was the first to enter Bayeux on June 7, 1944, and therefore became the first to liberate a town in France. As the men were not provided with many conveniences, our kitchen was soon crowded to the doors with men who had come to fetch shaving water or to press their trousers. Needless to say, Angelle had been hanging out the window to observe this collection of tents and activity in the park. Our house, with the flag over the door, stood out on the street, and soon the officers called on us. It was interesting to talk to them and to find out their reactions on returning to Normandy. They invited us to attend the ceremony that was to honour the men who had died in the battle. The cathedral was hung with regimental flags and banners, the bishop, in his fine robes, led the service, and there was magnificent choral singing. It was an honour to be there. A plaque was unveiled with a speech and a special prayer, and we then attended another service in the cemetery outside Bayeux where there were five thousand British graves.

In the evening we gave a party for the officers, inviting Antoinette and our other women friends in the French Red Cross. We all had a wonderful time; Mademoiselle Guilbert stayed with us as usual and knitted a long scarf that evening.

During our stay in Bayeux, there had been a number of Normandy-Canada ceremonies in various towns to honour the Canadians who had liberated them. Since there were very few Canadians left in the area, we were always invited to attend. We had been too busy to accept these invitations, but decided that we should attend the ceremony taking place at Graye sur Mer, as this was close to one of the main Canadian landing beaches.

We thought we had been invited as observers of the celebration, but to our astonishment found that we were the Canadian delegation, and of course expected to participate. The population of about two hundred had been awaiting our arrival. They formed a parade, headed by the band and the firemen in their brass hats, the women in their lovely Norman costumes with exquisite lace hats and brocade jackets, and several boys holding standards with banners and flags. We were placed in the front of the parade, which led us to the church. Here we attended a two-hour high mass complete with organ and violin music and lovely singing. There was a moving sermon extolling the bravery of the Canadians.

After mass, we lined up again in the streets and marched to the nearby beach. This time the priest in his colourful robes and the altar boys accompanied us. When we had reached the beach, Colonel Livrey Laval, an extraordinary Frenchman who had a distinguished war career, gave an eloquent and moving speech praising Canada's war effort and calling us the most stable country in the world. When he had finished, the priest blessed a wooden cross, which had been festooned with flowers, and we were ushered into an amphibious tank. The engine roared, we trundled down the beach and quite some distance out to sea. The colonel handed the wooden cross to Marion and she threw it on the sea over the watery graves.

As the flowers floated away, we circled back towards the beach. It was an extraordinary sight to see the Mulberry Harbour in the distance, while in front of us on the beach were the priest in his colourful robes, holding aloft a cross, the women in their beautiful costumes, and the crowd waiting silently for our return. When we had landed, the crowd sang "O Canada" and the "Marseillaise." We then went to the cenotaph where a wreath was laid, there were more speeches by the mayor, and the Canadian flag was hoisted. I felt a responsibility to respond to all this eloquence; fortunately I was able to adapt my speech to the occasion. Then we again marched through the streets in parade formation to a centre where a lavish banquet lasting two hours was served. This was followed by a visit to the local museum where there were a few relics and photos of the landings. Finally, we drove home feeling just a bit weary.

During the celebration, I had met the daughter of Colonel Livrey Laval. She was a lovely girl about twenty-five years old, who during the war, had been an agent in the Resistance. She lived at her father's home, the Château d' Audrieu, where nineteen Canadian airmen, prisoners of war, had been deliberately shot by the Germans. This became a "cause" in the annals of war crime and was still being investigated when we were there. Mackenzie King made a special visit to the château when he was in Normandy and unveiled a plaque to their memory.

The young girl who had witnessed the mass murder was caught trying to escape with the information and was deported to Buchenwald where she remained for over a year. She was liberated by the Russians, but was ill treated and escaped to France. She had a calm, serene manner and a sweet, lovely face; it was difficult to imagine that she had experienced such a traumatic event.

We were invited to attend a ceremony in Paris on November 7th in the Hôtel des Invalides, the site of Napoleon's tomb. This was a very moving experience as we were among a large group of people, over three hundred, receiving various decorations for service to France. There were Americans and British; we three were the only Canadians. Many of those present had been in the Resistance movement or active workers in the Red Cross. The ambassadors of the United States and Great Britain were present, as were General and Madame Vanier. There was martial music and a parade of flags. Marion was awarded the silver medal of the French Red Cross, and Marg and I were each awarded the bronze medal; "en temoignage de reconaissance" was inscribed on the document they gave us.

It was a bitter cold day, and after the ceremony, the Vaniers invited us back to the embassy for a warm drink and to review the day's events. We confided that we felt somewhat unworthy to have been among those receiving the croix de guerre for acts of bravery and courage. However, we agreed that we would consider our decorations to be a symbolic gesture of thanks to Canada for the quantity and quality of the relief supplics distributed in Normandy. We hoped that those in Canada who were responsible for the shipments would hear of this appreciation.

As December came to an end, it was time to leave. The warehouse was empty, the vehicles returned and our reports completed. On reflection, we agreed that our duties had been varied. Apart from the main task of personally distributing the relief supplies, our office had been an information centre and our home a haven. We had acted as social workers, official hostesses to visiting dignitaries, and had been Canadian representatives at official functions in Bayeux and other parts of Normandy.

Marion had faced all the surprising events we encountered with a calm manner and solved the many problems that came our way with wisdom and practical good sense. Marg had approached each task with gusto and a sense of humour, and delighted us with her infectious laugh. We were all three quite different in personality and style, but we complemented each other and had worked in harmony. Together we had faced a challenge and succeeded with the help of many people and the encouragement of Madame Vanier.

A farewell party was given for us and we said goodbye to our friends, the French and the British. Finally, we wanted to say farewell to our own countrymen. So we ordered a large floral wreath and took it to the Canadian Military Cemetery at Bretteville sur L'Aize.

I remember most vividly that it was a cold, grey, drizzly day. The cemetery looked bleak, a vast burial ground with white crosses as far as we could see, stretching over the horizon, the Canadian flag a bright red against the dark sky. The three of us were quite alone as we placed the wreath on the monument. The ribbon band on the wreath read "From the Canadian Red Cross—In Loving Memory." And so we left Normandy.

In May 1983, I went on a trip to France with my husband, my sister and brother-in-law, spending a week in Normandy where I had worked with Marion and Marg. We found our house in Bayeux; the street name had been changed to Place Charles de Gaulle, and a neighbour told me that Mademoiselle Guilbert had passed away. There were children playing under the trees in the park in front of the house where, in our time, there had been barren ground and military vehicles.

We walked along the cliffs overlooking the landing beaches: the Mulberry Harbour was gone, the sea calm; it looked quite different. We then visited the war museum in Arromanches where there was a large diorama depicting the British landings, with a model of the Mulberry Harbour, numerous charts, maps, photographs, and an excellent film. We later visited my friend, Antoinette, with whom I had corresponded for thirty years. The Château of St. Come had been sold; she now lived in a cottage on the edge of the estate. Here we were offered a wonderful lunch with champagne to toast our reunion, and a special toast to the memory of Marion and Marg, now both deceased.

Antoinette had been curator for twenty-five years in the museum at Arromanches and chief hostess when important visitors came, among them Queen Elizabeth II and Prince Philip. She told us of her acute embarrassment when Lord Mountbatten, one of the planners of D-Day visited the museum and was cornered by a local official who explained to him in great detail the strategy of the D-Day landings. On her retirement, Antoinette was awarded the Order of the British Empire by Britain, a special honour to a noncitizen; she displayed it with great pride. My friend's life had been filled with memories of war—as a young woman in the midst of the battle for Normandy, later in the French Red Cross, and finally as curator of the war museum.

We visited the Canadian cemetery at Breteville sur L'Aize. The grass was now a lush green. The crosses had been replaced by engraved headstones. There were flowers among the headstones, and it was evident that the cemetery was being tended with loving care.

Later we spent time in Caen, which had been completely rebuilt with local stone, giving it a golden glow. It was a masterpiece of reconstruction, following the original plan, and was now an elegant, bustling city risen like a phoenix from the ruins I remembered. We found lovely tree-lined squares and charming parks and an avenue lined by maple trees called Rue du Canada. Antoinette had told the archivist in Caen that I was in Normandy, and the archivist asked to interview me. Mainly it was to describe my impressions of the new city. This lady, who had always lived in Caen, told me she had lost her grandfather, her father and her husband to war. She said they were planning to open a museum in Caen in about five years to commemorate the battle for Normandy. I told her that on our travels through Normandy, we noticed that there were a number of young people visiting the battle area, possibly students, who had come to see where their fathers and other family members had fought in the war.

We had dinner in the Château d' Audrieu, which was now a three-star restaurant run by the former Mademoiselle Livrey Laval and her husband. Later, while walking in the grounds, we saw the plaque commemorating the airmen who had died there.

I had contacted Stani de Clermont Tonnerre, and my husband and I were invited to have coffee with him at the Château de Villers Bocage. Stani and I spoke together as if there had not been a passage of time, remembering the days when he had been our guide, and the happy times spent with his mother and father. Stani told me he still had the jeans given to him by the Canadian Red Cross in 1946. He was now mayor of Villers Bocage, which had also been completely rebuilt from the local stone, but in modern style. Stani was able to carry out his duties as mayor as well as manage the estate. It was a wonderful reunion.

In 1988, I was invited by the mayor of Caen to be present on June 6th at the official inauguration of the museum to commemorate the Battle of Normandy. Official representatives of Canada, the United States and all the Allied European countries had been invited as well as those from East and West Germany, Japan and the USSR. The invitation included representatives from all the regiments that had taken part in the battle, and citizens who had known Caen.

I could not attend, but I hoped that my friends whose memories of war filled much of their lives, would be there—Antoinette, Stani, Mademoiselle Livrey Laval and the lady archivist. The museum was to be called "MEMORIAL DE LA BATAILLE DE NORMANDIE — UN MUSEE POUR LA PAIX." Today it is simply called "Le Memorial," and it has special significance for all Canadians.

Dorothea Powell Wiens

*"My year in Japan and Korea was
an incredible, unforgettable experience"*

—

Dorothea (Powell) Wiens was born in Cranbrook, B.C. and grew up
in Creston, B.C. By 1950 she had earned a B.A. and B.S.W. from
the University of British Columbia. From 1950 to 1953 she
was the Director of Recreation for the Ontario CNIB
(Canadian National Institute for the Blind), after
which she went to Korea with the Canadian Red
Cross. She married in 1956 and has enjoyed
various overseas postings with her husband
and a career in social work in Canada.

In contrast to the Red Cross women who served in World War II, my memories are not of bombs and blackouts but more resemble the picture created by the television series *M*A*S*H,* as my service was in Korea and Japan. The movie was surprisingly realistic and brought back poignant and humorous memories to me and my husband, who also served at the "sharp end," as Korea was called by people who were posted there.

At the end of the Korean war on July 27, 1953, the armistice agreement established a demilitarized zone between the north and the south of the country at the 38th parallel. It was clear to the United Nations, however, that peace would not be maintained without surveillance of North Korea. As a result, one of the earliest of the United Nations' peace keeping efforts commenced. Many nations took part in this mission, including Britain, Australia, the United States, New Zealand and Canada. Most of the troops were stationed along the southern edge of the demilitarized zone.

The Canadian military, concerned about the morale of their troops guarding the zone, asked the Canadian Red Cross, which previously had a number of Red Cross workers in service hospitals during the war, to send a team of young women to the Far East for service in recreation facilities in Japan and Korea. These women, some from within Red Cross ranks and some from other areas, were carefully chosen and screened and were expected to observe a strict code of behaviour and deportment, strict even for that era. Most of the Red Cross team was deployed at servicemen's clubs and "R & R" (rest and recreation) centres in Japan, but a lucky few of us were also posted in Korea to the 25th Brigade headquarters at the demilitarized zone. There the Red Cross workers lived at the headquarters and worked at Maple Leaf Park, a recreation complex containing a 700-seat theatre, a large recreation Quonset hut, mess tents and administrative services. The complex was manned by a small detachment of officers and men who lived in tents on the premises. It was used by thousands of servicemen who came for a few hours at a time when off duty from their nearby military units in the field.

From 1953 to 1955 there were approximately twenty Red Cross

women in the Far East at any given time. Although selected by the Red Cross and deployed by them to the various areas, the military paid our salaries and we were responsible to them as well as to the Red Cross. We were given the rank of second lieutenant, since the military believed we might be better protected as officers if taken prisoner by the North Koreans. Our salaries were small but meals and accommodation were provided. Our tour of duty was one year, the same as that of the servicemen, so there was a steady flow of departures and replacements. My service, first in Japan and then Korea, was from February 1954 to March 1955.

I have sometimes been asked why I decided to go to the Far East. There were several reasons. An erudite friend, a psychiatrist by profession, once told me that I went to Asia because my mother had nursed in Salonica during World War I, and growing up with her stories of hardships and challenges had inspired me to try to do something similar in my own era. But there were other reasons. I went because the job promised to be a unique experience and a rare opportunity for a young Canadian woman. I went because I had, a couple of years previously, hitchhiked around Europe and I thought it would be interesting to compare and contrast the civilization and culture of Europe with that of the Far East. I went because I was a little fearful of committing myself to a year of experience so different from anything I had known, and I wanted to challenge that fear. More importantly, I went because I was told that there was a need for social workers to counsel, listen to and bring a touch of home to lonely young Canadian servicemen who, with the less demanding requirements of peacekeeping duties, had more time to think and worry about home and family than if a war were in progress.

My tour of duty began with a couple of days of rest and briefing in Tokyo. I was posted to a military complex on the outskirts of the small village of Hiro, located in the southern part of Japan's largest island, Honshu, near Kure, a large Japanese Naval base during World War II. A building in the Canadian military complex in Hiro was designated for recreation; it serviced soldiers on leave from Korea as well as those based locally. We were housed in a spacious "dorm" type of building, each with our own large room. Our "Girl Sans," as the Japanese women who served us were called, kept our rooms immaculate, put beautiful fresh flower arrangements in them daily and washed or pressed our clothes, even if we had worn some for a only a few minutes. They were happy, laughing, wonderful women; we became very fond of them and they of us. The Red Cross staff of five was responsible for planning and executing programmes which ranged from dances and social events to crafts and servicing a small library of Canadian newspapers and periodicals. The job also included talking with, and counselling, those soldiers who had concerns about family members and girlfriends at home, and helping to deal with the heartbreak of the many who received "Dear John" letters. It also included a form of marriage counselling.

Some of the soldiers wanted to marry Japanese women and bring them back to Canada. I found it extremely interesting and rewarding, as the social worker and area supervisor, to be involved in working with a serviceman and his bride-to-be for six months prior to their marriage. I believe that Canada's handling of the situation was superior to that of other countries, some of which allowed an immediate marriage with no counselling, while others refused permission absolutely. Canadian policy required that the serviceman and his fiancée have monthly interviews, some together, some separately, with the Red Cross social worker and the padre over a period of six months. At the end of that time, regardless of the recommendation of the social worker or padre, the couple was permitted to marry and to receive all military benefits of a married soldier, provided that the bride-to-be met certain medical requirements. Although the recommendations carried no weight, the six-month counselling requirement allowed either party time to change his or her mind; it also allowed the social worker to have some small part in discouraging marriages that might have been disastrous. In addition, it helped more stable couples to address and work through their problems so that their marriages might be successful.

Many of the women, who were interviewed with the assistance

of an interpreter, had a rosy, unrealistic picture of Canada and were due for a rude awakening. One example comes to mind: a young woman who was the well-educated daughter of a diplomat, trained in music and the arts. Her family had all been killed in the war, and she saw marriage to a Canadian as an escape from her difficult situation. The soldier she was engaged to marry had very little education. In Canada he lived with his parents, brothers and sisters and their children in a one-room house in the middle of nowhere. Fortunately in this case the Japanese fiancée decided against the proposed marriage.

In Japan I and the other Red Cross workers enjoyed relative freedom on days off. We were able to travel and see the country, visit our counterparts in Tokyo who served at the popular Maple Leaf Club there, enjoy the beautiful city of Kyoto, and explore and shop in our own local area. We were also allowed to visit Japanese homes to get to know the local people. We learned their customs, which included the removal of shoes at the door, eating with chopsticks, and sleeping on tatami mats (little futons) on the floor, separated from the rest of the house by lovely bamboo or ornately painted rice paper screens. We made a less pleasant outing to nearby Hiroshima. There was still no growth for miles around the area where the bomb had been dropped. Standing stark and cold in the midst of it was a large stone building, a memorial to the approximately 92,000 who died or were disabled for life. My feelings were much the same as those aroused by looking at Dachau or Auschwitz. Absolute horror. How could human beings treat other human beings in such a way?

Japan was a beautiful and gentle country, scenically and in atmosphere. We saw happy, playful children; proud, devoted parents; graceful, kimono-clad women; beautiful gardens and flower arrangements. It was difficult to imagine war in this environment.

My next seven months, which were spent in Korea as supervisor of a team of five workers, was a contrast in all respects. One could certainly imagine war and observe many of its after-effects. The country was not gentle like Japan, but harsh and rugged with spectacular, forbidding mountains and an austere landscape. I was flown over in a small military transport plane; as I sat in a hammock-type seat, frozen, despite wearing a military-issue parka and everything else I owned, I knew I was beginning another adventure.

We were met in Seoul and driven sixty miles north to the Canadian Brigade headquarters. It was just south of the DMZ (demilitarized zone) and nearly within shouting distance of the North Korean guns which guarded it to the north, as our guns did to the south. As we drove along, the driver pointed out our approach to "Death Valley" where the Gloucesters, a British Regiment, had been ambushed and suffered an enormous loss of life. Curiously, I had already sensed an ominous, sombre atmosphere as the jeep approached that deep ravine where so many were trapped and killed.

Arriving at my destination covered with a quarter inch of dust, I found that my abode was to be a double Quonset hut where five Red Cross girls occupied one side and three Korean girls, our domestics, occupied the other. There was a kitchen, a bathroom of sorts and a breezeway in between. It was far from elaborate but comfortable enough. The bathtub was not like home as there were no taps. There was a drain, however, and the Korean girls supplied water for the tub from buckets so one could wash off the dust. Washing one's hair was more difficult and it was not long before I asked a young soldier, who had been a barber on "civvy street," to do away with my long locks and give me a pixie cut. He did a good job. Since the bathroom did not contain a toilet, the soldiers were regularly amused to see Red Cross girls in an amazing array of warm clothing trekking out in sub-zero temperature to the outhouse.

The weather in Korea was in sharp contrast to Japan: freezing cold in winter, hot and very humid in summer, sheets of rain during the monsoons. For short periods in between it was glorious, particularly in the fall when the colours rivalled even those of eastern Canada and the red and green landscape stretched as far as the eye could see.

Compared with the relative freedom of movement permitted

in Japan, the Korean situation was rather like a prison. We were allowed to go nowhere, except with our own jeep and driver on assignments. We were not even allowed to go for walks, since the area was still mined. We were invited to, and attended, formal military functions where we were the only women present, but we did not go to dances (there were none) and did not date the servicemen. Our duties took us from our base only on rare occasions, such as when we were seeing troops off for Canada at the west coast seaport of Inchon.

Every few months we were permitted an overnight stay in Seoul. This brief vacation was strictly controlled by the military. An officer escort was mandatory; accommodation for the Red Cross worker was assigned, not chosen by her, and the officer escort was billeted elsewhere. We were allowed to choose our own escort, and there was much competition among the officers for the privilege, as they also had few opportunities to escape the base. I had two or three such trips, choosing as my escort an officer who was not only reliable in every sense but lots of fun as well. I recall us laughing and singing all the way to Seoul on those occasions and enjoying dinner and dancing at a local hotel.

We did not meet the Korean people to the same extent that we met the Japanese. The area in which we were serving was considered a war zone and, except for the few employed at Brigade headquarters and at Maple Leaf Park, all Koreans had been evacuated from the environs of the demilitarized zone. Those few Koreans we did know were friendly, laughing, happy people, covering well the heartache of lost homes, lost families, lost children and husbands listed as "whereabouts unknown."

Our job was also quite different from our job in Japan. Certainly it was more challenging, since morale was worse in Korea and soldiers serving there felt more isolated. There was no possibility of planning dances or mixed social events since there were no local people nearby. There were no marriages and no marriage counselling for the same reason. We put together what programmes we could, and the men enjoyed card games, ping-pong, Canadian reading material, crafts and gatherings to celebrate all manner of occasions. Our Red Cross craft specialists did a wonderful job in that area with men who had hitherto thought crafts were "sissy" activities. We celebrated birthdays, Christmas, repatriation and any special occasion with zeal, imagination and a wealth of ingenious, made-on-the-spot equipment and decorations.

All of our Red Cross work time was spent at the recreation centre where, at all times, there would be four or five of the Red Cross team present. The girls put in long hours because they loved the work and there was very little else to do. There would be about a hundred soldiers at any given time and, while it would seem impossible with this ratio to think in terms of a one-to-one listening counselling situation, this indeed happened. Most of my time was spent dealing with low morale, uncertainties, domestic concerns and homesickness of young men, many of whom were not yet twenty years of age. It was important just to be there socially with the men and talk about anything they wanted to talk about. If there was a serious illness in the family of one of the soldiers—a wife for example—I could let the Red Cross in Canada know that this man was worried about his family. They would check out the situation and, if it was necessary, he could be sent home.

One of the more dramatic incidents of the tour in Korea happened when a gun-happy Korean shot at the jeep in which I was a passenger. There was a sharp sound and I thought a rock had bounced off the jeep, but my officer escort took off in a cloud of dust as a bullet hit the fender. On another occasion a Korean guard stopped the jeep and asked my officer escort, "How much for the girl?" The officer had difficulty containing his mirth long enough to get the point across that a Red Cross girl's "services" were "not for sale" and, indeed, her services in the area he had in mind were available to no one, at any price. We all had a chuckle over that.

But less funny was an event that could have been disastrous. It was mid-December and, always late with my Christmas cards, I had at two o'clock in the morning just written the last one. As I took my slippers off in preparation for bed I was astonished to find the floor was hot. It was sub-zero weather and, as the Quonset hut sat

Red Cross staff, Korea, September 1954. Dorothea is second from right.

above the ground on blocks, the floors were usually ice cold. Looking up, I saw flames licking along the outer wall of my room and realized a fire was raging underneath the building that could very rapidly destroy both huts. I awoke our girls, who quickly evacuated the hut, carrying an intriguing assortment of their most precious and easy-to-reach belongings. For one, her camera and photos were the most important; for another, an early Christmas parcel from home; for yet another, letters and photos from her family in Canada.

I had no time to think of what to take with me, going immediately to phone in the alarm to the camp below and to wake up the Korean domestics in the adjoining hut. As the siren wailed in the camp below we huddled together, teeth chattering, talking about the treasures from our travels that we had left inside. The soldiers were on the spot in record time, however. Our treasures were saved and we were allowed to re-enter our damaged but welcoming abode.

So, although no war raged, there were moments of excitement

and times of tension. There was a real sense of contribution in an area of need. It was challenging, exciting, fascinating and heart-warming. For anyone interested in psychology and in people, as I was, it was a great learning experience, since I mixed with, and came to know, Japanese, Koreans, Kiwis, Brits as well as Canadians from all walks of life and all parts of the country. It was a learning experience also in working with an army on foreign soil in a war-torn country, watching military maneuvers and observing an army installation in a war zone. There was a real sense of poignancy, seeing ecstatic young men homeward bound waving from their vehicles. There was sadness for the losses and trauma suffered by the Korean people. There was knowledge gained of two very different Far East cultures. There was the feeling of warmth and affection for a multitude of conscientious, courageous, humorous, fun-loving, serious, charming young men serving their country abroad, making me feel proud and humble to be their compatriot. And there are all the memories, wonderful memories that now seem a dream, of a time and place long ago and far away. In short, my year in Japan and Korea was an incredible, unforgettable experience.

Yes, the rewards were many and, through the mysterious marvel of serendipity, not the least rewarding aspect of the year abroad was meeting my husband-to-be, my favourite officer escort with whom I have continued to enjoy the adventures of life for the past four decades. We have two delightful daughters who also have wandered the globe—Europe, India, Japan, the Caribbean, Mexico, Alaska, Australia—but never with greater enthusiasm, challenge and enjoyment than did I in Japan and Korea.

Florence Bell

*"Quite suddenly I was
whisked off to Korea"*

—

Florence Bell was born in the USA and moved to Montreal at the age of
three. She received her B.A. from McGill University and then in 1941
her Social Work Diploma from U.B.C., after which she worked with
the Children's Aid Society of Ottawa. During WW II she worked
for the Department of National Defence, and afterwards with
the Department of Veterans Affairs. On returning
from her posting in Korea, she worked
with the Social Planning Council
of Metropolitan Toronto.

After I received my Master of Social Work at the University of Chicago in 1954, I attended an international conference in Toronto where I had a number of pre-arranged interviews for positions of senior responsibility in social work. These were mainly executive directorships of small agencies or branch operations of national organizations. It turned out that they had a specific rather than a generalized focus and this didn't appeal to me. I was rather discouraged about what was available. In voicing this to a social work colleague from my days at the Department of Veteran Affairs, she told me that the Red Cross had organized a team of social workers and other professionals to provide recreational activities and other services to the troops in South Korea. The war was over by this time, and these men were no longer engaged in combat in Korea but were awaiting orders to return to Canada. In the meantime, they were supervising the orderly takeover of their positions by troops from the Republic of South Korea. Social work in Korea sounded very much more to my liking, and although it did not appear to have anything to do with professional advancement, it sounded like fun. I asked how to make an application and proceeded to apply that very day.

The Red Cross practically guaranteed that I would be accepted because they had not had many people with my lengthy experience and a degree in social work. They were also happy to hear that I had been president of International House in Chicago while a post-graduate student in the School of Social Service Administration, since this kind of leadership was one of the things they were looking for. In negotiating our arrangements, I advised them that I planned to visit my family in Vancouver where my mother as well as my sister and her family were living. I was assured that this would not be a problem since they would not be sending anyone to Korea or Japan until September. I could have all my shots done in Vancouver at the Military Medical Centre, and when the Red Cross knew the date of departure, they would pay for my return to Toronto where I would receive my uniform and have an orientation session prior to departure.

While in Vancouver, I heard from the Red Cross, but it was to tell me that they would not be sending me after all because all the troops would be returning in the near future. This was very disappointing—I couldn't believe it. However, I told them I would have to travel back east in any case because there were more employment opportunities there than in the west and I would do so at my own expense. First I returned to Kingston and gave the Red Cross my address in case there should be any change in plans. Then I went off to Ottawa to various interviews. On the day I returned to Kingston, my landlady met me in great excitement and told me to phone the Red Cross in Toronto immediately as they had been trying to reach me. They had said that unless I phoned them before four o'clock, there wasn't any point in calling them back. Naturally I phoned them right away and found out that one of the people they had planned to send had withdrawn because she had become engaged to be married. The Red Cross wanted to send me in her place because I had my passport, all my shots and could be at their headquarters by nine o'clock the next morning.

As you can imagine, this took some doing. It was already after the bank's closing hours, but I phoned the bank to see if I could withdraw some money. When I told the bank why, they were very interested in my plans and said of course they could open the bank for me. They did so and I withdrew what I needed to buy my ticket to Toronto and cover other personal expenses. My friends all helped with the packing, which took until about midnight. After a few hours of sleep, I was ready to board the 5 a.m. train to Toronto.

After arriving at the Red Cross headquarters on time, I tried on all the uniforms they had in stock. Unfortunately they were all too big. The nearest fit was the one that had just been returned by my friend who had told me about Korea. Not only was it not in very good shape, the skirt was much too long. But as it was the best they could do, they insisted that I travel in it. Even though I would have preferred to wear my own clothes and have the uniform altered before wearing, I had to go off in an outfit which made me look like a bag lady. I just hoped that no one thought of me as being representative of the Red Cross.

After two weeks in Vancouver waiting for my visa, I flew to Japan and began a series of interviews with the coordinator of the Red Cross team. This was when I first learned about the expectations they had of the Far East team members. They did not want social workers to use their counselling skills to treat or solve the problems of soldiers who might confide in them, but to limit their relationship to being a friendly listener. If there were a serious problem that needed a solution, they were to refer the person to the personnel officer who was the only person with authority to do anything, such as arrange compassionate leave or give advice. Our main role was to provide recreational activities, especially in Korea where it was essential that morale be maintained.

My tour of duty with the Far East Welfare Team began in mid-September 1954. After five days at Ebisu Camp in Tokyo, I was posted to Hiro on the Inland Sea. I enjoyed my two-week stay in this beautiful part of Japan, but two weeks is all it turned out to be. Quite suddenly I was whisked off to Korea, where I worked for the next seven months.

I joined five other Red Cross team members at Brigade headquarters on the banks of the Imjin River. We were part of the brigade officers' mess, but worked at Maple Leaf Park, where the recreation centre for all the Canadian military units was situated. We commuted by jeep with a driver and an officer escort along a road which followed the side of a valley. On the opposite side of the valley were the ROK (Republic of Korea) positions. Although supposedly allies, they felt that any moving target was fair game for target practice. We habitually broke the speed limit on these trips.

Within a few weeks, the brigade and most of the Canadian units had left for Canada. We moved into new quarters at Maple Leaf Park where the Queen's Own Rifles, and the Red Cross team became the holding unit on the 38th parallel opposite the North Korean Forces on the other side of the demilitarized zone.

The commanding officer made it clear to us that he did not want a lot of depressed soldiers "weeping into their beer" during the Christmas season. His hope was that the Red Cross contingent

Dorothy Wiens (l) and Florence Bell (r) at 38th Parallel, Korea, Fall 1954.

could keep them cheered up. With this in mind, I asked each soldier I met at the reception desk about his ability to play an instrument, sing or tell stories. Of course, none admitted to having any talent, but all knew someone who did and were quite willing to share this knowledge with me.

When I had a list of potential performers, I got them together. The ones with musical talent started practising as a group and soon showed signs of becoming an orchestra of sorts; the script writers of skits were busy, too. When the colonel heard the musicians practising one day, and learned that I hoped to have the men do a Christmas show, he was interested and eager to help.

Being an impressario with no previous experience, I shared all my problems with him. As a result, he assigned an experienced sergeant to take over as production manager, excused all participants from regular duties for the duration, gave me his own wellingtons for our Santa, $100.00 to buy small gifts to fill Santa's sack, and scheduled the opening in the 700-seat theatre for the evening of December 24th.

On opening night the curtain rose on a typical Korean village scene. A skilfully painted backdrop showed a small house with a straw roof under blue skies. In the farm yard (the stage) was a large straw stack and in the surrounding yard several live chickens pecking in the mixture of straw, dirt and corn. On a trumpet note, the orchestra rose up from the straw stack playing country music. The chickens were the stars of the evening. They perched on the instruments, got under foot on stage while skits were being performed or country songs being sung, and did what chickens do, unpredictably. The show was a "success foux" as they say in the reviews. The soldiers were prepared to make a theatrical career on Broadway. All they got, however, was a chance to repeat the performance at a hospital in Seoul and at Commonwealth Divisional headquarters.

The unit held Education Upgrading Programmes for the next few weeks. The Red Cross team members were invited to volunteer as teachers, if they wished to do so, on a part-time basis. I did this and enjoyed it immensely. I had a class of fifteen or so in a programme at grade two level. Actually, the men could do grade five arithmetic, but their reading and writing skills were negligible. They were terrible at spelling or writing anything and could hardly read at all, but because of my experience in social work I wasn't shocked. The men all did their assignments enthusiastically since they were aware of the value of being able to read work instructions, employment applications, etc. But one chap said he couldn't do the assignments I gave them, because he could not understand the questions. After he made quite a few excuses I became suspicious of his motives and asked him if he needed individual help. When he said yes, I arranged for one of the chaplains to give him extra help. When he learned this, he decided he could do the assignments after all.

We had a problem with a misprint in a reader. It was a reference to there being too many of something or too few of something else. The reader spelled "to" with only one "o," and I said there should be two "o's." One chap said, "Oh, that can't be right." I asked, "Why, what do you think?" He said, "It should be

Lower Bunker at Exercise Nightmare Range, Korea, 1954.

Arrival of troops from Canada, Inchon, Korea, 1954.

one "o" for too few and two "o's" for too many. That's what my wife told me." This gave me an opportunity to teach them the various uses of homonyms.

The men were very helpful in the classes which were held in a Quonset hut—not a nice new Quonset hut, but one of those old huts where the windows had been broken and covered with brown paper to keep the wind out. There was a potbelly stove in the middle of the hut. These stoves would become red hot, and sometimes they'd explode, so when I'd see it heating up I would say, "Well, I may be a teacher, but I'm not very good at heating equipment. How do you people turn it down so it won't explode and send us all up in the air?" The men felt very happy that they could do something useful.

At the end of the entire session, I took a picture of the men, and they were pleased and proud. I told them, "When you finish these tests, I'll turn them in to the education officer, and if you've passed them, I will recommend that you go on to the next level. But if you haven't done well, I'll suggest you do it over again." So after each test they all wanted to know how they had done. It was quite touching.

Soon after this, rumours circulated that the unit was slated to leave the Far East, and in early April we moved to Ebisu in Tokyo, there to await instructions. Our tour of duty in Korea was over.

Transportation arrangements for Canadian Forces were dependent on the United States, since ships from Yokohama to Seattle were under U.S. command. It was a time of waiting. United Kingdom troop movements were between Kure, Japan and London with many ports-of-call in between. A limited number of Red Cross members were given the opportunity to use that service, subject to the possibility of being bumped for higher priority officer dependants. It was necessary for each member to have $1,000.00 as a backup insurance against being stranded at some foreign port. Four of us elected to go this route. We sailed from Kure on April 27, 1955. Our adventures along the way would be another story.

Jacqueline Robitaille Van Campen

"It changed my life forever"

—

Jacqueline Robitaille Van Campen was born and raised in Quebec City.
After earning her B.A., she studied social work at Laval University.
In 1953, while preparing her M.A. thesis, she decided to go to
Japan and Korea with the Red Cross. After her tour of duty,
she travelled to Australia, South Africa and Europe. On
her return she took an M.A. in Linguistics and
taught at Royal Roads Military College.

In the spring of 1953, I walked into the office of one of my professors at Laval University's School of Social Work. I had graduated the year before and was now coming to ask for help in putting the finishing touches on my Master's thesis. I also complained to the professor that after working for six or seven months my boss had refused to give me four months' leave to go to Europe. She smiled and handed me a letter, and that is how my life was changed forever.

The Canadian Red Cross was recruiting a group of social workers and handicraft workers to go to Japan and Korea, at the request of National Defence, I presume. They had written to my school of social work because they desperately needed French-speaking girls. My professor never thought that I would take the letter seriously because the Korean War was still on, I didn't speak English, I hadn't finished my thesis, and it was so far from my family—no one in her right mind would go that far from Quebec. Well, it was not for nothing that my ancestors were "coureurs de bois." After all, in the beginning they had not spoken any of the native languages either. So I asked a friend who knew some English to write to the Red Cross on my behalf. In September 1953, unilingual and a little bit frightened, I landed in that marvellous country, Japan—having never in my wildest dreams imagined that I would ever find myself there.

There were some amusing episodes on the way from Quebec to Tokyo. For one thing, in the process of being interviewed for the job, I got drunk. My interviewer was to arrive in Quebec on one of the oceanliners which at that time came regularly from Europe. I had been given his name and was on the dock to greet him a good few hours before the ship was due to land. I had had breakfast, but no lunch. When the ship arrived in late afternoon, I anxiously waited for the passengers to disembark. I found the interviewer's luggage on the pier and stood guard over it as I had no idea what the man looked like; I was not even sure that he knew that he had the job of assessing me on arrival.

I was right. He came out, past suppertime, having had a few with the captain. After the first few minutes of greetings, he instructed me to follow him to the waiting train where he would interview me before the train left. He began by offering me some Scotch with ice provided by the train steward. I drank like a trooper, and that is how I got to Japan—no doubt, based on my ability to down the stuff. It certainly was not because of my communication skills. I had no sooner gulped down the first few glasses than the train made a move. I ran out like a startled rabbit. I can't even remember saying goodbye to my future boss. To my great surprise I had hardly put my feet on the ground when it was meeting me halfway. This was the first time I had tasted whisky; it was also the first and last time I ever got drunk.

I travelled most of the way to Japan with the famous Red Cross beret under my arm as I didn't know which way it went on my head—even with the advice of my numerous uncles, aunts and cousins. I arrived in Tokyo with two other girls, another social worker from Toronto and a Red Cross worker from Montreal who spoke French. I thought that in Japan I would be given some time to learn to speak English, but it was not meant to be. As soon as I arrived, the resident French Canadian girl in Tokyo was sent away to the South of Japan and I became "it."

I'll never forget my first day at the Maple Leaf Club in Tokyo where I was to work for the next six months. I had understood that I would be doing social work for the Canadian troops in the Far East, but nothing had prepared me for the club. The Maple Leaf Club was an R & R (rest and relaxation) centre for Canadian soldiers on leave in Tokyo. It had a lounge with music, books and papers on one side and, to my horror, a beer parlour on the other side. For me, naive as I was, I couldn't believe that I was expected to go *there* and speak to the boys.

No, my job was not what I thought it would be, but I soon realized the importance of what I was doing. My role was to make the men feel more at ease by talking with them over coffee, discussing the news and helping them make the most of their R & R in Tokyo. For the French Canadians, I was someone with whom they could talk in their own language. Some of the soldiers had really heartbreaking stories. As I listened to the men, I realized that the women of the Red Cross represented home. The men talked to us as if we were their sisters. The club was a meeting place—a social club where members of the armed forces came to relax and have fun. However, they were often very homesick and some of them were struggling with drinking problems.

I also met soldiers from other parts of the world. In fact, the first men that I met were two Kiwis, a Maori and an Australian sergeant with one of the biggest mustaches I had ever seen. I wonder what we talked about? Initially I was not able to say very much in English, but I soon became bilingual. I even acquired an Australian accent. For the first few days I felt so bad about my inability to speak English that I wanted to go home. But after two weeks, I was ready for an extension of my stay.

I had been hired before the Korean war ended, but on July 27, 1953, an armistice came into effect. My social life took a marvellous turn. With the war over, the servicemen were coming to Tokyo to have a good time, and the best clubs and hotels were reserved for the United Nations troops. In my position with the Red Cross I did not have military rank, but I enjoyed all the privileges of an officer. Japan was exotic, and my life was certainly more exciting than at the Family Welfare Agency where I had worked back home. And here I felt more appreciated and useful.

I stayed in Japan (Tokyo, Kure and Hiro) for fifteen months. Kure was the administrative centre of the Canadian Brigade and Kobe was an R&R centre for American troops, as well as one of their administrative centres. I was lucky enough to be re-posted often and introduced to different parts of Japan. In each of these places, my responsibilities were the same. As well as encouraging the men to talk, I wrote letters and did shopping for them. When I wasn't working, I was able to go out and learn more about the Japanese culture, which was a wonderful experience for a young woman who had never before been outside of Quebec.

After fifteen months in Japan, I was transferred to Korea near the Armistice line on the 38th parallel and the Imjin River. I was there for three months, and it was very different from my experience in Japan. Even though the war was over, there was still a

Jacqueline playing piano at Maple Leaf Club, Tokyo, December 1953.

strong sense of danger. At night we had to drive without lights because we were close to the military zone. I remember one time when two of us were being driven from work to where we were staying. Suddenly a soldier jumped out of the bush and demanded that the jeep stop. We were really scared, but fortunately the soldier turned out to be one of ours. Curiously enough, the Republic of Korea, the United Nations and countries such as Canada which fought under its aegis are still officially at war with North Korea. An official peace treaty between the two sides was never signed.

Of all the places where I lived in the Far East, I liked Tokyo the best because of the friendliness of the people, and because I was free to explore on my own. My activities were more restricted at the other bases in Japan. It was even rougher in Korea. There was no social life except at the officers' mess. The Koreans wanted us to leave them alone. If we tried to approach them to take photographs, they would chase us away. They seemed to hate the United Nations troops and that always puzzled me. In Japan, by contrast, we were treated with great courtesy.

Years later when I watched *M*A*S*H* on TV, it would take me back to the headquarters of the Canadian Brigade in Korea and our quarters on "Retreat Hill," so named because it was the Quonset hut suburb where we lived with the chaplains as neighbours. There were army trucks everywhere—it was a completely isolated military life.

In Tokyo, we could counteract the army environment by going out to see the sights and talking to other people. I was not an "Army girl"—military ranks and titles meant nothing to me. Members of the armed forces were all just people to me. I think most of us in the Red Cross felt the same way.

When I look back on the period of my life with the Red Cross, I consider myself very lucky to have been one of no more than fifty or sixty girls who were selected to work for the Red Cross in the Far East. It changed my life forever. I had grown up as a "Quebecer," but as soon as I arrived in Japan I wanted to be known as a Canadian. When I was practising my English, I noticed that people thought that I was Australian, so I made a special effort to learn the Canadian pronunciation of words like "car." Then I made a point of using the word "car" in conversations so people would say, "Oh, she's not Australian, she must be from Canada."

In Quebec, I had been to university, but as far as life was concerned, I was actually quite naive and protected by my community. In Asia, I developed a stronger sense of identity and decided that first of all I was Canadian. I felt even more special when I recognized that I represented two cultures and could speak two languages.

The curious thing, however, is that I never thought of Korea as a "cause." I did not see myself as going over to help the people of Korea. Of course, the Korean War was over by the time I got there, and perhaps I was too preoccupied with my own life at that time. In addition, I remember the poverty of the people in Japan: when going to night-clubs and restaurants, we passed people sleeping in doorways with their children. I never did anything to help them and I'm not too proud of myself at that age.

I wish that I could say that I did great things for Canada and the

world when I was in the Far East. Had I been in a hospital or acting as a social worker like some of my colleagues, perhaps I could
claim such accomplishments. Nevertheless, I agree with the lads
of the Royal Engineers, who said, "The Red Cross are the best
bunch of girls we have ever met! God bless them all." We were a
good group of Canadian girls representing home and family for
the servicemen from Canada and the Commonwealth, and that,
maybe, was enough.

As for myself, when I arrived in the land of the "Rising Sun," I
became a real Canadian instead of just a Quebecer. I gained a
great sense of my country which has never left me. Et Voilà—a
wonderful episode in my life!

Three and a half years after my time in the Far East, I finally
returned home. I had travelled to Australia, South Africa and
Europe, working my way from country to country. I was married in
1960 and we have three sons—all married now. My husband and I
never stopped travelling. I returned to university and earned an
M.A. in Linguistics at Simon Fraser, and then taught at Royal
Roads Military College. Now that both my husband and I are
retired, we spend most of our time travelling and doing volunteer
work. And I have just started learning to play the cello.

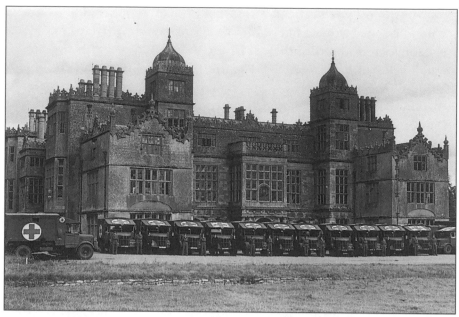

Red Cross ambulances at Charlton Park, England, before embarking for the continent, 1945.

Red Cross Corps members with recovering soldiers in Occupational Therapy, England, 1944.

AFTERWORD

After reading these memoirs, we might reflect on how these young and somewhat sheltered women could have "heard the call" and become involved in the war. It was a time filled with adventure, yet devastating and emotionally tearing. Many of these Red Cross Corps women lost husbands, fiancés and boy friends in the war. Each knew that she had to set aside her grief for the time being because there was a war to be fought and peace to be won.

One of these women was Frances Martin Day. Thinking back on her wartime experience, she writes a postscript to her story. "I made a promise to myself that twenty-five years after World War II, I would return to Europe for a pilgrimage to the Berlin Canadian Cemetery where Norman Martin, my husband, was buried with his crew. After checking into a hotel in Berlin, I hailed a taxi to drive me to the Canadian Cemetery. Up a very long grassy slope I walked to where three tall arches framed the view that met me—a long lawn aisle that led to a beautiful fountain. On each side were many stone markers in rows. A soft-spoken caretaker approached me asking me to sign the visitors' book and then escorted me to the row where Norman and his crew were buried. The inscription on his marker was as his parents and I had requested many years ago—'Dearly loved and deeply missed.' Leaving the cemetery in a reflective mood, I glanced over my shoulder once more to see the rows and rows of stone markers and felt a deep sadness for the loss of so many young men."

The Berlin Canadian Cemetery is just one of many memorial cemeteries where our 109,980 Canadian servicemen and women of the First and Second World Wars are either buried or commemorated. In Tang-gok, a suburb of Pusan, 387 Canadians are among the 1,588 Commonwealth soldiers buried in Korea.

It is important to remember that out of two devastating world wars, two great peace initiatives were established. When the armistice that declared the end of World War I was signed on November 11, 1918, many nations saw the need to plan together to maintain peace throughout the world. The League of Nations was founded by Woodrow Wilson, President of the United States, as he sought a way to end all wars. He formulated the plan of "all for one and one for all" which guaranteed that if one nation was under attack, other nations would come to its aid—and this became known as "collective security." The League was, however, unable to stop the assaults on European countries by Hitler. In 1945 the League of Nations was replaced by the United Nations, with its headquarters in New York City. Since then the United Nations has grown in strength and stature in its pursuit of world peace.

But world peace is still a fragile vision. In order to keep this vision intact, we must remember the servicemen and women who sacrificed their lives in the cause of peace. In her story, Claire Watson Fisher tells of a memorial in a museum overlooking Caen and the beaches of Normandy, named simply Le Memorial. It was created to study the causes of war, the development of human rights and the pursuit of peace. Although visitors to the museum can experience the effects of war through films and photographs of human suffering and devastation, they can also feel the hope for peace in the twenty-first century. Le Memorial is striving to prevent future wars by educating young people about the horrors of war and making them aware of the huge numbers of servicemen and women who died in the pursuit of peace and freedom. Scholarships are being established so that students will have an opportunity to visit Le Memorial, which includes a library and document centre.

While institutions such as the United Nations and Le Memorial are vital initiatives in the quest for world peace, first-hand accounts of the experience of war, such as the stories in *Women Overseas*, are also important as they bring to life the dry facts and figures of history books. Facts and figures become real women and men who affirm the spirit and courage of "ordinary" people. Several of the women in this book recall driving through the devastated countryside and seeing crumpled tanks, charred trees and shattered dwellings. But they also saw poppies growing among the ruins. And as one of them remembers, "the fields of red poppies lifted our spirits." Through the remembrances of the Canadian Red Cross Corps our spirits are lifted as they remind us of the power of individuals to make a contribution towards the continuing quest for world peace.

ABOUT THE EDITORS

FRANCES MARTIN DAY is a former member of the Canadian Red Cross Corps and has been a member of the Overseas Club, Victoria Branch, for many years. Over ten years ago, she suggested that the members discuss their wartime experiences, and her collection of their stories formed the basis for this book. Since her overseas experience she has studied art, fashion and drawing in Montreal and is well known for her paintings, which include landscapes and portraits of children and animals.

PHYLLIS SPENCE studied sociology and psychology at the University of Victoria, graduating in 1989. While at university she and Barbara Ladouceur became interested in oral histories and this eventually led to their collaboration in the bestseller, *Blackouts to Bright Lights: Canadian War Bride Stories* (1995). Phyllis currently works in a hospital staffing department and an evening program for seniors in Victoria.

BARBARA LADOUCEUR earned a BA in English and Women's Studies at the University of Victoria in 1989. She then travelled to York, England to study women's life writings in the Women's Studies programme at the University of York. In 1990 she graduated with an MA in Women's Studies and returned to Canada. She now resides in Vancouver where she works as an ESL teacher and a freelance editor.

FURTHER READING

Andrews, Allen. *Brave Soldiers, Proud Regiments: Canada's Military Heritage*. Vancouver: Ronsdale Press, 1997.

Broadfoot, Barry. *Six War Years, 1939–1945: Memories of Canadians at Home and Abroad*. Toronto: Doubleday, 1974.

Bruce, Jean. *Back the Attack!: Canadian Women During the Second War—at Home and Abroad*. Toronto: Macmillan of Canada, 1985.

Conrod, W. Hugh. *Athene, Goddess of War: The Canadian Women's Army Corps—Their Story*. Dartmouth, N.S.: Writing and Editorial Services, 1984.

Ellis, Jean MacLachlan with Isabel Dingman. *Face Powder and Gunpowder*. Toronto: S. J. Reginald Saunders, 1947.

Gillis, John Graham. *"A Lovely Letter From Cecie," in The 1907–1915 Vancouver Diary and World War I Letters of Wallace Chambers*. Vancouver: Peanut Butter Publishing, 1998.

Gordon, P. H. *Fifty Years in the Canadian Red Cross*. [n.p., 19—].

Gossage, Carolyn. *Greatcoats and Glamour Boots: Canadian Women at War (1939–1945)*. Toronto: Dundurn Press, 1991.

Greer, Rosamond "Fiddy." *The Girls of the King's Navy*. Victoria, B.C.: Sono Nis Press, 1983.

Gwyn, Sandra. *Tapestry of War: A Private View of Canadians in the Great War*. Toronto: HarperCollins, 1992.

Hibbert, Joyce. *The War Brides*. Toronto: PMA Books, 1978.

Ladouceur, Barbara and Phyllis Spence, editors. *Blackouts to Bright Lights: Canadian War Bride Stories*. Vancouver: Ronsdale Press, 1995.

Landells, E. A., editor. *The Military Nurses of Canada: Recollections of Canadian Military Nurses*. White Rock, B.C.: [E. A. Landells] with the assistance of Co-Publishing, 1995.

Latta, Ruth. *The Memory of All That: Canadian Women Remember World War II.* Burnstown: General Store Publishing House, 1992.

Mitchell, Miriam C. and Florence C. Deacon. *641: A Story of the Canadian Red Cross Corps, Overseas.* St. Catharine's, Ontario: Advance Printing Inc., 1978.

Nicholson, G. W. L. *Canada's Nursing Sisters.* Toronto: Hakkert & Company, 1975.

Pierson, Ruth Roach. *They're Still Women After All: The Second World War and Canadian Womanhood.* Toronto: McClelland and Stewart, 1986.

Prentice, Alison, et al. *Canadian Women: A History.* Toronto: Harcourt Brace Jovanovich, 1988.

Robson Roe, Kathleen. *War Letters from the C.W.A.C.* Toronto: Kakabeka Publishing Co., 1975.

Sterner, Captain Doris M. *In and Out of Harm's Way: A History of the Navy Nurse Corps.* Seattle: Peanut Butter Publishing, 1997.

Wicks, Ben. *Promise You'll Take Care of My Daughter: The Remarkable War Brides of World War II.* Toronto: Stoddart, 1992.

INDEX